CW00539972

Sovereignty Revisited

This book explores the new debates on Basque sovereignty and statehood that have emerged in the post-violence Basque political scenario. It deciphers how sovereignty is understood or imagined by a revitalized civil society after the unilateral cessation of operations by ETA (Basque Homeland and Freedom). The contributors to this book investigate the new political field developing in the nexus between conventional party politics, established socio-cultural and linguistic organizations, creative civil society initiatives and innovative activism.

This is a book for graduate students, scholars and professionals in political science, social anthropology, European studies, political philosophy, transnational studies, sociology, political geography and global studies. It will also be of interest to academic specialists in Basque studies, specialists working on sovereignty, nationalism and globalization, and professionals in governance, international relations, foreign affairs, European politics and diplomacy.

Åshild Kolås is a social anthropologist and research professor at the Peace Research Institute Oslo (PRIO) and was the head of PRIO's Conflict Resolution and Peacebuilding Program from 2005 to 2011. She has conducted long-term fieldwork in multi-ethnic communities in India and China and has written on Tibet, Nepal, Inner Mongolia and Northeast India with a focus on governance and governmentality, identity politics, discourse and representation. Her latest books are *Basque Nationhood: Towards a Democratic Scenario* (co-edited with Pedro Ibarra Güell) and *Reclaiming the Forest: The Ewenki Reindeer Herders of Aoluguya* (co-edited with Yuanyuan Xie). She is also the author of *Tourism and Tibetan Culture in Transition: A Place Called Shangrila* and *On the Margins of Tibet: Cultural Survival on the Sino-Tibetan Frontier* (with Monika P. Thowsen). Since 2006, Åshild Kolås has coordinated an institutional cooperation between PRIO and the Institute for Defence Studies and Analyses (IDSA) in New Delhi. Her current research is on gender, peacebuilding and conflict management in Northeast India and Myanmar.

Pedro Ibarra Güell is a professor of political science at the University of the Basque Country (UPV/EHU), where he served as director of the Department of Political Science and Public Administration. During the end of Francoism and the transition to democracy in Spain, Dr. Güell worked as a labour lawyer and advocate for political prisoners. He later founded and directed Parte Hartuz, a consolidated research group on participatory democracy based at the University of the Basque Country. He has been a visiting professor at universities in Bordeaux (France), Barcelona (Spain) and Reno, Nevada (USA). His main areas of research are theories of collective action, political participation, social movements and nationalism, in which he has conducted numerous research projects and published extensively. In addition to his academic work, he is known for his association with various Basque social movements.

Routledge Studies in Radical History and Politics

Series editors: Thomas Linehan, *Brunel University*, and John Roberts, *Brunel University*

www.routledge.com/Routledge-Studies-in-Radical-History-and-Politics/book-series/ RSRHP

The series *Routledge Studies in Radical History and Politics* has two areas of interest. Firstly, this series aims to publish books which focus on the history of movements of the radical left. 'Movement of the radical left' is here interpreted in its broadest sense as encompassing those past movements for radical change which operated in the mainstream political arena as with political parties, and past movements for change which operated more outside the mainstream as with millenarian movements, anarchist groups, utopian socialist communities, and trade unions. Secondly, this series aims to publish books which focus on more contemporary expressions of radical left-wing politics. Recent years have been witness to the emergence of a multitude of new radical movements adept at getting their voices in the public sphere. From those participating in the Arab Spring, the Occupy movement, community unionism, social media forums, independent media outlets, local voluntary organisations campaigning for progressive change, and so on, it seems to be the case that innovative networks of radicalism are being constructed in civil society that operate in different public forms.

The series very much welcomes titles with a British focus, but is not limited to any particular national context or region. The series will encourage scholars who contribute to this series to draw on perspectives and insights from other disciplines.

Titles include:

An East End Legacy
Essays in Memory of William J Fishman
Colin Holmes and Anne J Kershen

Sovereignty Revisited
The Basque Case
Edited by Åshild Kolås and Pedro Ibarra Güell

Forthcoming

John Lilburne and The Levellers
Reappraising the Roots of English Radicalism 400 Years On
Edited by John Rees

Sovereignty Revisited

The Basque case

**Edited by Åshild Kolås
and Pedro Ibarra Güell**

LONDON AND NEW YORK

First published 2018
by Routledge
2 Park Square, Milton Park, Abingdon, Oxon OX14 4RN

and by Routledge
711 Third Avenue, New York, NY 10017

Routledge is an imprint of the Taylor & Francis Group, an informa business

British Library Cataloguing-in-Publication Data
A catalogue record for this book is available from the British Library

Library of Congress Cataloging-in-Publication Data
A catalog record for this book has been requested

ISBN: 978-1-138-06804-9 (hbk)
ISBN: 978-1-315-15834-1 (ebk)

Typeset in Times New Roman
by Apex CoVantage, LLC

Printed and bound in Great Britain by
TJ International Ltd, Padstow, Cornwall

Contents

Figures

Tables

Map of the Basque country

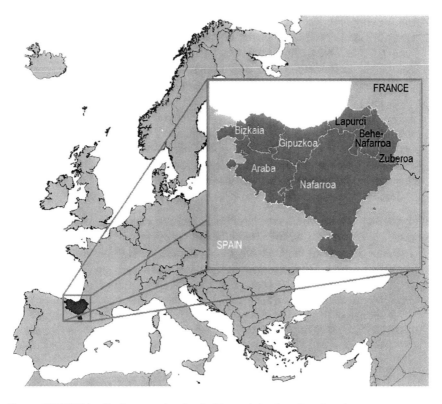

Source: PRIO/Wikimedia Commons (reprinted with permission from Peter Lang)

Contributors

Pablo Aguiar is a researcher at the International Catalan Institute for Peace (Institut Català Internacional per la Pau) in Barcelona. He has taught international relations at the Autonomous University of Barcelona (Universitat Autònoma de Barcelona) and was formerly responsible for studies, projects and programs at the Office of Peace and Human Rights (Oficina de promoció de la pau i dels drets humans) of the Generalitat of Cataluña. Pablo Aguiar is a postgraduate in Cooperation for Development from Barcelona Centre for International Affairs (Centre de Documentació Internacional de Barcelona) and graduated in political science from Complutense University in Madrid. His latest publications are on the implications of drone warfare for international relations and international law, human security and peacebuilding in Colombia.

Igor Ahedo holds an MA degree in political sociology and a PhD in political science. He is currently a professor at the University of the Basque Country and serves as director of the Department of Political Science and Administration. His core research interest is to study diverse processes of change and political conflict at the local, national and international levels, with a special focus on changing identities. Igor Ahedo's works on the French Basque country have been published in English (by the University of Nevada, USA), French and German.

Javier Alcalde is a research fellow at the Center of Social Movements Studies (COSMOS) of the Scuola Normale Superiore in Florence. He has worked as a researcher at the International Catalan Institute for Peace in Barcelona and at the Center of Advanced Studies on Social Sciences, Juan March Institute, Madrid. As an expert on disarmament he has participated in a number of international negotiations on treaties such as the ban on cluster bombs and arms trade treaty. He has taught at different institutions, including Universitat Autònoma de Barcelona, Universitat Oberta de Cataluña, and Univeritat Pompeu Fabra, as well as the Florence campus of the Arcadia University. He holds a PhD in social and political sciences from the European University Institute (2009) and an executive master's degree in diplomacy and foreign affairs from the Pompeu Fabra University (2015). Javier Alcalde has published extensively on different topics of peace research, such as refugees, human security, arms trade, transnational activism, media and social movements, pacifism, the Esperanto movement, linguistic justice and linguistic conflicts. His work has appeared in peer-reviewed international journals such as *Global Policy, European Political Science, Language Problems and Language Planning, Partecipazione e Conflitto, Hamburg Review of Social Sciences, Revista Internacional de Sociología, Revista Española de Investigaciones Sociológicas* and *Relaciones Internacionales.*

Daniele Conversi received his PhD from the London School of Economics and has since taught at Cornell and Syracuse University, as well as at the Central European University in Budapest. He is currently a research professor at the University of the Basque Country, Bilbao and the Ikerbasque Foundation for Science. His first book, *The Basques, the Catalans, and Spain*, was acclaimed by political scientists, historians and sociologists alike and has been reviewed in nearly forty international journals. His edited volume *Ethnonationalism in the Contemporary World: Walker Connor and the Study of Nationalism* is a collection of essays by some of the leading international scholars of nationalism. Daniele Conversi has published for *Democratization, Ethnic and Racial Studies, Nations and Nationalism* and other well-known journals. His article 'Modernism and nationalism' in the *Journal of Political Ideologies* is ranked as the journal's most read article.

Iban Galletebeitia Gabiola holds a PhD in Political Science and Master's degrees in Basque Nationalism, Innovation and Knowledge Management, and Participation and Community Development, all from the University of the Basque Country (UPV/EHU). He is a researcher at LANKI, Research Hub on Cooperative Studies at Mondragón University, where he explores the rethinking of sovereignty and territory in the European Union and its implications for the Mondragón Experience in the province of Gipuzkoa (Basque country). Galletebeitia is co-author of the book *Euskal Herriko pentsamenduaren gida* [*Guide to Basque Critical Thinking*], and a contributor to *Basque Nationhood: Towards a Democratic Scenario.*

Jule Goikoetxea graduated from the University of Cambridge (St. Edmund's College-King's College) and University of the Basque Country, where she obtained her PhD in philosophy in 2009. She has been an associate researcher at the University of London, Edinburgh University and Lancaster University. An awardee of several fellowships, she has worked as a post-doctoral research fellow at the University of Cambridge (POLIS) and Queen's University in Canada. Since 2014, Jule Goikoetxea has served as lecturer in political philosophy at the University of the Basque Country and academic director of the MA in Governance and Political Studies. Her latest articles have been published in journals such as *Ethnopolitics, Regional and Federal Studies, Nationalities Paper, The University of Cambridge Journal of Politics* and *Cambridge University United Nations Journal.*

Pedro Ibarra Güell is a professor of political science at the University of the Basque Country (UPV/EHU), where he served as director of the Department of Political Science and Public Administration. During the end of Francoism and the transition to democracy in Spain, Dr. Güell worked as a labour lawyer and advocate for political prisoners. He later founded and directed Parte Hartuz, a consolidated research group on participatory democracy based at the University of the Basque Country. He has been a visiting professor at universities in Bordeaux (France), Barcelona (Spain) and Reno, Nevada (USA). His main areas of research are theories of collective action, political participation, social movements and nationalism, in which he has conducted numerous research projects and published extensively. In addition to his academic work, he is known for his association with various Basque social movements.

Xabier Itçaina is a Centre National de la Recherche Scientifique research fellow in political science at Sciences Po Bordeaux and a former Marie Curie Fellow (2012–2013) at the European University Institute, Florence. His research interests are Catholicism and territorial politics, territorial dynamics of the social economy, and identity politics. He has conducted fieldwork in French, Spanish and Italian territories and published extensively on territorial identity and farmers' economic activism and mobilization in the French Basque country, the implementation of the EU agricultural reforms, discourse and practices of the Catholic Church on the Basque issue, and immigration in Spain. Xabier Itçaina is the co-editor (with François Foret) of *Politics of Religion in Western Europe: Modernities in Conflict?*

Åshild Kolås is a social anthropologist and research professor at the Peace Research Institute Oslo (PRIO) and was the head of PRIO's Conflict Resolution and Peacebuilding Program from 2005 to 2011. She has conducted long-term fieldwork in multi-ethnic communities in India and China and has written on Tibet, Nepal, Inner Mongolia and Northeast India with a focus on governance and governmentality, identity politics, discourse and representation. Her latest books are *Basque Nationhood: Towards a Democratic Scenario* (co-edited with Pedro Ibarra Güell) and *Reclaiming the Forest: The Ewenki Reindeer Herders of Aoluguya* (co-edited with Yuanyuan Xie). She is also the author of *Tourism and Tibetan Culture in Transition: A Place Called Shangrila* and *On the Margins of Tibet: Cultural Survival on the Sino-Tibetan Frontier* (with Monika P. Thowsen). Since 2006, Åshild Kolås has coordinated an institutional cooperation between PRIO and the Institute for Defence Studies and Analyses (IDSA) in New Delhi. Her current research is on gender, peacebuilding and conflict management in Northeast India and Myanmar.

Pedro J. Oiarzabal is a researcher of migration studies at the Human Rights Institute, University of Deusto (Spain), and Jon Bilbao Research Fellow on the Basque Diaspora at the University of Nevada, Reno (USA). His interdisciplinary research examines diaspora communities' interaction with digital technologies, diasporic citizenship, return migration and memory and oral history, with particular emphasis on the Basque case. Pedro J. Oiarzabal has conducted extensive fieldwork in North America and Europe. Among his publications are *La Identidad Vasca en el Mundo* [*The Basque Identity in the World*], *A Candle in the Night: Basque Studies at the University of Nevada, 1967–2007*, *Gardeners of Identity: Basques in the San Francisco Bay Area*, *Diasporas in the New Media Age: Identity, Politics, and Community* and *The Basque Diaspora Webscape: Identity, Nation, and Homeland, 1990s–2010s*. He has also produced the oral history video *Fragments of Our Lives*.

Mario Zubiaga graduated in law from the University of the Basque Country, holds a PhD in political science and is a professor at the University of the Basque Country's Department of Political Science. He has authored numerous articles, mainly on Basque nationalism and social protest in the Basque country. His current research interests include state- and nation-building and the study of contemporary trends in political theory related to political change, conflict resolution, hegemony and populism. In addition to his academic work, Mario Zubiaga is known for his association with various Basque social movements, especially the movement Gure Esku Dago (It's in Our Hands) related to the call for the Basque people's 'right to decide'. He has contributed to the volume *Towards a Basque State. Nation-building and Institutions* (IparHegoa Foundation), and is also the coordinator of the 'socio-political structure' thematic area of the Society of Basque Studies, Eusko Ikaskuntza.

Abbreviations

ACBC	Autonomous Community of the Basque Country (Comunidad Autónoma del País Vasco)
ADV	Asociación Diáspora Vasca (Basque Diaspora Association)
AEK	Alfabetatze Euskalduntze Koordinakundea (Coordinator of Basque Literacy)
APLI	Association des Producteurs de lait Indépendants et en Colère (Association of Angry Independent Milk Producers)
BLE	Biharko Lurraren Elkartea (Association for the Land of Tomorrow)
CAL	Coordinadora d'Associacions per la Llengua Catalana (Coordinator of Associations for the Catalan Language)
CCN	Chartered Community of Navarre (Comunidad Foral de Navarra)
CIU	Convergència i Unió (Convergence and Union)
CLEFE	Clubs Locaux des Femmes qui Entreprennent (Club of Local Female Entrepreneurs)
CLEJE	Comités locaux d'épargne pour les jeunes (Local youth savings committees)
EAJ-PNV	Eusko Alberdi Jeltzalea-Partido Nacionalista Vasco (Basque Nationalist Party)
EE	Euskadiko Ezkerra (Basque Left)
EH Bildu	Euskal Herria Bildu (Basque Country Reunite)
EHLG	Euskal Herriko Laborantza Ganbara (Chamber of Agriculture of the Basque Country)
EHNE	Euskal Herriko Nekazarien Elkartasuna (Farmers' Solidarity of the Basque Country)
EHU	Euskal Herriko Unibertsitatea (University of the Basque Country)
ELA	Euskal Langileen Alkartasuna (Basque Workers' Solidarity)

ELB	Euskal Herriko Laborarien Batasuna
	(Union of Basque Country Peasants)
ETA	Euskadi 'ta Askatasuna
	(Basque Homeland and Freedom)
ETA-m	ETA militar
	(ETA military)
ETA-pm	ETA político-militar
	(ETA political-military)
EU	European Union
FEVA	Federación de Entidades Vasco-Argentinas
	(Federation of Basque-Argentinean Entities)
FDSEA	Fédération Départementale des Syndicats d'Exploitants Agricoles
	(Departmental Federation of Farming Trade Unions)
GAL	Grupos Antiterroristas de Liberación
	(Anti-Terrorist Liberation Groups)
GED	Gure Esku Dago
	(It's in Our Hands)
GFAM	Groupement Foncier Agricole Mutuel
	(Mutual Agricultural Land Grouping)
GWT	Global War on Terror
ICAPB	Institut de Concertation Agricole du Pays Basque
	(Institut de Concertation Agricole du Pays Basque)
ICB	Institut Culturel Basque
	(Basque Cultural Institute)
LAB	Langile Abertzaleen Btazordeak
	(Patriotic Workers' Committee)
MLNV	Movimiento de Liberación Nacional Vasco
	(Basque National Liberation Movement)
MRJC	Mouvement Rural de Jeunesse Chrétienne
	(Movement of Rural Christian Youth)
NABO	North American Basque Organizations
OECD	Organisation for Economic Co-operation and Development
OPLB	Office Public de la Langue Basque
	(Public Office for the Basque Language)
PNV	Partido Nacionalista Vasco
	(Basque Nationalist Party)
PP	Partido Popular
	(People's Party)
PSE-EE	Partido Socialista de Euskadi-Euskadiko Ezkerra
	(Basque Socialist Party-Basque Left)
PSOE	Partido Socialista Obrero Español
	(Spanish Socialist Workers' Party)
SCMO	Sustainable Community Movement Organizations
SCOP	Société Coopérative Ouvrière de Production
	(Workers' Cooperative Production Company)

TAV   Tren de Alta Velocidad
             (High-Speed Train)
UPV   Universidad del País Vasco
             (University of the Basque Country)

Acknowledgements

This book is an output of the research project 'Imagined Sovereignties: Frontiers of Statehood and Globalization', funded by the Research Council of Norway (RCN) and hosted by the Peace Research Institute Oslo (PRIO). 'Imagined Sovereignties' (2013–17) studied sovereignty contestations in three main field sites: the Basque country, Cyprus and Northeast India. Research on the Basque case was carried out by researchers from the University of the Basque Country (Basque: Euskal Herriko Unibertsitatea, EHU; Spanish: Universidad del País Vasco, UPV; UPV/EHU), the International Catalan Institute for Peace (Catalan: Institut Català Internacional per la Pau; Spanish: Instituto Catalán Internacional para la Paz, ICIP) and PRIO.

The editors would like to thank our colleagues in Oslo, Barcelona, Guwahati, Nicosia and the Basque country and especially Covi Morales Bertrand, who coordinated the work on the Basque case, the contributors to this volume and all the participants in the project's conferences and seminars.

Introduction

Basque sovereignty revisited

Åshild Kolås

On 8 April 2017, BBC's Lyce Doucet informed viewers that 'the last insurgency in Europe is coming to an end'. The news story continued:[1]

> Who are ETA? Founded during General Franco's dictatorship, ETA wanted an independent Basque state in northern Spain and southern France. Bombings, assassinations and kidnapping were their most frequent tactics. In 1973, they killed Spain's Prime Minister, Admiral Louis Carrero Blanco. In 1997, they kidnapped and killed a Basque councillor, Miguel Angel Blanco. An estimated 6 million Spaniards took to the streets to protest. Considered a terrorist group by the EU, more than 800 people were killed by ETA over more than 40 years. The group announced a permanent ceasefire in 2011. Now ETA is handing over all its weapons, according to a letter obtained by the BBC.

ETA (Euskadi 'ta Askatasuna; Basque Homeland and Freedom) disarmed in the French city of Bayonne in a unilateral process that was dismissed by Spanish authorities as inconsequential. Madrid has remained unwilling to enter into negotiations, even on a more limited set of issues than those discussed in earlier peace talks in 1998–99 and 2006–07. Nevertheless, the Basque patriotic left (*ezkerra abertzale*) has achieved a victory of sorts in the reemergence of a meaningful debate on Basque sovereignty, which was practically impossible under the constant threat of violence. ETA's cessation of operations has inspired Basque civil society to engage in new, much more lively and open debates, revisiting the meaning of Basque sovereignty and nationhood.

As the home of the 'last insurgency in Europe', what makes the Basque country unique? How was Basque militant nationalism different from other nationalist projects in Europe, and why did the militarized struggle last so long? In post-Cold War Eastern Europe, scholars hypothesized that Communist autocracies had held down a 'simmering cauldron' or 'ticking bomb' of ethno-nationalist conflict, which erupted only after the erstwhile authoritarian regimes left the scene and democracy took the stage. By those standards, why did ETA take up arms during the authoritarian regime of Francisco Franco, and why did the group continue after the end of the Franco regime, as Spain made its transition to democracy?

As different from Eastern Europe, there was no post-authoritarian civil war in the Basque country. Nor was there any disruption in the continuity of the Spanish security establishment, since a blanket amnesty was granted to officers and officials of Franco's military dictatorship. In fact, there is continuity in the forces of the Spanish security establishment ever since the end of the Spanish Civil War and throughout World War II, with Spain often described as the 'forgotten' Axis power. In the other Axis countries of Europe, Germany and Italy, the wartime dictatorships and the security states that underpinned them were effectively discontinued at the end of World War II. Nevertheless, Germany and Italy both experienced post-war violent, left-wing extremism. If we compare the nature of militarized political violence in the three countries, the difference is obviously the nationalist nature of the Basque conflict and the mobilization potential offered by ethno-nationalism when repression can be attributed to ethnic identity rather than ideology. It seems that the formula for violent insurgency contains two basic ingredients: a pro-active, offensive security establishment targeting a population based on ethnic profiling, and an identity-based movement capable of armed resistance. Both ingredients were present in Eastern Europe after the fall of the Soviet Union, in Northern Ireland prior to the Good Friday agreement and in the Basque country until ETA's cessation of operations. The central role of the security establishment is undeniable, but without an armed resistance, how long can a militarized conflict last?

When ETA announced its permanent cessation of operations, the strategy of violence had in fact been debated within the Basque radical movement for decades. The debate became more intense after 11 September 2001, as the use of violence was associated with Al Qaeda and Islamist terrorism. When the 2006–07 peace talks were again held in top-secret locations, tightly sealed from the public, there were complaints from Basque civil society that the talks should be inclusive and transparent. There was a mounting tension, rooted in the contradiction between the strategy of violence and the freedom and self-determination it was supposed to accomplish. After the talks broke down, ETA leaders finally came to realize that the right to decide belongs to the people, and that violence is useless as a means to achieving independence in any meaningful sense of the word.

In the post-militancy scenario, the debate on Basque sovereignty has flourished with a fresh sense of opportunity and unprecedented openness to new ideas and innovative political formats. Novel social media platforms and artistic modalities have been employed, bringing politics to the people in a completely new fashion. Self-determination is at the core of the new wave of Basque politics. The medium is really the message (McLuhan 1967), and both the message and medium of the new Basque political scene come across in a burst of artistic, pluralistic, colorful, spontaneous, creative energy. Innovative forms of mobilization and organization have appeared on the Basque stage, together with new means of communicating ideas through creative multimedia expressions.

The tired compartmentalization of formal institutions has been challenged. The political itself has been laid out for grabs, as a free-for-all of popular recreation. At the center of it all, the concept of self-determination and its links to Basque identity have been unshackled. The new scenario has offered an opportunity to reimagine the meaning of sovereignty and the 'right to decide' – a key demand of Basque and Catalan nationalists alike. Similar debates have taken place in the French Basque country (Iparralde), where there has also been a creative surge of new Basque identity politics.

Scholars of Basque nationalism have often returned to the historical chartered rights and privileges, the mediaeval 'foral codes' (*los fueros*) as a pillar of Basque political identity, as described in the following pages (see also Conversi, this volume). While *los fueros* have an undeniable place in Basque political history, evidence based on ancient law has gradually lost relevance, as have arguments about self-determination as a right of a people. For some, this is a question of realism, or 'de facto realities of power' (Wallerstein 2004: 44), while others come to a similar conclusion from a constructivist perspective, viewing sovereignty as socially constructed, contingent and ever-changing (Biersteker and Weber 1996; Weber 1995). Sovereignty is no doubt a concept in flux, influenced not only by the immediate concerns of superpower politics but also by the gradual evolution of international norms and institutions, novel governance techniques, mounting transnational migration and ever more globalized markets. Changing visions of state legitimacy, political representation, citizenship and territoriality all influence the imagination of what 'sovereignty' might mean. Globally, transmutations of the 'sovereignty order' are evident in the evolution of sovereignty sharing, social sovereignty and supra-state sovereignty, as seen in institutions and frameworks for cooperation ranging from the Arctic Council to the European Central Bank.

From an anthropological perspective, sovereignty can be understood as imagined in similar ways as the 'imagined communities' (Anderson 1983; Liu 2003) that make up the 'people' of sovereignty demands. Rapidly changing governance practices and new means of contestation affect this imagination, with implications for the sovereignty claims of state agents as well as their contenders. For mediators in peace talks, quickly changing governance techniques and practices makes sovereignty a 'moving target' (Kolås 2016). Considering the importance of sovereignty demands in a range of twenty-first-century conflicts, theorists of peace and conflict resolution should revisit contemporary imaginations of sovereignty, as they are grounded in new socio-political contexts. This is the approach taken in the chapters of this book, as we revisit Basque debates about self-determination, the complexities of defining the Basque 'self', and the rethinking of 'sovereignty' as a concept. The contours of the evolving global sovereignty order can also be seen when contemporary debates on Basque sovereignty are viewed from this perspective.

Histories of independence and Basque identity

Notions of a Basque polity and a distinct Basque identity have existed for centuries, as evidenced in historical work on the 'foral' (or chartered) rights and privileges (Spanish: *fueros*, Basque: *foruak*) codified in mediaeval times (see for instance Heiberg 1989; Zia 2005). As an organized political movement, Basque nationalism has its roots in the founding of the Basque Nationalist Party (Partido Nacionalista Vasco, PNV) by Sabino Arana in 1895, at a time when rapid industrialization brought a sudden influx of migrant workers to the region (Sullivan 1988: 1).

Contemporary discourse on Basque nationhood and independence continues to revolve around the idea of the Basque Country (Basque: Euskal Herria) as a unified territory spanning the Pyrenean Mountains and the border between Spain and France. The Basque territories of Spain, or the 'southern Basque Country' (Basque: Hego Euskal Herria; Hegoalde) comprises the Chartered Community of Navarre (Comunidad Foral de Navarra, Basque: Nafarroako Foru Komunitatea) and the three provinces of the present-day Autonomous Community of the Basque Country (Comunidad Autónoma del País Vasco; Basque: Euskal Autonomia Erkidegoa): Alava (Araba), Vizcaya (Bizkaia), and Guipúzcoa (Gipuzkoa). The French part of the Basque country (Basque: Iparralde) consists of Labourd (Lapurdi), Soule (Zuberoa; Xiberoa) and Basse-Navarre (Nafarroa Beherea; Nafarroa Baxenabarre), all in the département des Pyrénées-Atlantiques (previously known as Basses-Pyrénées). Basque nationalists have long called for the unification of all these regions under one Basque sovereign domain.

The four Basque territories in Spain, Navarra, Araba, Bizkaia and Gipuzkoa, carry the epithet of 'the four in one' (Basque: *laurak bat*). While nationalists insist on the unity of the four, they are also attributed unique political histories. Spanning the Pyrenean mountain range, Navarra was founded in the ninth century after a rebellion against Frankish authority and remained a sovereign kingdom until 1512, when it was occupied by the troops of Ferdinand the Catholic of Aragon, husband of Queen Isabella of Castile. After the invasion, Navarra was divided and a viceroyalty was established in Navarra south of the Pyrenees, while the territory north of the mountains (Basse-Navarre) remained as a kingdom.

Bizkaia was established in 1072 as a lordship (Basque: *jaurerria*). As a major Atlantic port, Bizkaia had its own customs offices in Balmaseda and Urduña, and a consulate in Bruges. Since the fourteenth century, Bizkaia, Araba and Gipuzkoa each had their own representative assembly (Basque: *batzar nagusiak*; Spanish: *juntas generales*). In 1379, King John I of Castile became Lord of Bizkaia (Spanish: *Señorío de Vizcaya*), and the lordship was thereby integrated into the Crown of Castile and eventually the kingdom of Spain. Nevertheless, the three provinces managed to retain a virtually independent status until the nineteenth century, with the rights and privileges of each province codified in charters known as *fueros*. The earliest example of this is the Old Law (Spanish: *Fuero Viejo*), which was passed in Bizkaia in 1452. This was made famous in the Anglophone world by William Wordsworth's poem 'The Oak of Guernica' (1810), which tells the story of the assembly of Bizkaian lawmakers gathered under an old oak tree. Wordsworth described the lawmakers as 'Guardians of Biscay's ancient liberty'. Basque historians have reiterated this view, maintaining that the Old Law was based on established Basque customs and codes that provided extraordinary individual and collective liberties (Zallo 2007; Zia 2005).

Another important aspect of Basque national identity is related to the claim to universal nobility (see Totoricaguena 2004; Woodworth 2002). Historians have asserted that the doctrine of universal nobility was made official in 1526, when the Bizkaian General Assembly (*Juntas Generales*) approved the New Law of Bizkaia (*Fuero Nuevo de Bizkaia*), 'by which the status of nobility was applied to all native residents of the territory' (Muro 2013: 31). In 1610, a similar law passed in Gipuzkoa was to give citizens similar rights to fiscal benefits, exemption from military service beyond the Basque country and representation in the General Assembly.

The French Basque country (Basque: Iparralde; literally 'northern side') is also accredited with a unique history. Along with Gascony, the territories of Labourd and Soule came under English rule in 1152 with the marriage of Eleanor of Aquitane to Henry Plantagenet, also known as King Henry II of England. According to royal practice at the time, a monetary compensation secured the autonomy of these territories, re-codified by King Edward II of England in 1311 (Jacob 1994: 4). In 1451, at the end of the Hundred Years' War, Labourd and Soule passed to the Crown of France with the Treaty of Ayherre. Hence, both of these territories became French provinces (French: *pays d'état*), though royal charters codified customary rights and privileges. The *Coutume* (custom) of Labourd (1514) covered the right to bear arms, free travel and transport of goods, and rights of free assembly to deal with matters of common interest (Jacob 1994: 15). Labourd was also exempt from a number of taxes, duties and obligations known elsewhere in France (ibid.: 6), while the *Coutume* of Soule (1520) similarly protected citizens from servile obligations and granted freedom of movement, the right to carry arms, right of political assembly and unrestricted hunting and fishing privileges (ibid.: 5).

The third Basque territory in France, Basse-Navarre (Lower Navarre), made up the northernmost district of the Kingdom of Navarra until the polity was divided in 1512. When King Henry III of Navarre succeeded to the throne of France in 1589, he was also the direct agnatic descendant of Louis IX of France. He was therefore proclaimed king under the name of Henry IV of France and Navarre. In 1620–24, during the reign of Henry's son Louis XIII, critical powers of the parliament and courts of Basse-Navarre were transferred to the French Crown.

During the French Revolution, all the Basque areas of France (Basse-Navarre, Labourd and Soule) were incorporated into Basses-Pyrénées, one of the original departments of the French Republic established in 1790. Two years later the monarchy was abolished, and the last 'King of France and Navarre', Louis XVI, was executed. The French Republic discontinued all codified customs and agreements with local regimes. Beginning in the nineteenth century, Basque communities in Spain were also struggling to hold on to chartered privileges and powers of autonomy. After the First Carlist War, Navarra negotiated the *Ley Paccionada* (Compromise Act) of 1841, granting administrative and fiscal privileges against acceptance of the transformation of the viceroyalty of Navarra into a province. The other Basque polities clung to their autonomy throughout the Carlist Wars (1833–76), supporting the Carlist pretender to the throne. In 1876, the troops of Alfonso XII defeated the Carlists, and Basque charters were hence reduced to Economic Agreements.

The Basque Nationalist Party was founded in the 1890s, in the aftermath of a popular protest centered in Navarra, known as the Gamazada Uprising. Among the key goals of the nationalists was to create a unified political status for the

Basque territories. In 1923, however, General Miguel Primo de Rivera established military rule in Spain. This eventually provoked an anti-monarchist campaign to overthrow the dictatorship, launched in the Basque city of Donostia (also known as San Sebastián) with the August 1930 signing of the Pact of San Sebastián. When the Second Republic of Spain was proclaimed in April 1931, the Spanish King Alfonso XIII went into exile. The Republicans then drafted a new constitution, approved in December 1931, creating a secular democratic system in which both the Spanish head of state and the head of government were to be elected. The new constitution introduced equal rights for all citizens, a wide range of civil liberties, female suffrage, free secular education for all, and civil marriage and divorce. The Republican constitution also included provisions for regional autonomy. In 1932, a statue of autonomy for Cataluña was approved, while the Republicans started negotiations with Andalucía, Aragón, and Galicia. In the Basque country, efforts were first made to draft a single statute for Navarra and the three Basque provinces (*provincias Vascongadas*). After the Navarrese withdrew support, the 'Statute of Estella' was presented in 1932, modelled on the Catalan statute. However, when the statute was finally approved in 1936, it could only be implemented in Bizkaia due to the outbreak of the Spanish Civil War.

During the Civil War (1936–39), the Basque region was again divided. The local governments of Araba and Navarra sided with the fascist 'rebels' under General Francisco Franco. They were hence able to retain a considerable degree of autonomy, running independent telephone companies, police forces and public road works, and maintaining taxation rights. Meanwhile, Basque nationalists supporting the Republicans ruled Bizkaia and Gipuzkoa. In 1937, their troops were forced to surrender to General Franco, and the Provisional Basque Government under Lehendakari (President) José Antonio Aguirre sought refuge in Barcelona. Two years later, in 1939, the Basque government left Barcelona for American exile.

General Franco's defeat of the Republicans was followed by suppression of Basque culture, including a ban on the public use of the Basque language. In 1959, young nationalists (Basque: *abertzaleak*) founded the separatist group Euskadi 'ta Askatasuna (ETA). Starting with non-violent activism, ETA adopted violence after the repression of Basque activists during the mid-1960s, inspired by Marxist revolutionary theory. The ensuing spiral of armed conflict was driven by the violent actions and reactions of ETA and Spanish security forces, eventually giving rise to paramilitary agencies such as GAL (Grupos Antiterroristas de Liberación, Anti-Terrorist Liberation Groups).

After the death of Franco in 1975, Spain began a process of transition to democracy led by King Juan Carlos I, the first reigning Spanish monarch since 1931. Subsequent to the approval by referendum of a new Constitution in 1978, self-governing communities (Spanish: *comunidades autónomas*) were established, and special powers were devolved to the new 'autonomous' areas. The Constitution of 1978 acknowledged the national and cultural plurality of Spain and recognized the right to self-government of the country's 'nationalities':

> The Constitution is based on the indissoluble unity of the Spanish Nation, the common and indivisible homeland of all Spaniards; it recognizes and

guarantees the right to self-government of the nationalities and regions of which it is composed and the solidarity among them all.
(Preliminary Title, Section 2, English translation of the Spanish Constitution)[2]

The Constitution's Chapter III on Self-governing Communities spells out the implications of the right to self-government. Section 143.1 grants the right to 'accede to self-government and form Self-governing Communities' and identifies the holders of this right as 'bordering provinces with common historic, cultural and economic characteristics, insular territories and provinces with a historic regional status'. While the right to self-government is thus in itself quite broadly defined, Section 145.1 draws a clear limit to this right by stating, 'Under no circumstances shall a federation of Self-governing Communities be allowed'. It is important to note that the Constitution describes a process through which a Statute of Autonomy can be drawn up, approved and amended, and it lists a set of competences that Self-governing Communities may assume and ways in which they can be funded, both by taxation and other means. It does not, however, refer to any particular community, nationality or region that might become a Self-governing Community under the new Constitution (such as the Basque or Catalan). This essentially left the Spanish map of autonomous regions open, as autonomy became available to any Spanish region that demanded it, which also served to delink autonomy from recognition of a separate identity. According to a popular expression, there was 'coffee for everybody' (Spanish: *café para todos*) until a political settlement outlined the territorial division of Spain in 1982 (see Elvira 2011).

The fourth Transitional Provision of the Constitution opened up for the incorporation of Navarra into the Basque Autonomous Community:

[I]n the case of Navarra, and for the purpose of its integration into the General Basque Council or into the autonomous Basque institutions which may replace it, the procedure contemplated by section 143 of this Constitution shall not apply. The initiative shall lie instead with the appropriate historic institution (órgano foral), whose decision must be taken by the majority of its members. The initiative shall further require for its validity the ratification by a referendum expressly held to this end and approval by the majority of votes validly cast.
(Transitional Provisions, English translation of the Spanish Constitution)[3]

Despite this provision, two separate Autonomous Communities were subsequently created in Hegoalde. The Statute of Autonomy of the Basque Country was passed in 1979[4] and thereafter approved by referendum, while the Statute of Autonomy of Navarre was approved in 1992 by a unique procedure,[5] as an Improvement of the Ancient Legal Charter and without a referendum. The Statute of Autonomy of the Basque Country was drafted with a view to gain all powers and competencies not reserved for the State, including education, health, welfare and public safety, and to give the Autonomous Community almost full financial autonomy (Urrutia and Nikolas 2016). Powers held historically by the chartered governments were hence returned to the new governments of the Autonomous Community of the

Basque Country (ACBC) and Chartered Community of Navarre. The chartered governments (Spanish: *diputación foral*, Basque: *foru aldundia*) were thus partially restored.

New frontiers of sovereignty

As the Statute of Autonomy of Navarre was finally approved, Basque identity politics was overshadowed by major developments on the European political scene. In 1992, members of the European Economic Community (EEC) signed the Treaty on European Union, mandating the creation of seven key institutions: the European Parliament, the European Council, the Council of the European Union, the European Commission, the Court of Justice of the European Union, the European Central Bank and the Court of Auditors. The Schengen Agreement took effect in 1995, a decade after it was initially signed. Restrictions on cross-border travel and communication between France and Spain were thereby lifted. This greatly facilitated cross-border communication between the northern and southern parts of the Basque country.

Over the years, EU policymaking has had increasing impact on local socio-economic conditions across Europe, as evidenced by the growing number of EU programs, regulations and institutional mechanisms. In 1999, Spain and France were among the nineteen EU member states that joined the monetary union adopting the Euro (€) as the common currency. Another major landmark was the signing of the Lisbon Treaty, which came into force in December 2009 after approval by all twenty-seven national parliaments of EU member states. Difficult negotiations preceded the agreement, especially on the original proposal to create a European Constitution, accept the supremacy of EU law over national law and give vast powers to a European Union 'foreign minister'. The 2009 Lisbon Treaty provided the European Central Bank with the powers of a full-fledged central bank and brought nearly all policy areas including the budget under the co-decision procedure, hence increasing the power of the European Parliament.

In 2010, then-President of the European Council Herman Van Rompuy created intense controversy when he claimed that 'the age of the nation state is over'.[6] Mounting integration among EU countries, increasing freedom of movement and loss of national legislative powers has sparked fierce debates on statehood, sovereignty and democracy across Europe. In 2014, citizens of Bulgaria and Romania gained full access to the EU labor market, fuelling Western European concerns about a potential surge of welfare immigration. In the United Kingdom, the controversy triggered David Cameron's 2015 campaign promise to renegotiate British membership in the EU, and later hold a referendum on exiting or staying in the Union ('Brexit').

Despite the claim that the EU is primarily about economic integration and 'managing the European marketplace' (Dinan 2004: 9), there is mounting controversy over freedom of movement and migration, and a widening gap between decision-makers and the general public. Issues of sovereignty are thus at the heart of continuous disagreements between 'nationalists' and proponents of Europeanization, as became clear in the 'Brexit' referendum (United Kingdom European Union membership referendum 2016). Old and new sovereignty demands are also emerging at the sub-state level, as evidenced by the 2014 Scottish referendum, the Catalan popular consultation in 2014, and its follow-up in 2017.

The pan-European tension over nationhood and integration has not left the debate about Basque sovereignty and self-determination unaffected. New practices and tools of governance and changing regulations on citizenship and mobility within the Eurozone have essentially created new conditions for exercising state sovereignty. This has informed current debates in the Basque country, where we find a growing recognition of the complexity of Basque identity and a new attention to the 'self' of self-determination and to the holder of the 'right to decide'.

The state is still the blueprint for sovereignty in the contemporary world order, despite the predictions of globalization scholars on its imminent demise (Agnew 2009; Evans 1997; Everard 1999; Hansen and Stepputat 2005; Sidaway 2003). State boundaries continue to define the political map of the world, while militaries are preoccupied with 'securing' territories. The capacity for power of contemporary states is also what makes state- and nationhood so fiercely contested.

Despite the importance of the state as a blueprint or a vehicle of sovereignty, it is also true that statehood is a risky business, exercised under increasingly precarious conditions. State sovereignty is under pressure from increasing global interconnectedness and interdependence of markets and business conglomerates, and the development of new international mechanisms and technologies of governance (Barber 1995; Batliwala and Brown 2006; Gabel and Bruner 2003; Roht-Arriaza 2006). The changes are not simply about the acceleration of globalization or the development of new autonomy arrangements and forms of consultation to protect indigenous rights, improved federal structures and devolution of powers.

What is at stake in these transformations is not so much the role of the state as an organizational unit in the global order but the very idea of the significance of 'statehood', or the links between sovereignty and the state. The nature of sovereignty itself is in a process of transformation, especially as sovereign powers and functions are taken over by public-private partnerships of state and non-state structures. Civil society has entered the scene in unprecedented ways. One example is the Arctic Council, which has evolved as a novel mechanism for sovereignty sharing (Dingman 2011; Grant 2010) and an example of 'social sovereignty' (Latham 2000) by including state and non-state actors in its organizational structure. As Latham (2000: 3) points out, what is at stake in the new approach is not the status of the agent, 'but of a body of relations that shape spheres of life operating within or even across state boundaries'.

The Basque case revisited

The creation of a democratic, multi-national Spanish state has occurred in parallel with changing practices and notions of sovereignty, simultaneously encouraging and disappointing the two 'nationalities' in Spain with the strongest sense of nationhood, namely the Basques and the Catalans. This eventually resulted in two clear proposals to reconsider the relationship of these two 'nationalities' with Spain in an effort to create independent states. Why did a system of autonomous regions, created specifically to accommodate the autonomy demands of diverse communities turn into a source of tension if not outright conflict? To explain this paradox, we need to look beyond contemporary identity construction in the peripheries, or the 'idea of Spain' and its multi-national state-building since 1975. What is needed is to shift our focus to the logics of sovereignty over time and the rationalization of power that has simultaneously opened up spaces for its contestation.

For the sake of this analysis, we can imagine globalization as a continuum of societal interconnectedness, complexity and interdependence, though by no means a linear history. Focusing on key events of importance to sovereignty as exercised or practiced, Table 0.1 below draws up a very rough timeline or chronology of events. The Treaty of Westphalia (1648) and the French Revolution (1789–99) are included as key landmarks in European history. According to scholars, the origins of the modern international system of states, multinational corporations and organizations are all associated with the Peace of Westphalia (Gabel and Bruner 2003: 2). The French Revolution is similarly considered important, not only for the transition of France from a monarchy to a republic but also in creating a new blueprint for sovereignty rooted in the people as opposed to the regent. This established democracy as popular rule, or rule by the will of the people, as the basis for legitimate governance poses a major challenge to the prevailing doctrine of royal absolutism. As our chronology illustrates, however, the Treaty of Westphalia and French Revolution do not fit into a progressive linear history of gradual evolution from religious and royal absolutism towards secular and popular democratic versions of sovereignty. In fact, many European democracies remain constitutional monarchies. In Spain, anti-monarchism gave impetus to the 1931 Republic, but the Civil War soon followed, resulting in almost four decades of dictatorship. Today, Spain is again a monarchy, but now also a democracy. Ironically, the King of Navarra lives on despite the demise of the Kingdom of Navarra centuries ago. What this history highlights is the complexity and contingency of contemporary notions of sovereignty, not just in the postcolonial peripheries but in the very heartland of Westphalian Europe.

After the end of the Cold War and the subsequent reunification of Germany, scholars have reached for 'neo-medievalist' metaphors and models from the age of Empire, as they attempted to elucidate the new sovereignty order of 'post-wall' Europe (Wæver 1997; Østergaard 1997; Sassen 2006). Others used the metaphor of Empire when describing the global role of the USA (Hardt and Negri 2000, 2004). At the same time, sovereignty was becoming increasingly illusive with the rise of multinationals and global integration shaped by corporate power. As described by Gabel and Bruner (2003), of the world's hundred largest economies at the turn of the millennium, half were corporations, controlling most of the world's energy, technology, food, banks, industry and media. For some, sovereignty appears more and more like 'organized hypocracy' (Krasner 1999).

Table 0.1 Chronology of sovereignty-related events

Year	Event
602	'Wasconia' set up by Franks as a frontier duchy during wars with Visigoths
660	Felix of Aquitaine becomes Duke of both Vasconia and Aquitaine
732	The Battle of Tours allows the Duchy of Vasconia to expand south of the Pyrenees
824	Kingdom of Pamplona founded after rebellion against Frankish authority
1072	Lordship of Bizkaia established
1152	Gascony, Labourd, Soule become English with marriage of Henry II to Eleanor of Aquitane
1379	John I of Castile becomes Lord of Bizkaia, integrating Bizkaia into Castile
1451	Treaty of Ayherre ends Hundred Years' War; France absorbs Labourd and Soule
1452	'Old Law' of Bizkaia passed at Gernika (Guernica)
1512	Castilian Crown invades Kingdom of Navarra, sets up viceroyalty south of the Pyrenees
1514	'Custom' of Labourd codified
1520	'Custom' of Soule codified
1526	'New Law' of Bizkaia passed
1589	Henry III of Navarre succeeds to the throne of France as Henry IV
1618	Beginning of Thirty Years' War, pitting Roman Catholics against Protestants
1624	Basse-Navarre loses critical powers to the Crown of France under King Louis XIII
1648	Treaty of Westphalia allegedly establishes sovereign statehood based on territorial integrity
1789	French Revolution begins
1790	Basses-Pyrénées founded as one of eighty-three French departments
1792	Crown of France formally abolished
1841	First Carlist War ends; Navarra viceroyalty becomes Spanish province
1876	Carlists defeated in Spain; Basque charters reduced to Economic Agreements
1893	Gamazada Uprising breaks out in Navarra
1895	Basque Nationalist Party founded in Spain
1923	Military rule established in Spain
1931	Second Republic of Spain proclaimed; King Alfonso XIII exiled
1936	Civil War breaks out in Spain
1939	Provisional Basque Government under Lehendakari Aguirre leaves Barcelona for exile
1944	Bretton Woods Conference gathers in New Hampshire, USA
1955	General Franco's Spain is accepted into the United Nations
1957	Treaty of Rome establishes the European Economic Community (EEC)
1959	ETA formation announced
1975	Franco dies; transition to democracy starts under King Juan Carlos I
1978	New Spanish constitution approved, offering regional autonomy
1979	Provisional Basque Government-in-exile dissolved
1986	Spain enters the EEC
1992	The Treaty on European Union is signed by EEC members
1999	Monetary union of EU member states adopts the Euro (€) as common currency

(Continued)

Table 0.1 (Continued)

Year	Event
2003	The Ibarretxe Plan is approved by the Basque Government
2004	The Madrid terror attack; Crown Prince Felipe joins a government-organized protest
2005	The Ibarretxe Plan is rejected by the Spanish Parliament
2011	ETA declares the definitive end to its armed activity
2014	Felipe VI becomes King of Spain following the abdication of his father Juan Carlos I
2014	Catalan 'referendum' on secession from Spain; of 2.3 million voters, eighty per cent favor independence

Terms like contingent sovereignty, social sovereignty, shared sovereignty, graduated sovereignty, fragmented sovereignty and qualified sovereignty have all been used to try to grasp the new global order. Innovative topics such as consumer sovereignty and food sovereignty have also emerged (see Conversi, this volume), showing up the antagonism between concerns for bare survival and fantasies of global governance. Cosmopolitanism and hypermodernity coexist with neo-tribalism and the search for roots. Slavery has by no means disappeared; it has become part and parcel of Sovereignty Inc. While new models and blueprints are developing, ranging from the post-Imperialism of the Eurozone to the public-private partnership of the Arctic Council, old ideas and notions of sovereignty still live on in the popular imagination, whether in stories of the *Juntas Generales* and the Oak of Guernica or fairytales about kings and queens.

The chapters of this book

The overall concept of this volume takes an anthropological perspective on the contestation of Basque sovereignty, or the sovereignty-state equation, as it is contested and negotiated not only within conventional party politics but also in grassroots activism and everyday life.

Our focus is therefore on sovereignty as practiced, experienced, imagined and understood from grassroots perspectives. Nevertheless, the contributions to this volume display a diversity of perspectives, including geographical, institutional and disciplinary, covering expressions of Basque identity and related debates in the Basque communities of the diaspora as well as Spain and France.

In the first chapter, Daniele Conversi describes 'sovereignty in a changing world', tracing the shifting meaning of the concept of sovereignty from the premodern age to the era of globalization and applying it to the evolution of radical nationalism in the Basque country. Conversi first detects the term's epochal semantic shifts and its centrality in the configuration of the modern age, particularly the international relations system, then tracks the development of grassroots concepts of Basque national sovereignty since the foundation of ETA (1959), through the democratic transition (1975–80) and up to the current peace process. As described here, changing practices of governance are reflected in shifting perceptions and discourses of sovereignty from the transition to the peace process, culminating in the 2011 international conference at Aiete which marked the end of ETA's violence. These changes include the way sovereignty and territoriality are imagined and debated, through evolving visions of political legitimacy and political representation. The notion of *liquid sovereignty* is introduced as a possible framework for analysis, but this is set against rapid changes in the concept of sovereignty as a consequence of the unfolding environmental global emergency. The chapter finally ventures into theorizing the surfacing of new forms of sovereignty centred on aliments, nutrition and survival, namely *food sovereignty*, often emerging in opposition to the seizure of land by corporate and market-related forces. Conversi questions whether these emerging notions of sovereignty can fully reflect the adaptation of the term to new and unforeseen circumstances.

The following chapter, authored by Iban Galletebeitia and Pedro Ibarra Güell, describes changes in the Basque sovereignty demand over the same time period, with a focus on how the demand has been constructed. It does so in a dynamic and evolutionary form, considering the social context and collective consciousness that has given rise to imagined conceptions of sovereignty, including political, cultural, economic and institutional factors – and their corresponding mobilizations – causing the demand for sovereignty to advance or retreat. Finally, the chapter describes how these factors have in turn defined different types of sovereign national consciousness as Basque actors have reoriented their discourse on the nature of sovereignty to encompass new recognitions of the complexity of multiple identities and reflections on the changing implications of nationhood and citizenship under transnational impacts.

In the next chapter, Mario Zubiaga returns to the evolution of Basque nationalism in Spain, arguing that the demand for Basque self-government coincided with the process of democratization that began after the end of the Franco regime. Importantly, however, Basque nationalists were not homogeneous in positioning themselves to the transition of Spain to democracy. While the moderate faction, articulated around the Basque Nationalist Party, opted to negotiate an autonomous institutional framework within the Spanish constitutional system established in 1978, the more radical sectors headed by the *ezkerra abertzale* (patriotic left) rejected this autonomy model and advocated a break-away stance backed by the armed action of ETA. This strategic divergence within Basque nationalism meant that demands for sovereignty made by the two great *abertzale* 'families' were configured differently. Speeches that upheld those demands, their scope, the specific proposals linked with them, and the ways of manifesting them both through institutional action and collective mobilization, have been largely at cross-purposes with one another. Thus, the nationalist contention was played out on a dual stage. On the one hand, the Basque political assertion in both its manifestations – institutional and anti-system – confronted the agents of the Spanish political system. On the other hand, on the internal stage, the two ways of making the demand for sovereignty interacted with one another contentiously. On the first stage and with regard to the main state agents, no changes of note are apparent in the conceptualization of sovereignty. However, from the early 1990s onwards, the evolution in theoretical terms that has taken place in the concept of sovereignty and in stateless nations' ways of asserting it, and the emergence of opportunities and threats in both the international and national contexts, have favoured a certain process of discursive convergence on the internal stage, always mediated by certain actors/brokers and conditioned by the party political competence existing within Basque nationalism. This strategic convergence, even though relative and fluctuating, can be understood as a manifestation consistent with the logic of the internal democratization process, insofar as the contemporary Basque nationalist contention is inseparable from that process – so much so that there is an actual overlap between state-, nation- and democracy-building in the Basque sphere.

The identity politics of the Basque diaspora is the topic of the following chapter, penned by Pedro J. Oiarzabal. The Basque diaspora has an institutional presence, centennial in some cases, in over twenty countries. This chapter presents findings from a study of institutional relations between the Basque government and the Basque diaspora worldwide since the 1980s. The study is based on in-depth interviews with Basque policymakers and diaspora leaders, and participant observation in diaspora community events and activities. In this chapter, Oiarzabal explores the ways that Basque diaspora communities and their institutions live, experience, imagine and deal with the highly contested meanings of identity, nationhood and homeland. This sheds light on the role that diaspora communities play in the daily reconstruction and renegotiation of ideas of nationhood and homeland, embedded in local as well as transnational practices. Though the Basque homeland is currently divided into three political administrations under France and Spain, the government of the Basque Autonomous Community has assumed much (if not all) the institutional representation in the diaspora since Spain's return to democracy in 1978. The government of the Basque Autonomous Community has undeniably served as the main homeland institutional reference for the Basque diaspora for the last decades, just as it was during the period of the Basque government-in-exile (1937–78). Nevertheless, this chapter highlights the complexity and multi-directionality of diaspora-homeland relations, the irregular impact of the diaspora on homeland affairs, and the uneven commitment of homeland politicians to the diaspora. In sum, it presents a fine-grained analysis of the complex relationship of the Basque diaspora with its homeland.

In the literature on peripheral nationalism, the French Basque country (Iparralde) is often seen as a case of 'failed' political nationalism, in contrast to the 'success' of its southern counterpart. As Xabier Itçaina points out in the following chapter of this volume, such a view tends to reduce identity politics to its electoral, party-political, and 'non-conventional' (or violent) expressions. In particular, it excludes civil society mobilizations that are perceived as relatively distant from the sphere of electoral politics. Since the 1970s, mobilizations concerning Basque language and culture, sustainable farming and social and solidarity-based economic activity have been important for the notion of a shared territorial destiny in Iparralde. Such mobilizations are diverse and do not operate according to a unified ideological pattern. Nevertheless, they should not be considered as constituting the mere cultural, social or economic aspects of Basque nationalism. This chapter argues that, in a Europeanized and globalized context, territorial *and* sectorial dimensions generate specific sets of constraints and resources for each of these mobilizations. In concrete terms, each one of the above-mentioned sectors (language and culture, sustainable farming, social- and solidarity-based economy) are subject to different (macro, meso and micro) scales of governance. Therefore, their daily experiences of sovereignty will vary according to the way each sector is governed. This chapter assumes that a reinforced Basque territorial autonomy is crucial for the social movement promoting Basque language and culture, while it has few consequences for milk producers depending on EU policy-making and global markets. Other small farmers, in turn, are demanding specific institutions for Basque farming, thus trying to establish horizontal alliances with consumers and environmentalists. Similarly, activists of the social and solidarity-based economy are developing social innovations such as the *Eusko* local currency in order to generate small-scale economic spaces and networks, and a circulation of goods *within* the boundaries of Iparralde. Case studies allow us to address the way multiple conceptions of sovereignty are experienced in the daily life of citizens of the Basque country in France, in their respective sectors and 'infra-territories'. The argument of this chapter unfolds following a historical-sequential approach by distinguishing (a) political, cultural and economic protest movements in the 1970s and 1980s; (b) the partial institutionalization of civil society mobilizations within the new territorial governance of the French Basque country in the 1990s and (c) the current multiplicity of 'imagined sovereignties' at work within the pluralistic civil society mobilizations involving cultural and socio-economic affairs.

The following chapter, authored by Jule Goikoetxea, describes Basque identity and sovereignty within a European context. To understand the current Basque political identity and its coupling with sovereignty demands, Goikoetxea maintains that it is necessary to analyze the general preconditions for a nation to survive as a *demos* in twenty-first-century Europe. In other words, what is required from a Basque identity for it to survive as a political identity? This chapter argues that in the Basque case, some of the conditions are absent, and that the absence of these conditions is precisely what gives rise to sovereignty demands. Goikoetxea enquires how particular institutional and political workings give concrete meaning to key terms such as 'nation', 'identity', 'sovereignty' and 'democratic governance', which articulate both nationalist and democratic practices, discourses and identities, including political demands. She argues that the 2004 Basque Project for a New Statute of Autonomy arose not from a nineteenth-century ethno-centric Basque nationalism, but from a twenty-first-century federal political entity that had shaped and most effectively met the needs of its population, and hence managed to uphold its claim to the monopoly of authoritative law-making more successfully than the Spanish state itself. Through this discussion, Goikoetxea makes clear why the dominant Basque political parties (representing more than sixty per cent of voters at the time) insisted on laying out new constitutional futures for the Basque Autonomous Community. The main objectives were, firstly, to show the empirical connections that existed in the Autonomous Community of the Basque Country (ACBC) between sovereignty, democracy and identity, and secondly, to explain why these connections take on such a highly contentious character in political communities that do not control their own state, such as the Basque community, and in states that do not include their different political communities in the governance of the polity, such as the Spanish state.

The concluding chapter of this volume is a collaborative effort by the Basque scholars Pedro Ibarra Güell, Iban Galletebeitia, Jule Goikoetxea, Mario Zubiaga and Igor Ahedo, together with two colleagues from Cataluña, Javier Alcalde and Pablo Aguiar. In itself an experiment in democratic sovereignty-sharing, this chapter revisits the contemporary Basque demand for sovereignty in an attempt to bring back together the fragments and pieces of deconstructed concepts and retell the story of Basque sovereignty for the twenty-first century.

Notes

1 The video can be viewed online at: www.bbc.com/news/world-europe-39540081
2 Online at: www.lamoncloa.gob.es/lang/en/espana/leyfundamental/Paginas/index.aspx
3 Online at: www.congreso.es/portal/page/portal/Congreso/Congreso/Hist_Normas/Norm/const_espa_texto_ingles_0.pdf
4 Organic Law 3/1979, on the Statute of Autonomy for the Basque Country (18 December 1979).
5 Organic Law 13/1982, on Reintegration and Improvement of the Foral Regime of Navarre (10 August 1982).
6 See Daniel Martin, Nation states are dead: EU chief says the belief that countries can stand alone is a 'lie and an illusion', MailOnline 11 November 2010, available at: www.dailymail.co.uk/news/article-1328568/Nation-states-dead-EU-chief-says-belief-countries-stand-lie.html#ixzz3ZFvjcAv3

References

Agnew, J. 2009. *Globalisation and Sovereignty*. Lanham: Rowman and Littlefield.
Anderson, B. 1983. *Imagined Communities*. New York: Verso.
Barber, B. R. 1995. *Jihad vs. McWorld: How Globalism and Tribalism Are Reshaping the World*. New York, NY: Ballantine Books.
Batliwala, S., and Brown, D. L., eds. 2006. *Transnational Civil Society: An Introduction*. Bloomfield, CT: Kumarian Press.
Biersteker, T., and Weber, C., eds. 1996. *State Sovereignty as Social Construct*. Cambridge Studies in International Relations. Cambridge: Cambridge University Press.
Dinan, D. 2004. *Europe Recast: A History of European Union*. Boulder, CO: Lynne Rienner Publishers.
Dingman, E. 2011. 'Sovereignty Matters: States, Security and Climate Change in the Arctic', The World Policy Institute, New York, International Affairs Working Paper, 5 May, 2011.
Elvira, A. 2011. 'Spain', in D. Oliver and C. Fusaro, eds, *How Constitutions Change: A Comparative Study*. London: Bloomsbury Publishing.
Evans, P. 1997. 'The Eclipse of the State?', *World Politics*, 50: 62–87.
Everard, J. 1999. Virtual States: Globalisation, Inequality and the Internet. London: Routledge.
Gabel, M., and Bruner, H. 2003. *Global Inc.: An Atlas of the Multinational Corporation*. New York: The New Press.
Grant, S. 2010. *Polar Imperative: A History of Arctic Sovereignty in North America*. Vancouver: Douglas & McIntyre.
Hansen, T. B., and Stepputat, F., eds. 2005. *Sovereign Bodies: Citizens, Migrants, and States in the Postcolonial World*. Princeton, NJ: Princeton University Press.

Hardt, M., and Negri, A. 2000. *Empire*. London: Harvard University Press.

———. 2004. Multitude: War and Democracy in the Age of Empire. New York: Penguin.

Heiberg, M. 1989. *The Making of the Basque Nation*. Cambridge: Cambridge University Press.

Jacob, J. E. 1994. *Hills of Conflict: Basque Nationalism in France*. Reno, NV: University of Nevada Press.

Kolås, Å. 2016. 'Sovereignty at the Frontiers: Contests and Contradictions', in D. Gogoi, ed., *Unheeded Hinterland: Identity and Sovereignty in Northeast India*. New Delhi: Routledge India, pp. 17–29.

Krasner, S. D. 1999. *Sovereignty: Organized Hypocrisy*. Princeton, NJ: Princeton University Press.

Latham, R. 2000. 'Social Sovereignty', *Theory, Culture & Society*, 17(4): 1–18.

Liu, L. H. 2003. 'Desire and Sovereign Thinking', in J. Culler and P. Cheah, eds, *Grounds of Comparison: Around the Work of Benedict Anderson*. London: Routledge.

McLuhan, M. 1967. *The Medium Is the Massage: An Inventory of Effects*, illustrated by Quentin Fiore. London: Penguin Books.

Muro, D. 2013. *Ethnicity and Violence: The Case of Radical Basque Nationalism*. London: Routledge.

Østergaard, U. 1997. 'Nation-States and Empire in the Current Process of European Change', in O. Tunander, P. Baev and V. I. Einagel, eds, *Geopolitics in Post-Wall Europe: Security, Territory and Identity*. London: Sage, pp. 94–119.

Roht-Arriaza, N. 2006. *The Pinochet Effect: Transnational Justice in the Age of Human Rights*. Philadelphia, PA: University of Pennsylvania Press.

Sassen, S. 2006. *Territory, Authority, Rights: From Medieval to Global Assemblages*. Princeton, NJ: Princeton University Press.

Sidaway, J. 2003. 'Sovereign Excesses? Portraying Postcolonial Sovereigntyscapes', *Political Geography*, 22(2): 157–178.

Sullivan, J. 1988. ETA and Basque Nationalism: The Fight for Euskadi 1890–1986. London: Routledge.

Totoricaguena, G. P. 2004. *Identity, Culture, and Politics in the Basque Diaspora*. Reno, NV: University of Nevada Press.

Urrutia, I. and Nikolas, Z. 2016. 'Legal Limits of Decentralization in Spain: Accommodation or Secession?', in P. Ibarra Güell and Å. Kolås, eds, *Basque Nationhood. Towards a Democratic Scenario*. Oxford: Peter Lang, pp. 183–218.

Wæver, O. 1997. 'Imperial Metaphors: Emerging European Analogies to Pre-Nation-State Imperial Systems', in O. Tunander, P. Baev and V. I. Einagel, eds, *Geopolitics in Post-Wall Europe: Security, Territory and Identity*. London: Sage, pp. 59–93.

Wallerstein, I. (2004) *World-Systems Analysis: An Introduction*. Durham, NC: Duke University Press.

Weber, C. 1995. *Simulating Sovereignty: Intervention, the State, and Symbolic Exchange*. Cambridge: Cambridge University Press.

Woodworth, P. 2002. *Dirty War, Clean Hands: ETA, the GAL and Spanish Democracy*. New Haven, CT: Yale University Press.

Zallo, R. 2007. Basques, Today: Culture, History and Society in the Age of Diversity and Knowledge. Irun: Alberdania.

Zia, G. M., ed. 2005. The Old Law of Bizkaia (1452): Introductory Study and Critical Edition. Reno, NV: University of Nevada Press.

1 Sovereignty, boundaries and violence

Constructing the Basque national self (1959–2011)

Daniele Conversi

The modern notion of sovereignty developed in tandem with the post-Westphalian state system and with its systematic use of violence. It cannot be disentangled from violence itself. The shift from absolutist to popular sovereignty in the aftermath of the French Revolution implied an intensification of the modern state's violence and centralization, usually directed against both internal and external foes. In the logic of 'state-making and war-making as organize crime' (Tilly 1992, 2002), the modern state controlled, vetted, spied, imprisoned, persecuted, expelled and murdered its own citizens while reinforcing its boundaries with war. Amongst its internal victims, recalcitrant minorities stood out for specific forms of persecution going from assimilation to mass expulsion and elimination. The very existence of non-hegemonic groups, stateless nations and cultural, linguistic and religious minorities became incompatible with the homogenising visions that permeated the making of Western statehood. Cultural homogenization became the hallmark of the emergence and spread of the nation-state system (Conversi 2007, 2010) and the *conditio sine qua non* preluding to WWI, fascism and genocide. The latter would be unthinkable without the prior emergence of the former. Yet, is the relationship between sovereignty and violence only applicable to the state? Is the same relationship applicable, although perhaps to a lesser extent, to 'nations without a state'?

This chapter analyses the Basque case and sets it within the broader historical horizon of changing concepts of sovereignty. After briefly exploring the historical trajectory of the term 'sovereignty', this chapter considers some of the competing meanings currently associated with it. It does so first at a general theoretical level, and then at the level of transitional Basque politics. The time frame spans from 1959, when a 'rupture' within underground Basque nationalism gave rise to ETA (Euskadi 'ta Askatasuna; Basque Homeland and Freedom), until 2011, when ETA announced a definitive unilateral cessation of armed struggle. In the everyday Basque experience, the militancy associated with ETA has had a significant impact on perceptions of national sovereignty, with ETA raising the demand for Basque sovereignty as their key political objective. This has certainly had a great impact on the way 'sovereignty' began to be conceived, especially by the younger generations (Conversi 1997).

Sovereignty's semantic changes

The 'sovereign' was once a person within whom ultimate political authority resided and whose jurisdiction extended to, and was invested in, a specific territory. Charles Tilly identified 'fragmented sovereignty' as the dominant mode of governance in medieval and early modern Europe, with hundreds of city-states and minor principalities competing with empires and national states for territorial control – often over the same piece of land (Tilly 1992: 21, 31 and 40–41).[1]

Following the Reformation, religious conflict engulfed large swaths of the continent. According to the principle of *cuius regio, eius religio* ('whoever rules, his religion') adopted by the Peace of Augsburg (1555), the incumbent ruler's religious confession should apply to the whole citizenry within his territory, thus introducing state religion. The wars of religion took place also to make the state's territory more 'congruent' with the ruler's religious creed. Wars of religion constituted attempts at ideological rather than cultural homogenization: The former resulted in the expulsion and massacre of religious minorities, in which ideas of morality, righteousness and political legitimacy were all expressed through the adherence to an overarching shared religious idea and creed, while the latter would later result in the twentieth-century persecution of 'counter-entropic' minorities, in which common language, norms, traditions and set of behaviours, including dress and musical taste, were deemed to constitute a potential problem for, threat to, or deviance from patriotic loyalty Thus the move was from religious persecution to cultural homogenization.

After the wars of religion, the Peace of Westphalia (1648) recognized, among others, the principle of non-intervention into the internal affairs of all signatories. Westphalian sovereignty applied to specific territories, providing the foundation of the modern (i.e., Western) international state system, centred on the mutual respect of the principle of territorial integrity – thereby placing sovereignty in the hands of the ruler, as 'Power was circumscribed by whatever territory a ruler controlled' (Biersteker and Weber 1996). After the French Revolution, the entire edifice of absolutist legitimacy crumbled, and political authority became valid only if it reflected or embodied the will of the people (or nation). Since nationalism was predicated on the myth of a common origin, language provided the raw material and *prima facie* evidence of shared descent (i.e., nationhood). Yet, the state form was kept intact. Absolutist centralism became revolutionary centralism, and the principle of *cuius regio, eius religio* was replaced by that of *cuius regio, eius natio* ('whoever rules, his nation'). The relationship between Paris and the 'provinces' was not altered in form, but in intensity. And yet, the sovereign world order is a recent phenomenon and the 'pre-sovereign era' enveloped most of human history (Bellamy 2006). After the French Revolution, the state, as the key political institution, appropriated for itself the notion of sovereignty so that political legitimacy became increasingly based on national criteria. Modernity soon became articulated around the nation-state (Conversi 2012). Not only incumbent rulers and governments, but the entire state structure with its institutions had, at least nominally, to represent the 'people' they ruled, and these were defined on the basis of ethno-national criteria (Connor 2002). In the era of fiercely competing nation-states, popular sovereignty presupposed an internal cohesion and homogeneity (the 'people') that rarely, if ever, existed in reality. 'Counter-entropic' groups and individuals were eliminated through assimilation, discrimination, expulsion and mass murder (ethnic cleansing, genocide) (Mann 2005).

Sovereignty's meaning has shifted again since the inception of neoliberal globalisation. In most of the world, prevailing notions of sovereignty are being questioned after the social and political turmoil brought about by neo-liberal globalization since the 1980s (Conversi 2009). Already in the mid-1990s, Saskia Sassen described a 'de-sovereigntization' that later on became obvious and all pervasive:

> U.S. firms such as Ford, IBM, and Exxon now employ well over fifty percent of their workers overseas, rankling both domestic workers who argue that jobs are being exported while unemployment soars at home and activists who contend that wealthy corporations are exploiting low-wage workers in Third World nations. And as immigration levels soar, the very concept of citizenship has moved to the top of political agendas around the world.
>
> (Sassen 1996)

These changes have detracted legitimacy from the nation-state, as well as from specific governments, which are seen as no longer in charge, nor accountable. Walker Connor has underlined how political legitimacy became an essential attribute of modern governance and the very presence of a nationalist movement indicates how far a degree of political illegitimacy is vested in a particular 'host' state (Connor 2002). However, liberal pluri-national democracies cannot simply rest on mere majority rule (Conversi 2012), but require the successful involvement of all sections of society in the administrative process (Hannum 1996). The issue of sovereignty is therefore central to that of political legitimacy.

The next section charts the development of some of the above notions of sovereignty in the Basque context in the last about half a century.

Basque sovereignty and violence (1959–80)

At its inception, Basque nationalism was radical, but not violent. The choice of political violence was the distillation of long debates turning around mere survival and hopes of regeneration in one of the darkest hours of Basque history. ETA (Euskadi 'ta Askatasuna; Basque Homeland and Freedom) was founded on 31 July 1959, and its initial activities consisted largely of study meetings, producing a first assessment of the possibility to articulate a mass movement for Basque sovereignty and statehood. This was also the year that the Spanish economic policy changed into one of fast development (*desarrollismo*). Urbanization had begun to move vast numbers of people from Spain's countryside into Bilbao and other cities.

ETA's evolution accompanied, and reflected, all these developments. Initial public actions, while limited to the display of *ikurriñas* (Basque flags) and hand-daubing slogans and other graffiti, already implied the vision of a sovereign Basque homeland to be achieved through statehood. Amongst ETA's militants and supporters, ideals of sovereignty were visualised in a project of political independence. As we shall see, a class dimension was slowly added with the declared goal of a sovereign *socialist* republic.[2]

Whereas the early nationalism of Sabino Arana Goiri (1865–1903) focused on the centrality of race and religion (integral Catholicism), ETA was secularly oriented and rejected racism (Clark 1979, 1984; Garmendia 1979: 23; Gurrutxaga 1989; Ibarra Güell 1987; Letamendia Belzunde 1977; Pérez-Agote 1984, 1987). In their place, language emerged as the cornerstone of Basque identity. But, with the number of Basque speakers rapidly declining, the language-centred approach revealed a new anxiety about language shift and the possible eclipse of Basque identity. Gurutz Jáuregui Bereciartu uses what is, I believe, one of the clearest and most concise concepts coined for the study of Basque nationalism in general and in particular the feelings and attitudes prevailing in those years: '*sentimiento agónico*' or 'a feeling of agony' (Jáuregui Bereciartu 1981, 1996).[3] One of ETA's internal communiqués alarmingly declared that 'once language is lost', race could not sustain Basque identity.[4] This approach anticipates the more recent argument about the 'morality and mortality of nations' (Abulof 2015). Yet, these were largely the reflections of a highly conscious elite. How could violence arise from this?

It is crucial to consider that ETA was born as a political movement articulated around cultural concerns, first of all the fate of Euskera and local culture (Pérez-Agote 1984: 91). Since its beginning, the achievement of Basque independence went hand in hand with the revival of Basque culture and language. Given such cultural orientation, ETA remained for a long time partly at the margins of Basque society, counting on a few hundred activists and sympathizers. It remained so until state intervention and repression changed the social dynamics and cemented a shared sense of grievance within Basque society as a whole.

Although occasional acts of political violence had occurred already in 1961,[5] still in 1962 there was no agreement on the use of violence within ETA.[6] The first direct, armed attack occurred in 1965 (a robbery of a bank courier), and the first premeditated political killing was carried out in 1968 (the police commissioner Melitón Manzanas).

ETA's First Assembly (1962)[7] oriented the organization towards a 'revolutionary movement for national liberation' (Garmendia 1979: 19–21). In the book *Vasconia* (1963) by Federico Krutwig Sagredo (1921–98), a sovereign Basque imaginary was associated with a more clearly defined political, ideological and military programme (Krutwig Sagredo 1973).[8] Already in 1956, Krutwig had argued that, considering the decline of Euskera and other elements of Basque distinctiveness, 'violence' had become necessary to create a Basque nation (Krutwig Sagredo 1987). At that time, notions of sovereignty were couched in vague terms, and Krutwig envisaged it mostly on the basis of a federalist (or cantonalist) union of Basque territories. However, a map sketched in *Vasconia* incorporated a much broader territory than usual, including portions of the French region of Gascony (French: *Gascogne*, Spanish: *Gascuña*). Race was replaced by the concept of *ethnos*, as manifested through language and culture. Embracing stern anti-clericalism, religion was replaced by nationalism and the movement redefined as a-confessional and patriotic (Letamendia Belzunde 1975: 279). Krutwig's idea of politics as a vocation owed much to Ernest Renan's (1823–92) voluntarist view of the nation as a 'daily plebiscite' (Jáuregui Bereciartu 1981: 152). In fact, the stress on voluntary participation was, and remains, central to Left Basque nationalism. The strategic choice of guerrilla war as the only means to liberate Euskadi was inspired by the Algerian and Cuban revolutions, largely absorbed through the readings of Franz Fanon (1925–61). Anti-colonial violence was promulgated as a liberating force, essential to the psychological well-being of the 'oppressed' (Conversi 1993). The decision to embark on a violent path was confirmed in a forty-six-page booklet, *Insurrección en Euskadi*, written by José Luís Zalbide under the pseudonym of 'Zunbeltz' (Zalbide 1963). Entirely devoted to armed struggle, the pamphlet soon began to be used like a guerrilla manual, reiterating Krutwig's military strategy and emphasizing the Maoist aphorism of the guerrilla fighter who moves among his people as a 'fish in the water' (Krutwig Sagredo 1973: 330). Krutwig's and Zalbide's theses were approved in ETA's Second Assembly (1963), in which armed struggle was perceived as the only method of liberating Euskadi from its political shackles and cultural chains.

The Third Assembly (1964) saw a further shift towards the theorization of political violence, defining ETA as an anti-imperialist and anti-capitalist organization working for Euskadi's freedom, as well as for the emancipation of the working class.[9] The Fourth Assembly (1965) further stressed the programmatic link between social and national sovereignty, between class struggle and Basque liberation. Zalbide's theory of the 'cycle of action/repression/action' was approved by ETA as an article of faith (Zalbide 1963). It held that, where popular protest against injustices met with oppression, the revolutionary forces should act to punish the oppressor. The occupying forces would then retaliate with indiscriminate violence, since they would not know who the revolutionaries were, causing the population to respond with increased protest and support for the resistance in an upward spiral of resistance to the dictatorship. This theory was to provide the overall framework of ETA's strategy throughout its long evolution, turning it into a paramilitary organization. On the one hand, the revolutionary hypothesis rested on spurious empirical grounds, being largely imported from extra-European, non-liberal contexts. On the other hand, the relationship between state repression and the escalation of violence has been recently confirmed by social movement studies and political violence research (della Porta 2014).

Trotskyist, Third-Worldist (*tercermundista*), Maoist and 'culturalist' factions, the latter chiefly concerned with the survival of euskera and other elements of Basque culture, pursued their own visions of a sovereign state, which in turn reflected their respective ideological inclinations. The Fifth Assembly (1966–67) employed the concept of *Pueblo Trabajador Vasco* (Basque Working People) and vowed to combine nationalist with class struggle by joining labour unions' disputes, including direct support for the *Comisiónes Obreras*, the pro-Communist clandestine labour union (Garmendia 1979). Intense ideological debate took place in an atmosphere of confrontation polarized by secrecy and the fear of police intrusions. These conditions demanded one simple and unchallenged ideological choice. But this in turn led to excommunication and the proliferation of splinter groups and sub-groups in an unceasing process of self-definition. Yet, most people in Euskadi were oblivious to such internal conflicts and saw ETA as a homogeneous entity.

As mentioned earlier, political murders and assassinations began in June to August 1968. Despite hundreds of arrests and exiles, ETA continued to grow. In 1970, the Burgos Trial against sixteen ETA cadres (*etarras*) charged with the murder of Manzanas became a potential catalyst for Spain's democratic opposition, as well as an international standard to be invoked amongst left socialists worldwide (Halimi 1971). In all cases, Euskadi was conceived both as an internal colony and as an urban society in which the working class should play a decisive role in the building of Basque socialism. As most workers were immigrants from other regions of Spain, the emphasis had to be on class, rather than ethnic, conflict – pushing ETA's ideology further to the left. Indeed, ETA's radicals quickly found out that the immigrants were more likely to be involved whenever actions prevailed over theory and over 'abstract' debates on Basque identity (Zabalo et al. 2013).

Within Basque nationalism, the cultural nationalists played a key role in reinvigorating political nationalism by attempting to build up an inter-class alliance amongst all nationalist forces and focusing on visions of 'cultural sovereignty', that is, by pursuing the goal of an independent society articulated around the defence of a threatened cultural identity. Around 1971, the 'culturalists' within ETA proposed a *frente nacional* ('national front') to reunite all Basque nationalists from Left to Right in a common struggle to defend Basque identity and culture. The difference between ETA's Marxist leaders and 'bourgeois' nationalists was still problematic.

As regards Basque language, the early 1970s also saw an unprecedented revival through the expansion of the *ikastolak*, the primary and secondary schools where Euskera was the (main or only) medium of instruction. Although they had spread to most cities and villages, these efforts were heavily repressed under Francoism. The desire to protect and revive Basque culture, particularly language, transcended nationalism, and the non-nationalist Left played a key role in setting up the first *ikastolak*. While the spiral of violence grew, central authorities identified the entire cultural movement, including the *ikastolak*, as a receptacle for terrorism. The idea of a separate cultural sphere of sovereignty, however, was intrinsically tied to notions of political sovereignty, as culture and politics could not be easily disentangled.

During late Francoism, ETA reached a period of unequalled expansion, in which a fusion between Marxism and nationalism proved to be highly attractive. In this expansion, a new kind of sovereign imaginary linked up with the traditional stress on Basque egalitarianism and craving for social justice (Conversi 1997: 180; Hess 2009: ch. 1), whose roots can be traced back to the egalitarian 'familism' of the *baserritarrak*, that is, people whose livelihood is centred on the traditional Basque farmhouse or *baserri* (Zulaika 1988: 127).[10] Basque sovereignty was thus ideally conceived as reflecting a just and democratic space rooted in a clearly demarcated territory comprising all of its seven 'provinces' across the Pyrenees.

With the killing of the expected successor of Franco, Admiral Carrero Blanco (December 1973), ETA's star among their followers reached its pinnacle. Yet, internal fragmentation led ETA's fronts to act autonomously and in mutual competition, as did different sub-factions within them.[11] In 1974, an important split took place between ETA-m (ETA militar) and ETA-pm (ETA político-militar), while new mass protests prompted further states of emergency.

After the death of Francisco Franco (20 November 1975), Juan Carlos de Borbón was crowned King of Spain and immediately proclaimed a first general amnesty for about 15,000 political prisoners and exiles. Demands for a total amnesty deeply conditioned the relations between Basque activism and Madrid throughout the 'Transition'. As democratization continued, so did nationalism, the two being tightly bound up. Beyond free and fair elections, lifting the veil of censorship offered to many Basques their first opportunity for unrestricted expression. Notions of sovereignty were articulated and solidified in a context of weak state legitimacy and mounting popular mobilizations.

In 1976, under a King-appointed cabinet led by Adolfo Suárez, most political parties were legalized. Since the 1980 regional elections there has been considerable electoral stability with little transfer of votes between the two main blocks (nationalists and non-nationalists), and constant nationalist hegemony by the Basque National Party, PNV (Partido Nacionalista Vasco, or Eusko Alberdi Jeltzalea-Partido Nacionalista Vasco, EAJ-PNV). With around forty per cent of the votes, the moderate nationalists have thus remained consistently ahead of other parties.

Changing practices of Basque governance and national sovereignty

While the very visions of Spanish sovereignty seemed to mutate with the Transition, so did visions of Basque sovereignty. Immediately after the 1977 general elections, the new elites rapidly embarked in the *proceso constituyente* (constitution-making), and a new constitution was approved in 1978. Although the Constitution maintained the state's unitary form (that is, it did not formally accept federalism or historical rights), it still granted and recognized the right to autonomy. However, constitution-making encountered difficulties in the Basque Country, where most nationalists opposed, or abstained from approving, the existing text of the Spanish Constitution on the ground that it did not recognize the specific historic rights of the region (Gunther et al. 1988: 123–24).

Violence had begun to decline after the approval of the Statute of Autonomy in 1980: ETA-pm abandoned violence postulating in favour of a negotiated settlement and pardons through political participation, chiefly joining the Euskadiko Ezkerra coalition (EE, Basque Left, founded 1977).

As a theoretical and methodological approach, *historical institutionalism* focuses on institutions, particularly the state, as the most suitable agent in the solidification of sub-state identities. Since institutions are normatively and cognitively 'internalized', 'human agency is embedded in the institutional contest' (Lecours 2007: 13). Although institutions cannot provide the sole explanatory variable, various levels of personal and collective sovereignty can be attached to them through their 'identity-generating potential'. Moreover, institutions can 'launch and sustain a process of identity construction quite independently of agency' (Lecours 2007: 15). For instance, Cantabria was officially 'invented' during the transition to democracy when the Castilian province of Santander (La Montaña) was given a separate status among Spain's seventeen autonomous communities (Conversi 2000, 2002). Endowed with a set of symbols, landmarks and myths including a colourful flag, a powerful geographical context (the Cordillera Cantábrica or Cantabrian Mountains) and even an associated ethnonym (the tribal Cantabri confederacy mentioned first by Strabo and then by Julius Caesar in his *De Bello Gallico*), Cantabria's autonomy statute (1981) pushed local intellectuals on the path of developing a regional identity. This led to new claims, for instance the claim that Cantabrian was a distinct language. In short, a new regional identity was developed after autonomous Cantabrian institutions had been set up. However, not everything can be said to be determined by institutions, as shown by the birth and development of Asturian nationalism during the pre-autonomy years – including the existence between 1976 and 1982 of a radical branch with ETA links (Zimmerman 2012).

Coming back to our key argument, Basque institutions (Gasteiz government, provincial *diputaciones*, their associated departments, like health, education, welfare, etc.) have contributed to solidify a sense of distinctive Basque sovereignty.

A pure institutionalist approach would seem to counter much of the recent literature on the impossibility of artificially creating distinctive ethnic identities, a view most profoundly articulated by Anthony D. Smith's ethno-symbolist approach (Smith 1996, 1998, 2009). According to this view, the case of 'millennial' Basque resilience reveals that institutions can make identities, but cannot break them.[12]

The 'war on terror' and declining Spanish sovereignty

A turning point occurred under José Maria Aznar's mandate, particularly during Spain's incorporation into the US-led 'Global War on Terror' (GWT), when 'the political climate in the Basque country was the most volatile and tense it had been since the end of the dictatorship' (Lecours 2007: 2). At the same time, the confluence of international and domestic policies under Aznar contributed to radicalize public opinion in Cataluña, where the dominant narrative of the 'war on terror' seemed to converge with broader perceptions of a recurring and inveterate Spanish nationalism (Beilin 2012).

Aznar's adherence to the unpopular US-led campaign was received with disappointment and apprehension by an overwhelming majority of Spaniards, with opposition voiced across the political spectrum, despite that reactions within the conservative Partido Popular were most often muted. Surveys at the time of the Iraq war (2002–03) showed an overwhelming ninety-one per cent opposition to the GWT across Spain (Tremlett and Arie 2003), which indicates that a majority of the rank and file within the Partido Popular privately opposed the war. Within the Basque country and in the diaspora, the rationale of the 'global war on terror' has been submitted to robust critical assessment (Aretxaga 2002, 2005; Zirakzadeh 2010; Zulaika 2010a, 2010b; Zulaika and Alonso 2009; Zulaika and Douglass 2008). Re-cast as part of the Bush administration's remapping of the world order into 'good' and 'evil', an internationally emboldened Spanish nationalism had *de facto* put a halt on decades of progress towards deepened political participation, risking a regression to the dark days of authoritarianism. Aznar referred to all possible negotiations as 'appeasement' to terrorism (Mees 2003: 116).

The brief return of the Socialists in power (March 2004) led to great expectations of a 'second transition' to democracy (Encarnación 2008). However, massive demonstrations against terrorism had already created a more suitable environment for ETA's 'permanent ceasefire' in March 2006, and the subsequent Donostia-San Sebastián International Peace Conference in Aiete (17–20 October 2011), which resulted in ETA's 'definitive cessation of armed activity'. Over a decade of pressure from peace groups and civil society organizations had yielded positive results in terms of peacemaking independently of the government's persistent refusal to deal with ETA. However, Madrid's initiatives and progresses in many realms had been insignificant and did not outlast the Partido Popular's return to power after the 2011 Spanish general election. The overwhelming victory of Partido Popular, and ensuing methods of governance informed by Spanish-centred majoritarianism (Conversi 2012), precipitated a descent into mutually recriminating nationalisms, particularly radicalizing the conflict between Cataluña and Madrid (Guibernau 2013).[13]

In the Basque country, the edifice of political legitimacy built around ETA was beginning to dissolve. Discourses that offered legitimation to violence encountered an increasingly more vocal, less muted reception. Such discourses had previously been associated with the 'dirty war' conducted by the central state in the 1980s, and reflected a fall of its overall political legitimacy (Encarnación 2007). The discursive apparatus used to legitimate violent action was among a range of oppositional practices and expressions manifesting themselves side by side with mainstream political culture. As a result, the Basque country became fragmented along three political and social cultures: the nationalist, the radical left and the Spanish constitutionalist.

The role of the 'war on terror' on Spain's politics is important. Joseba Zulaika perceptively applies Giorgio Agamben's notion of the 'paradox of sovereignty' to the 'war on terror' and its accompanying 'states of exception' (Zulaika 2010b: ch. 7; 2011). Significantly, in the USA as in other countries drawn into this 'global war', the 'sovereign' placed himself 'at the same time, outside and inside the judicial order' so that, in this way, counter-terrorism discourse could be effort-lessly twisted to legitimate authoritarianism and unaccountability – a drift exem-plified in the USA by the Guantanamo Bay detention camp and the suspension of *habeas corpus* (Zulaika 2010b: 32). In a democratic world, this leads not only to contestations of the legitimacy of political order, but also to questions about the legitimacy of judicial power itself and the associated system of norms and laws. Following the GWT, the 'counter-terror' bio-political machine has shaped new geographies of exception through the imposition of a new nomos, 'within which decision is produced by a permanent state of exception, and where law exists only through its endless strategic (dis)application' (Minca 2007).

While Zulaika largely refers to the USA, the implications of the new 'paradox of sovereignty' have not been lost to critics of Madrid's harsh neo-liberal poli-tics. Indirectly, this critique has also been seized by pro-independence movements in Cataluña. These have progressed in the legitimacy vacuum opening up with Madrid's slow disengagement from flexible dialogue through a stern 'winner-takes-all' majoritarianism (Conversi 2012). The accompanying regurgitation of Spanish nationalism verged on the partial dismantling of the pacts and agreements that had shaped the transition to democracy.

In the Basque country, the historical relationship with Madrid is perhaps best described as *pacted sovereignty*. Pactism (*pactismo*, a reliance on signed agree-ments) has deep historical roots, enshrined in local rights (*fueros*) and parliamen-tary institutions. As an historical doctrine, *pactismo* developed in the kingdoms of Aragon and Navarre, serving efficiently as an ideological alibi for limiting the absolute power of the monarch. Joseba Agirreazkuenaga (2012: 35–36) rightly encourages us to 'rethink and to inquire into different forms of sovereignty', focusing on valid traditional models of complex interdependence. According to Agirreazkuenaga (2012), this is pertinent even today, for the debate about how to build future models of 'diversity in unity'.

Land and soul: the territorial articulation of national sovereignty

In the nationalist worldview, territory is the single most important element of national sovereignty: No sovereignty can be imagined without a territory attached to it and constantly experienced through a collective imaginary, re-enacted in daily life rituals. Still, because the ultimate actor of this territorial entrenchment is the Westphalian state itself, stateless nations can hardly escape its iron cage. Nations without a state provide no exception to the logic of territoriality, since they manifest themselves and operate in an international system of states. This system is far from having lost its main prerogatives: 'Invested with a kind of meta-capital, the state remains a crucial presence, a screen for political desires and identifications as well as fears' (Aretxaga 2003: 393).

The main theorist of this relationship between sovereignty and violence was Carl Schmitt (1888–85), sometimes identified as the organic intellectual of the Nazi regime although his influence outlasted the demise of the regime. Schmitt argued that sovereign authority is indispensable for a smooth functioning of the legal order. Because sovereignty is inextricably bound to a territory, for Schmitt it is 'unthinkable without an "outside"' (Bauman 2003: 288). Schmitt's vision is thus 'as "localized" as the sovereignty whose mystery it aims to unravel' (ibid.) and 'does not step beyond the practice and cognitive horizon of the made-in-heaven wedlock of territory and power'. However, 'the power of exemption would not be a mark of sovereignty, were the sovereign power not wedded first to the territory' (Bauman 2003: 288). This leads inevitably to an exclusivist dimension. The main targets of the era of ascending 'nation-statism' were indeed stateless nations, peoples and territories, the 'dirty monsters' whose fearing semblance were mobilized by the ruler to chip away ever more rights and culture from their terrorised populations: in the words of Zygmunt Bauman (2003: 289), 'sovereignty being the power to define the limits of humanity, the lives of those humans who have fallen or have been thrown outside those limits are unworthy of being lived'. And here we can also return to Agamben's vision of the *homo sacer*, who is banned and can be killed by anybody with impunity, though he cannot be sacrificed for religious rituals (Agamben 1998). Giorgio Agamben also traces exclusion and inclusion to Schmitt's work. For Agamben (2005: 35), 'Schmitt's concept of sovereignty derives [. . .] from the state of exception, and not vice versa'.

There are grounds for scepticism in the face of a state purporting to act as paladin of ecological sovereignty. The growing bio-political management of citizens parallels state- and market-led political claims to sovereignty over the natural world – at a time when Schmitt's states of exception, unable to uphold the singularity of each individual human being, are becoming, in Agamben's words, a global bio-political norm (Smith 2009).

Although the territory is sacrosanct, its boundaries are subjected to change. In the Basque case, the territorial imaginary mutated from Arana's earlier focus on Bizkaia in *Bizkaia por su independencia* (Arana Goiri 1980) to his synthetic motto *zazpiak-bat* (seven in one)[14] and the equally concise formula '*4 + 3 = 1*' (four plus three equals one). These shifts continued later on, for instance with Krutwig's inclusion of the French region of Guascony in his Vasconia (Krutwig Sagredo 1973). However, the realm of the seven provinces has firmly established itself in the *abertzale* sovereign worldview, as visible in virtually all nationalist maps and logos: 'Seven (provinces) in one' alludes to the three provinces and Navarre on the Spanish side (Hegoalde) and the three *départements* on the French side (Iparralde). In the aspirations of most nationalists, the seven areas are imagined as, and will one day be, autonomous participants in a free and sovereign Euskal Herria.

Important rituals have been established to link and bond the territory: since 1980, the *Korrika* running race aligns the entire territory of Euskal Herria, with a popular defence of the Basque language, Euskera (Valle 1994).[15] This groundbreaking initiative has spanned replicas and emulative runs in the defence of other European minority languages.[16] Since the early twentieth century (and 1935), but truly beginning in 1980, championships of *bertsolariak* (singers of *bertso*, improvised musical verse) are held four times annually in each of the seven provinces, along with other annual gatherings and sparring matches of *bertsolarism*, including amongst the Basque diaspora (Aulestia 2000). Basque oral poetry is declaimed in popular Euskera, allowing for much more flexibility and spontaneity than with the standard *batua*. These developments occurred in the same years when the Statute of Autonomy (ratified in 1979) begun to be put into practice through the transferral of administrative competences (*transferencias de competencias administrativas*). This seems to indicate a direct linkage between the establishment of semi-sovereign institutions and cultural revival. Imagined sovereignties overlap with the sovereignties of ordinary daily life through the impact of really existing institutions. The competing levels of everyday enactments of sovereignty correspond to the overlapping layers of multi-level governance (municipal, provincial, regional), as well as the imagined supra-layer of the Euskal Herria imaginary.

The next section addresses the ultimate consequences of sovereignty's semantic shift from the nested pluralism of the Middle Ages to the complex plasticity of the 'postmodern' condition.

Liquid sovereignty

The idea that we have moved into a post-sovereign world order is by now acknowledged in most disciplines from different angles and perspectives. It cannot be easily denied that the notion of sovereignty has entered a deep, perhaps terminal, crisis – whether or not the state is part of the crisis (Walker 1992).[17] Not only 'post-sovereignty' is enshrined by most institutions and through multiple governance levels within the EU, but the UN and a host of other international bodies supervise and have a say in many 'domestic' policies. North Korea, a country whose constitution explicitly enshrines 'sovereignty' in its pursuance of reunification with the South, is certainly an exception rather than the rule. Indeed, multiple overlapping sovereignties may have become the rule, rather than the exception, in what is increasingly recognized in international relations and political philosophy as a post-Westphalian world order.

What exceptions can there be? Putin's Russia has tried simultaneously to hold on to older conceptions of national sovereignty, while acting as patron and supporter of separatist movements and quasi-states in the 'near abroad' – in Abkhazia, South Ossetia, Transnistria and, more recently, in Crimea and Eastern Ukraine with the self-declared Donetsk and Lugansk thug 'Republics' (Bonnot 2014). All these areas are characterized by a dense post-sovereignty. In India, the Hindutva movement pushes for a homogenizing vision of greater Hindustan, threatening Christian, Muslim and other minorities while retaining a parvence of pluralism in its approach to the multiple manifestations of Hinduism, whose alleged 330 million deities are increasingly conceptualized as expressions of one Supreme Being. Even in highly centralized China, transnational environmental advocacy merged with Tibetan nationalism, revealing the 'competing entanglements' of Chinese, Indian, and Tibetan sovereignties (Yeh 2012). Probably the most conspicuous manifestation of obstinate Westphalian state sovereignty is the 'wall' Israel has built around itself as part of a process of Palestinians' 'dispossession and containment' (Bowman 2007).

Yet, experiments with a post-sovereign new order have also expanded, the EU providing perhaps its most advanced arena (Conversi 2014a). Neil MacCormick described Europe as a 'non-sovereign confederal' space (MacCormick 1999). This concept of post-sovereignty is in turn reflected amongst nations without a state. For Michael Keating, statehood is no longer the leading goal among sub-state nationalisms (Keating 2001). In fact, sub-state nations have a gamut of possible options that they can choose to determine their relationships with both the central government and the wider world. Within the EU, Basque politics has spawned its own goal of shared sovereignty through the *Ibarretxe Plan* for Basque 'co-sovereignty' or 'free association', which includes the right to self-determination (Keating and Bray 2006; Lecours 2007).[18] In Québec the term 'sovereignty' has been in use since at least the 1960s and 1970s, and from Québec the term *souveranisme* or 'sovereignism' has expanded to other stateless nations, entering into the Catalan vocabulary as *soberanisme* and then into Castilian as *soberanismo*.[19]

Zygmunt Bauman associates the notion of *Liquid Modernity* (Bauman 2000, 2010) with a word that cannot stand still and, like liquid, is in perpetual movement. It is a world permeated by precariousness, uncertainty (Bauman 2005), fear (Bauman 2006) and the frailty of human bonds (Bauman 2003). Could we also speak of *liquid sovereignty*? As an expression of late modernity, liquid modernity is configured by a shifting relationship with a specific (or 'solid') territory, rather than a staying and grounded relationship with it, while human, social and political relationships become increasingly characterized by provisional, rather than permanent, commitment. In this fluctuating environment, it becomes next to impossible to speak about sovereignty in its post-Westphalian, state-centred meaning. If globalisation has led to a decline of state sovereignty, then its ultimate consequence is likely to be at further erosion of state sovereignty, seemingly verging towards the implosion of the very notion of sovereignty.

The short circuit produced by neoliberal globalization is visible in the ultimate challenge posed by climate change as the eventual terminator and dismantler of state sovereignty in any meaningful sense. *Liquification*, rather than liquidity, becomes a suitable description of the melting state at the edges of the neo-liberal *cul-de-sac*. Incidentally, the fact that neither neo-liberal ideology nor consumer behaviour have been able to reform themselves during and after the 2010's economic recession is a powerful reminder that they are unlikely as a political economic system to be able to face the unprecedented challenges posed by climate change. The answers will probably have to come from beyond the spent and out-dated mental map of neo-liberalism (Moreno and Conversi 2017a, 2017b).

Ulrich Beck describes the formation of 'cosmopolitan communities of climate risk' as a global effort to avoid a consumerism-induced cataclysm. These are defined as 'new transnational constellations of social actors, arising from common experiences of mediated climatic threats, organized around pragmatic reasoning of causal relations and responsibilities' (Beck et al. 2013: 2). Thus, Ulrich Beck prefigures the optimist vista of a 'globalized change of consciousness and practice' and a 'reorientation towards "*cosmopolitization*"' (Beck et al. 2013). But, behind this optimism, one can still discern the undisclosed chain of calamities looming ahead. Climate change's impact on any form of sovereignty is likely to be devastating, while the current global plunder already reveals an overall lack of state control inherited by both the Westphalian and post-Westphalian orders. In fact, both reproduce incrementally, each in its own way, the developmentalist drive of the Western modernist, state-centred world order. Only recently, a wholesale alternative to state- and market-centred developmental modernism has begun to emerge. This has implicated, and has been reflected in, a new notion of sovereignty that is explored in the next section.

Back to basics: land grabs vs. food sovereignty

'We are what we eat', goes the old adagio. In fact, food not only affects our physical being and quality of life, but it also exercises a deep impact on our personal and collective identity – at both the individual and collective level. Unlike language, which is composed of, and conveyed by, symbols (sounds and letters), food is physically graspable, materially grounded and directly consumable. As the culinary historian Massimo Montanari has shown, 'everything having to do with food – its capture, cultivation, preparation, and consumption – represents a cultural act'; in other words, 'food is culture' (Montanari 2004, 2006). It is therefore not surprising that food has been under attack by the forces of unregulated globalization, which have dispensed with traditional agriculture by forcing standardized modes of production and consumption upon millions of people. The response to agro-business' relentless march has been a proliferation of initiatives centred on the need to reassert sovereignty over food. The 'food sovereignty' (*soberania alimentaria*) movement was launched in 1996 by *Via Campesina* ('Peasants' Way'), an international network of peasant organizations. The whole idea is centred on the notion of food as a basic human right. 'Food sovereignty' is about popular sovereignty rather than the sovereignty of the state, which sets it against 'food security' as a national (or state) security issue (Conversi 2016).

The movement was also spawned by the ultimate form of sovereignty obliteration, 'land grabs', which have massively expanded since the 2007–08 global food-price crisis. Patterns of territorial acquisition and enclosure within alleged development schemes have radically altered land use through a dramatic increase in large-scale land deals (Kish 2011). The very nucleus of sovereignty as a viable human condition has been subverted to the core by shifting public lands into the hands of foreign or domestic investors; in most of these cases the 'sovereign' state has surrendered its sovereignty to more powerful economic forces (Wolford et al. 2013).

This links us back to the passage to the nation state and imperial era, which was characterized by a process of annexation and border-building (Conversi 2014b). The seizing of territory remained its main scope, involving sweeping expropriation of property from its erstwhile usufructuaries (Levene and Conversi 2014). Since then, the modern era has been characterized by a frenetic rush to seize, re-size, bound, enclose and classify, all of which nourished an obsession with border-building and, subsequently, cultural homogenization. This rush is re-enacted with contemporary 'land-grab' mega-events, in which governments and global companies have connived to appropriate huge expanses of rural lands by exploiting legal niches, imprecise mapping, overlapping territorial claims, 'cycles of contentious politics' and vague or blurred acquisition processes (Neville and Dauvergne 2012). For many NGOs, these gerrymandering and appropriation practices exemplify the plunder, rapaciousness and spoils of applied neo-liberal ideology (Kish 2011; Oxfam 2011).[20] Large-scale deals shifted ownership from public lands to the hands of unscrupulous investors. Land grabs can be seen as a contemporary re-enactment of the British enclosure acts on a global scale (Levene and Conversi 2014). The role of the post-sovereign state is often shadowy and ambiguous and never operating with a single voice. Deals are often made secretively and away from the public gaze, while the mass media prefers to focus attention on less substantial events.

While seventeenth- and eighteenth-century colonial settler projects were already eliminationist acts of massive land grabs, we are now witnessing an epochal 'condensation of a series of linked crises' rapidly leading to 'an ecological tipping point' with profound new ontological implications (McMichael 2014). The response to these massive shifts of sovereign power has been articulated in various ways. Notwithstanding global media bowdlerization and expurgation, the 'climate transition' has begun to spawn a 'grand narrative' guided by its own cosmology in pursuit of a more resilient, sovereign future founded on agro-ecological production. The 'transition movement' includes intellectuals who have helped to shape an agenda for a global coalition based on international solidarity against nutritional impoverishment and the corporate greed and abuses of agro-food biotechnologies (Sage 2014). The emerging agrarian and peasant social movements amalgamate anti-globalization, pro-democracy and environmentalist agendas under the banner of global food sovereignty (Teubal 2009). This new political constellation reflects increasing needs to integrate agro-ecological science and indigenous knowledge systems (Altieri and Toledo 2011). In terms of sovereignty, what is propounded here is nothing less than a 'sovereignty model founded on practices of agrarian citizenship', in the awareness of how agriculture has been historically linked to successive 'metabolic ruptures between society and nature' (Wittman 2009).

As land grabbing rests on the previous identification of the most fertile areas, it also includes '*water grabbing*', just as water is becoming a scarcely available, vital supply for millions of peoples (Franco et al. 2013). The focus on alimentation is thus a focus on the very fundaments of human development, which incidentally includes water quality and water availability as keys to human survival – well beyond notions of 'sustainable sovereignty'.

While the looming reality of climate change begins to alter the deepest gist and significance of 'sovereignty' as a viable concept, *territoriality*, that is, the territorially entrenched nation state, provides a major stumbling block towards the achievement of an orderly retreat from the fossil-fuel-driven global economy (Kythreotis 2012). Repeatedly, states and governments have blocked any meaningful advance towards the abandonment of the hegemonic, fossil-fuel-energised economy of profit, being much keener to address the 'threat' of poorer countries' collapse onto 'us', rather than attempting to give serious consideration as to how the transition might be accomplished (Abbott et al. 2006: 28, Levene and Conversi 2014: 289, Parenti 2011: 14–20).

What is the impact of all of this on Basque society and sovereignty? How far has the notion of 'food sovereignty' penetrated everyday practices and images of Basque society? Within Basque society the concept found a fertile ground for experiencing new modes of agricultural self-organization and production: the creation of Euskal Herriko Laborantza Ganbara (EHLG, Chamber of Agriculture of the Basque Country) in January 2005 as a NGO depending on donations and local institutional support. The latter includes labour unions, town councils, civics associations and *udalbiltzak* from the seven Basque Provinces – the latter are associations of municipal elected officials, mayors and town councillors (Letamendia Belzunde 2006).[21]

Beside this, the labour union EHNE (Euskal Herriko Nekazarien Elkartasuna, Farmer's Solidarity of the Basque Country) is active in a series of campaigns designed to address issues of sustainability, safety and quality, articulated around the notion of food sovereignty (Mann 2014: 117–139). EHNE is part of a broader movement for union renovation deeply intermeshed with both radical Basque nationalism and the global movement of peasants' resistance (Elorrieta 2014). Founded in 1976, EHNE has acted in the defence of *baserritarriak* interests, initially supporting the creation of farmers' cooperatives and support for their productivity in front of the challenge posed by EU agrarian policies (Egaña 1996: 228). In May 1993, it participated in the foundational meeting of Via Campesina. According to Paul Nicholson, EHNE's European coordinator for Via Campesina, EHNE stresses food sovereignty as a 'new way of internal democracy' (Holt-Gimenez 2013: ch. 1). In recent years, EHNE has exposed the lack of consideration for the rural consequences of megaprojects like motorways and the controversial TAV (*Tren de Alta Velocidad*, High-Speed Train) with detailed reports listing previously underplayed collateral effects, like seizure of land, parcel fragmentation, loss of access, impact on human and animal health, building stability, consequences for adjoining plots of land, damage to landscape and cultural heritage and patrimonial devaluation (Barcena and Larrinaga 2009: 87–99). Other projects and activities include the Euskal Herriko Hazien Sarea (*Red de Semillas de Euskadi*, Seed Savers Exchange of the Basque Country), created in 1996 for the recovery of local seed varieties once the loss of this biodiversity heritage and culture became evident. It can count with over hundred partners and collaborators and acts as official interlocutor on issues of agro-biodiversity. Several other initiatives go hand in hand with the emerging notions of alimentary sovereignty, including local purchasing, local currency, *ferias de productos ecológicos* (ecological products fairs) and rural markets,

Beyond sovereignty? Emerging sovereign scenarios in Basque society

This chapter's methodological approach is historically grounded and theoretically oriented more than empirically anchored. The goal is to contribute to a political theory of 'sovereignty without a state' by addressing the changing perceptions of the sovereign *imaginaire* amongst Basque citizens in their everyday life, as well as to identify possible future trends of how, or if, sovereignty could be imagined and practiced in the future.

A minimal amount of empirical data has been used to support this chapter's main argument. A focus interview has been carried out amongst non-representative samples of the postgraduate student population at the Universidad del País Vasco (UPV, University of the Basque Country) with a focus group of six participants who addressed some conceptual issues raised by the multiple usages of the term 'sovereignty'. During the guided discussions, the possible multiple understandings of the meaning of sovereignty have been explored.

The results are as follows. Although some participants found the concept of sovereignty difficult to grasp, it was generally understood that the notion might refer to an internationally recognized, independent state. Yet, there was awareness that sovereignty is nowadays a fuzzy, nebulous and relative notion and that its achievement is not, or no longer, fully possible given an increasing inter-dependence at the global level. Some participants identified a personal layer of sovereignty akin to the philosophical notion of individual self-determination.

The notion of 'food sovereignty' emerged early on in the discussion group. Although this has not yet penetrated everyday practices, its significance was grasped promptly, perhaps more easily than the notion of political sovereignty. Its usage is still limited to a restricted niche, but it emerged early on in the focus group while discussing the intersection between personal and collective identities and focusing on how sovereignty can be put into practice with immediate effects. This contrast between personal and collective sovereignty is explored below.

There are several layers to which the concept of sovereignty can be applied. Amongst these, two main co-existing layers can be discerned: a personal and a collective one. At the *personal* level, any individual is potentially sovereign insofar as s/he can exercise different degrees of control over one or more domains of his/her life. At the *collective* level, a group is likely to enjoy sovereignty insofar as it maintains the capacity to control resources over a specific territory and exercise decision making over a set of policies within it. Therefore the territorial dimension of sovereignty becomes apparent at the collective level, although it is also incarnated in various ways at the personal level.

In philosophy, the concept of 'self-determination' similarly focuses on the individual through the idea that we are the ultimate arbiters of our destiny and through the exercise of 'free will' (Latin: *liberum arbitrium*). Immanuel Kant theorized the importance of 'individual self-determination' as the *personal* 'moral autonomy' that occurs when an individual's decision on a course of action stems from his respect of a moral duty. Amongst the theorists of nationalism, only Elie Kedourie identified Kant's principle as lying at the basis of *collective* national self-determination. Indeed, Kedourie himself argued that Kant's notion of individual self-determination lies at the root of nationalism (Kedourie 1993). In fact, one can also say that rational self-determination at both the individual and socio-political level was the goal of the Enlightenment project.[22] Despite being once a fundamental legitimating principle of the international system, its presence in public discourses and practices has sharply declined over the last half century.

Yet the passage from individual to collective identity needs a broader cultural context. Notions of cultural sovereignty, as introduced above while mentioning the cultural revival in both its pre-political and political forms, also emerged earlier on in the discussion, largely associated with the struggle to preserve Basque identity, with a particularly keen awareness of the memory of state repression against traditional Basque symbols and culture.

How do notions of culture and practices of cultural revival reflect on Basque sovereignty? The focus group provided a potential context in which to connect sovereignty with culture in the broader sense. However, the concept of *culture* appears to be even more weakly defined and difficult to grasp than the notion of sovereignty. Although 'culture' is often meant as 'language', some participants identified culture in other ways and, generally, as a lifestyle and set of inter-generationally inherited traditions.

On the other hand, notions of 'culture', as defined by the mobilized protagonists, articulate discourses on national sovereignty. Understanding the role of culture is, therefore, an important and often lost dimension needed to explain the dynamics of ethnic conflict de-escalation, political settlement, the establishment of peace and long-term stability. The contrasting dimensions of cultural loss and revival have permeated the entire discourse on Basque sovereignty since before the rise of nationalism. Cultural variables should therefore be identified as major determinants in violent vs. non-violent strategy choices in sovereignty disputes.

Conclusions: elements of sovereignty

Although sovereignty is an 'essentially contested' concept, there is general agreement that it is related to power.[23] Moreover it is *relational*: One is always sovereign in relationship with, and in respect to, another (person or group), and this sovereignty is bounded in space and grounded within a specific territory. I have begun by tracing the conceptual shifts in the notion of sovereignty throughout the modern age, from late-medieval Europe to the era of neo-liberal globalization. The contemporary international system works in such a way as to make the very exercise of sovereignty nearly unattainable. Sovereignty has thus become a largely obsolete concept in its analytical form, rarely applied to denote something substantial. Yet, the signifier has changed, but the signified has not: the image of sovereignty retains a powerfully evocative force, just as its promise of self-determination evaporates. Subsequently, the chapter has tracked the development of grassroots concepts of Basque sovereignty since the foundation of ETA (1959) through the democratic transition (1975–80) up to the current peace process (2011). During the transition to democracy, notions of sovereignty were articulated in the context of a process of falling state legitimacy and mounting popular mobilizations. Changing practices of governance were reflected in shifting perceptions and discourses of sovereignty from the implementation of the statute of autonomy to the peace process. These changes included the way sovereignty and territoriality were imagined and debated through evolving visions of political legitimacy and political representation. It may be argued that the four separate Basque provinces, Araba, Bizkaia, Gipuzkoa and Navarre,[24] have increasingly acted as *de facto* sovereign entities since the establishment of the autonomy statutes of the Basque Country and Navarre, and hence could be perceived as quasi-sovereign spaces and political units. The level of prerogatives, attributes, capacities and resources enjoyed by the Autonomous Communities and the *Diputaciones* or provincial governments is, at least in some respects, on a par with those of a *de iure* sovereign state.[25] In fact, this chapter has also illustrated how Basque sovereignty is currently imagined, not necessarily in a distant future, but as being enacted in the present moment. Yet, as we shall see, contemporary challenges do not allow for foregone conclusions.

Global political and economic shifts have been largely reflected in Basque political culture, where sovereignty remains a protean notion, rapidly adapting to changing macro circumstances. The concept of 'liquid sovereignty' highlights contemporary tensions, sorrows and distresses, leading us to question whether it can be applied to the case of Basque resilience. The following elements of sovereignty have been found to possess a relevant meaning in distinctive adaptations of political identity through successive stages in the evolution of Basque nationalism: political sovereignty, personal sovereignty, cultural sovereignty and food sovereignty.

At first sight, the inclusion of the last element may seem out of place, but one of the article's assumptions is that the new socio-economic conditions brought about by neo-liberal globalization (and its crisis) have inspired a vast array of responses that directly bear upon the very idea and perception of sovereignty. These have converged around notions of food sovereignty, where sovereignty is acquiring new meanings untypical of either the modern era of nation-states or the pre-modern era of overlapping sovereignties.

The chapter has finally moved the attention towards food sovereignty, which appears to be an eminently practical and feasible form of sovereignty (Conversi 2016). This is because, if we choose so, we can exercise at least some control over what we eat, provided that we have the legal-political resources, know-how and willingness to set free from food retailers' and agro-business' encroachment. The goal is partly to regain control over the channels of transmission or communication from where aliments are cultivated to where they are actually consumed. This is cogently felt precisely because it may not be a sovereign option in vast areas of the world, where the food chain is subjected to lack of redistributing power (hunger) or selective distribution (low-quality preheated, precooked, pre-packaged standardized foodstuffs sold via franchise operations, and overconsumption). Food sovereignty thus reunites many of the dimensions of sovereignty we have discussed so far – personal, cultural, political – and is certainly the less 'liquid' of all these forms. Opting for this notion of quotidian sovereignty, one can perform an act of sovereignty that is simultaneously political, cultural, territorial and personal.

In this way, the eco-political emergency propels us towards a new direction in which all of the above levels of sovereignty can be currently practiced and simultaneously present: from the political to the personal, from the consumer to the producer, while encompassing more hazy notions of malleable 'post-sovereignty'. In other words, all these forms are highly interconnected, and such interconnectedness is emphasized by the notion of food sovereignty.

To sum up, the Basque political scenario has not been immune from the conceptual turns associated with the meaning of sovereignty. While political violence has informed previous concepts of sovereignty, so did the end of violence, and this article has explored one of the possible directions in which sovereignty may develop at both the local and global level.

Notes

1 Between two and three hundred city-states were co-existing in Italy's territory in AD 1200 (Waley and Dean 2010), roughly the same number of ancient Greek city-states at the times of Pericles – most of them proudly independent, albeit under Athenian hegemony.

2 On Basque nationalist graffiti, see Chaffee (1993).

3 This reflects, I believe, the '*sentimiento trágico de la vida*' (tragic feeling of life) of Miguel de Unamuno or the '*sentimiento agónico de la existencia*' (agonizing feeling of existence) of Antonio Machado, by way of existentialism.

4 *Cuadernos de ETA*, as cited in Garmendia (1979: 22).

5 According to Txillardegi, by 1960 more than 300 militants had passed through its *cursillos de formación* (training courses): Interview with Txillardegi, reported in *Garaia*, vol. I, n° 1, 1976, pp. 24–25. The Basque linguist and writer José Luis Alvarez Enparantza, aka Txillardegi (1929–2012) was the most prominent figure within ETA's cultural branch.

6 *Zutik* still reported that 'between Gandhi's non-violence and a civil war there are intermediate methods of struggle [. . .] which we want to put in practice' (*Zutik*, n° 19 reported in *Documentos Y*, vol. 2, 229).

7 Although only four members of ETA remained then in Spain as a consequence of repression, this did not deter it from launching a series of frenetic activities, such as the adhesion to workers' struggle, the enrollment of women, the extension of activities in Navarre, printing, producing propaganda, etc. See ETA 1979–81, *Documentos Y*, vol. 2, page 5).

8 Krutwig was the son of a German industrialist living in Bilbao and an ex-secretary of the Basque Language Academy, never being a member of ETA.

9 By 1963, ETA had already participated in the organization of working-class strikes. In his *Carta a los intelectuales* (Letter to the intellectuals), Zalbide postulated the basic principles to be adopted by ETA. Reprinted in Garmendia (1979: 287–303).

10 *Baserritarrak* are those living on a *baserri*, the typical Basque house-barn farmhouse. *Familism* is 'a social pattern in which the family assumes a position of ascendance over individual interests' (see *Merriam-Webster Dictionary*, www.merriam-webster. com/dictionary/familism).

11 For instance, in 1974, the Labour/Workers and the Cultural fronts split off to form their own autonomous parties, LAIA and EHAS.

12 For an approach combining institutionalism with the *longue durée* of ethno-symbolism, see (Agirreazkuenaga 2004, 2012).

13 For the exploration of more general factors, see Crameri (2014) and Stegmann and Sancliment-Solé (2014).

38   *Daniele Conversi*

14 This motto was first used by the Navarrese Euskaros to replace the older *laurak-bat* (four in one), limited to the four provinces on the Spanish side..
15 The *Korrika* is organized by Alfabetatze Euskalduntze Koordinakundea (AEK), a grouping of *euskaltegis* (Euskera academies or centres for Basque language learning).
16 The Basque initiative provided a model for similar events in other regions of Europe, with Correlingua covering the Catalan-speaking areas across the Pyrenees (f. 1993), Correlingua in Galicia (est. 1997), Ar Redadeg running through Brittany's five *départements* (est. 2008) and Rith in support of the Irish language in Ireland (est. 2010). All these initiatives have been sponsored by their respective language-centered association, like the Coordinadora d'Associacions per la Llengua Catalana (CAL) or various Galician groups. Since 1993, the Correlingua is organized in combination with the Corsa d'Aran per sa Lengua in the Valley of Aran, where Aranese, a variety of Occitan, is spoken.
17 The idea has been around for a while. I have counted seven books titled 'beyond sovereignty' published since 1986: Soroos, Marvin S. (1986) *Beyond sovereignty: The challenge of global policy*. Columbia: University of South Carolina Press; Elkins, David J. (1995) *Beyond sovereignty: Territory and political economy in the twenty-first century*. Toronto: University of Toronto Press; Farer, Tom J. (ed.) (1996) *Beyond sovereignty: Collectively defending democracy in the Americas*. Baltimore: Johns Hopkins University Press; Cusimano, Maryann K. (ed.) (2000) *Beyond sovereignty: Issues for a global agenda*. Boston: Bedford /St. Martin's; Ieda, Osamu and Balázs Majtényi (eds.) (2006) *Beyond sovereignty: From status law to transnational citizenship?* Sapporo: Slavic Research Center, Hokkaido University; Grant, Kevin, Philippa Levine and Frank Trentmann (eds.) (2007) *Beyond sovereignty: Britain, empire and transnationalism, c. 1880–1950*. Basingstoke: Palgrave Macmillan; Leahy, D. G. (2010) *Beyond sovereignty. A new global ethics and morality*. Aurora, CO: Davies Group.
18 This owed much to the historical examples of Québec, adding the novel dimension of 'sustainable human development' (Ibarretxe Markuartu 2011, 2012). Also important was Puerto Rico's movement for 'sovereign free association', a more popular option than full 'independence', as revealed in the 2012 status referendum,
19 If one had to speak of political sovereignty within the international system, what minimal level would be acceptable? Probably the smallest nominally sovereign 'quasi state' in the world is the Sovereign Military Order of Malta (It., *Sovrano Militare Ordine di Malta*). It consists of a few buildings in the heart of a Rome, and its sovereignty is practiced by issuing stamps, coins (the Maltese *scudo*), passports and car license plates. Largely borrowing from the Vatican example of nested statehood, this kind of minimal attribution of sovereignty prerogatives can be defined as the 'Lateran' model of sovereignty. It is just one of the several multiple levels in which sovereignty can be circumstantially applied. It may not be satisfactory for some, but it may be for others.
20 In Guatemala, where at least forty-six per cent of smallholder lands have been seized by imported African palm plantations, drug-traffickers, cattle ranchers and international corporations, the military can be identified as the main 'shadow beneficiary' of a World Bank-induced agrarian reform (Grandia 2013). In Madagascar, government officials and elites routinely ignore the existing land laws in defence of local rights in front of agribusiness-led land appropriation (Burnod et al. 2013). However, in Costa Rica a popular movement against transnational mining concessions and land deals was articulated around notions of a bounded national territoriality threatened by obscure imperial forces (Graef 2013). At the same time, 'Chinese land-based interventions multiply across the African continent' (Buckley 2013).
21 See Euskal Herriko Laborantza Ganbara www.ehlgbai.org/en
22 Kedourie overlooked the wider impact of the French Revolution and preferred instead to describe nationalism as a sort of 'conspiracy' of German Romantic intellectuals.

23 On the notion of 'essentially contested concepts', see Collier et al. 2006 and Freeden 1996). The concept was originally introduced in an essay by W.B. Gallie (1955), reprinted in Gallie (1968).
24 Although, out of simplicity, I describe Navarre (*Nafarroa*) as a province, it is actually a 'Foral Community' (*Comunidad Foral de Navarra*, or *Nafarroako Foru Komunitatea*, approximately the 'chartered' Community of Navarre).
25 For an analysis of the impact of Basque semi-sovereign institutions, see Goikoetxea 2014.

References

Abbott, C., Rogers, P., and Sloboda, J. 2006. *Global Responses to Global Threats: Sustainable Security for the 21st Century*. Oxford: Oxford Research Group.
Abulof, U. 2015. *The Mortality and Morality of Nations*. Cambridge, MA: Cambridge University Press.
Agamben, G. 1998. *Homo Sacer: Sovereign Power and Bare Life*. Stanford, CA: Stanford University Press.
———. 2005. *State of Exception*. Chicago: University of Chicago Press.
Agirreazkuenaga, J. 2004. *Historia de Euskal Herria: Historia general de los Vascos*. Donostia-San Sebastian: Lur, 6 vols.
———. 2012. *The Making of the Basque Question: Experiencing Self- Government, 1793–1877*. Reno, NV: Center for Basque Studies, University of Nevada Press.
Alonso, A., and Zulaika, J. 2009. *Contraterrorismo USA: profecía y trampa*. Irun: Alberdania Editora.
Altieri, M. A., and Toledo, V. M. 2011. 'The Agroecological Revolution in Latin America: Rescuing Nature, Ensuring Food Sovereignty and Empowering Peasants', *The Journal of Peasant Studies*, 38(3): 587–612.
Arana Goiri, S. de. 1980. *Bizkaya por su independencia*. Bilbao: Geu (Reprod. facs Bilbao: Tipografía de Sebastiín de Amorrortu, 1892, 3 ed.).
Aretxaga, B. 2002. 'Terror as Thrill: First Thoughts on the "War on Terrorism"', *Anthropological Quarterly*, 75(1): 139–150.
———. 2003. 'Maddening States', *Annual Review of Anthropology*, 32: 393–410.
———, ed. 2005. *Empire and Terror: Nationalism/Postnationalism in the New Millennium*. Reno, NV: Center for Basque Studies, University of Nevada Press.
Aulestia, G. 2000. *The Basque Poetic Tradition*. Reno, NV: University of Nevada Press.
Barcena, I., and Larrinaga, J., eds. 2009. *TAV. Las Razones Del No*. Tafalla: Txalaparta.
Bauman, Z. 2000. *Liquid Modernity*. Cambridge: Polity Press.
———. 2003. *Liquid Love: On the Frailty of Human Bonds*. Cambridge: Polity Press.
———. 2005. *Liquid Life*. Cambridge: Polity Press.
———. 2006. *Liquid Fear*. Cambridge: Polity Press.
———. 2010. *44 Letters From the Liquid Modern World*. Cambridge: Polity Press.
Beck, U., Blok, A., Tyfield, D., and Zhang, J. Y. 2013. 'Cosmopolitan Communities of Climate Risk: Conceptual and Empirical Suggestions for a New Research Agenda', *Global Networks*, 13(1): 1–21.
Beilin, K. O. 2012. 'Bullfighting and the War on Terror: Debates on Culture and Torture in Spain, 2004–11', *International Journal of Iberian Studies*, 25(1): 61–72.
Bellamy, R. 2006. 'Sovereignty, Post-Sovereignty and Pre-Sovereignty: Three Models of the State, Democracy and Rights Within the EU', in R. Bellamy, ed., *Constitutionalism and Democracy*. Aldershot: Ashgate, pp. 167–190.

Biersteker, T. J., and Weber, C., eds. 1996. *State Sovereignty a Social Construct*. Cambridge, MA: Cambridge University Press.

Bonnot, M. 2014. *Des États de facto: Abkhazie, Somaliland, République turque de Chypre nord*. Paris: L'Harmattan.

Bowman, G. 2007. 'Israel's Wall and the Logic of Encystation: Sovereign Exception or Wild Sovereignty?', *European Journal of Anthropology*, 50: 127–135.

Buckley, L. 2013. 'Chinese Land-Based Interventions in Senegal', *Development and Change*, 44(2): 429–450.

Burnod, P., Gingembre, M., and Ratsialonana, R. A. 2013. 'Competition Over Authority and Access: International Land Deals in Madagascar', *Development and Change*, 44(2): 357–379.

Chaffee, L. G. 1993. *Political Protest and Street Art: Popular Tools for Democratization in Hispanic Countries*. Westport, CT: Greenwood Press.

Clark, R. P. 1979. *The Basques: The Franco Years and Beyond*. Reno, NV: University of Nevada Press.

———. 1984. *The Basque Insurgents: ETA, 1952–1980*. Madison, WI: University of Wisconsin Press.

Collier, D., Hidalgo, F. D., and Maciuceanu, A. O. 2006. 'Essentially Contested Concepts: Debates and Applications', *Journal of Political Ideologies*, 11(3): 211–246.

Connor, W. 2002. 'Nationalism and Political Illegitimacy', in D. Conversi, ed., *Ethnonationalism in the Contemporary World: Walker Connor and the Study of Nationalism*. London: Routledge, pp. 24–49.

Conversi, D. 1993. 'Domino Effect or Internal Developments? The Influences of International Events and Political Ideologies on Catalan and Basque Nationalism', *West European Politics*, 16(3): 245–270.

———. 1997. The Basques, the Catalans and Spain: Alternative Routes to Nationalist Mobilization. London: Hurst & Co.

———. 2000..'Autonomous Communities and the Ethnic Settlement in Spain', in Y. Ghai, ed., *Autonomy and Ethnicity. Negotiating Competing Claims in Multi-Ethnic States*. Cambridge: Cambridge University Press, pp. 122–144.

———. 2002. 'The Smooth Transition: Spain's 1978 Constitution and the Nationalities Question', *National Identities*, 4(3): 223–244.

———. 2007. 'Homogenisation, Nationalism and War: Should We Still Read Ernest Gellner?', *Nations and Nationalism,* 13(3): 371–394.

———. 2009 'Globalization, Ethnic Conflict, and Nationalism', in B. Turner, ed., *Handbook of Globalization Studies*. London: Routledge/ Taylor & Francis, 1st ed., pp. 346–366.

———. 2010. 'Cultural Homogenization, Ethnic Cleansing and Genocide', in R. A. Denemark, ed., *The International Studies Encyclopedia*. Boston, MA: Wiley-Blackwell, pp. 719–742.

———. 2012. 'Majoritarian Democracy and Globalization Versus Ethnic Diversity?', *Democratization*, 19(4): 789–811.

———. 2014a. 'Between the Hammer of Globalization and the Anvil of Nationalism: Is Europe's Complex Diversity Under Threat?', *Ethnicities*, 14(1): 25–49.

———. 2014b. 'Modernity, Globalization and Nationalism: The Age of Frenzied Boundary-Building', in J. Jackson and L. Molokotos-Liederman, eds, *Nationalism, Ethnicity and Boundaries: Conceptualising and Understanding Identity Through Boundary Approaches*. Abingdon: Routledge, pp. 57–82.

————. 2016 Sovereignty in a changing world: From Westphalia to food sovereignty', *Globalizations*, 13(4): 484–498.

Crameri, K. 2014. *Goodbye, Spain? The Question of Independence for Catalonia*. Sussex: Sussex Academic Press.

della Porta, D. 2014. 'On Violence and Repression: A Relational Approach', *Government and Opposition*, 49(2): 159–187.

Egaña, I. 1996. *Diccionario histórico-político de Euskal Herria*. Tafalla: Txalaparta.

Elorrieta, J. 2014. *Renovación sindical*. Tafalla: Txalaparta.

Encarnación, O. G. 2007. 'Democracy and Dirty Wars in Spain', *Human Rights Quarterly*, 29(4): 950–972.

————. 2008. *Spanish Politics: Democracy After Dictatorship*. Cambridge: Polity Press.

Franco, J., Mehta, L., and Veldwisch, G. J. 2013. 'The Global Politics of Water Grabbing', *Third World Quarterly*, 34(9): 1651–1675.

Freeden, M. 1996. *Ideologies and Political Theory: A Conceptual Approach*. Oxford: Clarendon Press.

Gallie, W. B. 1955. 'Essentially Contested Concepts', *Proceedings of the Aristotelian Society*, 56(1): 167–198.

————. 1968. *Philosophy and the Historical Understanding*. New York: Schocken Books.

Garmendia, J. M. 1979. *Historia de ETA*. Vol. 1. San Sebastian: Haranburu.

Goikoetxea, J. 2014. 'Nation and Democracy Building in Contemporary Europe: The Reproduction of the Basque Demos', *Nationalities Papers*, 42(1): 145–164.

Graef, D. J. 2013. 'Negotiating Environmental Sovereignty in Costa Rica', *Development and Change*, 44(2): 285–307.

Grandia, L. 2013. 'Road Mapping: Megaprojects and Land Grabs in the Northern Guatemalan Lowlands', *Development and Change*, 44(2): 233–259.

Guibernau, M. 2013. 'Secessionism in Catalonia: After Democracy', *Ethnopolitics*, 12(4): 368–393.

Gunther, R., Sani, G., and Shabad, G. 1988. *Spain After Franco: The Making of a Competitive Party System*. Berkeley, CA: University of California Press.

Gurrutxaga, A. 1989. *La refundacion del nacionalismo basco*. Bilbao: Servicio Editorial Universidad del Pais Vasco.

Halimi G. (1971) *Le procès de Burgos*. Paris: Gallimard (Préf. de Jean-Paul Sartre).

Hannum, H. 1996. *Autonomy, Sovereignty, and Self-Determination: The Accommodation of Conflicting Rights*. Philadelphia, PA: University of Pennsylvania Press.

Hess, A. 2009. *Reluctant Modernization: Plebeian Culture and Moral Economy in the Basque Country*. Bern: Peter Lang.

Holt-Gimenez, E., ed. 2013. *Food Movements Unite! Strategies to Transform Our Food System*. Oakland, CA: Food First Books.

Ibarra Güell, P. 1987. *La evolución estratégica de ETA: de la "Guerra revolucionaria" (1963) a la negociación (1987)*. Donostia: Kriselu.

Ibarretxe Markuartu, J. J. 2011. *The Basque Case: A Comprehensive Model of Sustainable Human Development*. Arlington, VA: The School for Conflict Analysis and Resolution/ George Mason University.

————. 2012. *El caso vasco: El desarrollo humano sostenible*. Bogotá: Editorial Oveja Negra/Centro Vasco Euskal Etxea.

Jáuregui Bereciartu, G. 1981. *Ideología y estrategia política de ETA: análisis de su evolución entre 1959 y 1968*. Madrid: Siglo Veintiuno Editores.

————. 1996. *Entre la tragedia y la esperanza: Vasconia ante el nuevo milenio*. Madrid: Editorial Ariel.

Keating, M. 2001. *Plurinational Democracy: Stateless Nations in a Post-Sovereignty Era.* Oxford: Oxford University Press.

Keating, M., and Bray, Z. 2006. 'Renegotiating Sovereignty: Basque Nationalism and the Rise and Fall of the Ibarretxe Plan', *Ethnopolitics*, 5(4): 347–364.

Kedourie, E. 1993. *Nationalism*, 4 ed. Oxford: Blackwell.

Kish, Z. 2011. 'Land Grab', in D. K. Chatterjee, ed., *Encyclopedia of Global Justice.* Dordrecht: Springer.

Krutwig Sagredo, F. 1973. *Vasconia*, 3 ed. Buenos Aires: Norbait (Originally published as Sarrailh de Ihartza, Fernando. *Vasconia*. Buenos Aires: Norbait, 1962).

———. 1987. 'El echo vasco, el euskera, y el territorio de Euskadi', *Euskal Batzar Orokorra. Congreso Mundial Vasco. 2° aniversario.* Vitoria: Gobierno Vasco, pp. 130–131.

Kythreotis, A. P. 2012. 'Progress in Global Climate Change Politics? Reasserting National State Territoriality in a "Post-Political" World', *Progress in Human Geography*, 36(4): 457–474.

Lecours, A. 2007. *Basque Nationalism and the Spanish State.* Reno, NV: University of Nevada Press.

Letamendia Belzunde, F. 1975. *Historia de Euskadi. El nacionalismo vasco y ETA.* Paris: Ruedo Ibérico.

———. 1977. Les Basques: Un peuple contre les états. Paris: Seuil.

———. 2006. 'Las organizaciones agrarias vascas: el ejemplo de Euskal Herriko Labo-rantza Ganbara', in F. L. Belzunde, ed., *Acción colectiva Hegoalde-Iparralde.* Madrid: Ed. Fundamentos, pp. 228–243.

Levene, M., and Conversi, D. 2014. 'Subsistence Societies, Globalisation, Climate Change and Genocide: Discourses of Vulnerability and Resilience', *International Journal of Human Rights*, 18(3): 279–295.

MacCormick, N. 1999. Questioning Sovereignty: Law State and Nation in the European Commonwealth. Oxford: Oxford University Press.

Mann, A. 2014. *Global Activism in Food Politics: Power Shift.* Basingstoke, Hampshire: Palgrave Macmillan.

Mann, M. 2005. *The Dark Side of Democracy: Explaining Ethnic Cleansing.* Cambridge, MA: Cambridge University Press.

McMichael, P. 2014. 'Rethinking Land Grab Ontology', *Rural Sociology*, 79(1): 34–55.

Mees, L. 2003. Nationalism, Violence and Democracy: The Basque Clash of Identities. New York: Palgrave Macmillan.

Minca, C. 2007. 'Agamben's Geographies of Modernity', *Political Geography*, 26(1): 78–97.

Montanari, M. 2004. *Il cibo come cultura*, 1 ed. Roma: GLF editori Laterza.

———. 2006. *Food Is Culture.* New York: Columbia University Press.

Moreno, L., and Conversi, D. 2017a. 'Modelo Social y Límites al Crecimiento en el Antro-poceno', *Eunomía*, (12): 310–314.

——— 2017b. 'Antropoceno, Cambio Climático y Modelo Social', Documentación Social (monográfico sobre '*Cambio climático y crisis socioambiental*'), (183): 13–30.

Neville, K. J., and Dauvergne, P. 2012. 'Biofuels and the Politics of Mapmaking', *Political Geography*, 31(5): 279–289.

Oxfam International. 2011. Land and Power: The Growing Scandal Surrounding the New Wave of Investments in Land. Oxford: Oxfam International.

Parenti, C. 2011. *Tropic of Chaos: Climate Change and the New Geography of Violence.* New York: Nation Books.

Pérez-Agote, A. 1984. *La reproducción del nacionalismo: el caso vasco.* Madrid: Centro de Investigaciones Sociológicas /Siglo XXI.

———. 1987. *El nacionalismo vasco a la salida del franquismo.* Madrid: Centro de Investigaciones Sociológicas.

Sage, C. 2014. 'The Transition Movement and Food Sovereignty: From Local Resilience to Global Engagement in Food System Transformation', *Journal of Consumer Culture,* 14(2): 254–275.

Sassen, S. 1996. *Losing Control? Sovereignty in an Age of Globalization.* New York: Columbia University Press.

Smith, A. D. 1996. *Nations and Nationalism in a Global Era.* Cambridge: Polity Press.

———. 1998. Nationalism and Modernism: A Critical Survey of Recent Theories of Nations and Nationalism. London: Routledge.

———. 2009. *Ethno-Symbolism and Nationalism: A Cultural Approach.* London: Routledge.

Smith, M. 2009. 'Against Ecological Sovereignty: Agamben, Politics and Globalisation', *Environmental Politics,* 18(1): 99–116.

Stegmann, T., and Sancliment-Solé, M., eds. 2014. *Katalonien: Der diskrete Charme der kleinen Staaten.* Münster: Lit Verlag.

Teubal, M. 2009. 'Agrarian Reform and Social Movements in the Age of Globalization: Latin America at the Dawn of the Twenty-First Century', *Latin American Perspectives,* 36(4): 9–20.

Tilly, C. 1992. *Coercion, Capital, and European States, AD. 990–1990,* 2 ed. Cambridge, MA: Blackwell.

———. 2002. 'War Making and State Making as Organized Crime', in C. L. Besteman, ed., *Violence: A Reader.* New York: New York University Press, pp. 35–60.

Tremlett, G., and Arie, S. 2003. 'Aznar Faces 91% Opposition to War', *The Guardian,* 29 March. www.guardian.co.uk/world/2003/mar/29/spain.iraq.

Valle, T. del. 1994. *Korrika: Basque Ritual for Ethnic Identity.* Reno, NV: University of Nevada Press.

Waley, D. P., and Dean, T. 2010. *The Italian City Republics.* Harlow: Longman.

Walker, R. B. J. 1992. *Inside/Outside: International Relations as Political Theory.* Cambridge, MA: Cambridge University Press.

Wittman, H. 2009. 'Reworking the Metabolic Rift: La Vía Campesina, Agrarian Citizenship, and Food Sovereignty', *The Journal of Peasant Studies,* 36(4): 805–826.

Wolford, W., Borras, S. M., Hall, R., Scoones, I., and White, B. 2013. 'Governing Global Land Deals: The Role of the State in the Rush for Land', *Development and Change,* 44(2): 189–210.

Yeh, E. T. 2012. 'Transnational Environmentalism and Entanglements of Sovereignty: The Tiger Campaign Across the Himalayas', *Political Geography,* 31(7): 408–418.

Zabalo, J., Mateos, T., and Iraola, I. 2013. 'Conflicting Nationalist Traditions and Immigration: The Basque Case From 1950 to 1980', *Nations and Nationalism,* 19(3): 513–531.

Zalbide, J. L. 1963. *La insurrección en Euskadi.* Bayonne: Goiztiri.

Zimmerman, P. W. 2012. 'The Conceyu Nacionalista Astur and the Delegitimization of Nationalist Violence in Post-Franco Asturias, 1976–82', *International Journal of Iberian Studies,* 25(1): 21–40.

Zirakzadeh, C. E. 2010. 'Joseba Zulaika's Terrorism: The Self-Fulfilling Prophecy', *Anthropological Quarterly,* 83(4): 931–936.

Zulaika, J. 1988. *Basque Violence: Metaphor and Sacrament.* Reno, NV: University of Nevada Press.

————. 2010a. 'The Terror/Counterterror Edge: When Non-Terror Becomes a Terrorism Problem and Real Terror Cannot Be Detected by Counterterrorism', *Critical Studies on Terrorism*, 3(2): 247–260.

————. 2010b. *Terrorism: The Self-Fulfilling Prophecy*. Chicago: University of Chicago Press.

————. 2011. 'The War on Terror and the Paradox of Sovereignty: Declining States and States of Exception', in C. J. Greenhouse, ed., *Ethnographies of Neoliberalism*. Philadelphia, PA: University of Pennsylvania Press.

Zulaika, J., and Douglass, W. A. 2008. 'The Terrorist Subject: Terrorism Studies and the Absent Subjectivity', *Critical Studies on Terrorism*, 1: 27–36.

2 Changes in the Basque sovereignty demand

Iban Galletebeitia and Pedro Ibarra Güell

This article analyzes how the affirmation of and demand for sovereignty has been constructed in the Basque country. It does so in a dynamic and evolutionary form, considering the social context and collective consciousness from which the conception of sovereignty has been set in motion. It also investigates the political, cultural, economic and institutional factors – and their corresponding mobilizations – that have caused the assertion of and demand for sovereignty to advance or retreat. And, finally, it considers how these factors have in turn influenced the definition of one or another type of sovereign national consciousness.

The broader aim of this study is to explore how Basque actors are reorienting their discussions on the nature of sovereignty to encompass new recognitions of the complexity of multiple identities, and reflections on the changing implications of nationhood and citizenship under transnational impacts, especially within the European Union (EU). The study further presents an opportunity to propose an analytical model which would take into account the confluence of multiple factors and contexts that combine to influence the emergence, consolidation and territorial spread of a determinate assertion of national sovereignty.

Euskadi: the Basque country and its political space

Our analysis will be focused on what we might call the 'political space' of the Basque Country (Euskal Herria), namely Euskadi. It is important to note that the Basque territory, known as Euskal Herria (literally 'Basque Country'), covers a larger geographic area than the specifically 'political space' of Euskadi. Euskal Herria is an area that defines a historical and cultural entity, sharing a significant heritage of art, culture, language, history, and identity. The collective subject of Euskal Herria is divided into three different political and juridical entities. Two of them – the Autonomous Community of the Basque Country (Euskadi) and the Foral Community of Navarre – form a part of the Spanish state. Together, these two areas are known as Hegoalde, the southern part of Euskal Herria. The northern part – Iparralde – belongs to the French Republic.

This chapter will focus exclusively on the question of sovereignty in Euskadi. It is in this specific community we find a level of political autonomy that is high enough to generate what we might call a consciousness of pre-sovereignty, or the perception of its viability. Moreover, it is only in this community, in the territory of Euskadi, that we find a Basque national consciousness that expresses itself as a nation, and makes a demand for sovereignty. For several decades, the political debate on the sovereignty of Euskadi was shaped by the actions of the militant group ETA (Euskadi 'ta Askatasuna – Basque Homeland and Freedom). After the cessation of armed activities by ETA in 2011, debates about the 'right to decide' (self-determination) were reinvigorated. In the current debates, the actors have realized the need to rethink the nature of sovereignty, taking into consideration the changing status of nationhood and citizenship within the EU.

We need to keep in mind that we are analyzing a part of Europe that is economically prosperous, having changed during the past two centuries from a rural and poor region to an urbanized society. Culturally, it has customary practices based on a high level of cooperation and solidarity. Technologically, this is again a developed society, with a strong industrial drive. Politically, the Basque case is also complex, presenting a pluralistic map with four big political parties: Partido Nacionalista Vasco (PNV, the Basque Nationalist Party), EH Bildu (a coalition of the Basque nationalist Left including Eusko Alkartasuna, Aralar and Alternatiba), Partido Socialista Obrero Español (PSOE, the Spanish Socialist Workers' Party) and its Basque branch, Partido Socialista de Euskadi-Euskadiko Ezkerra (PSE-EE), and finally Partido Popular (PP, the People's Party – which is currently the largest political party in Spain).

We are dealing in this case with experiences and processes of a transnational, or even post-global, construction of sovereignty, situated in a western European context where peace (at least between states), prosperity and democracy have formed the backdrop for seventy years. However, this Europe must be made and reproduced every day, as a process that is dynamic, complex and under construction in interdependent and asymmetrical ways. This means that each nation state of the European Community must adapt itself to the EU's institutional and organizational standards of governance and its new, networked citizenry. Modern European (and Basque) society is undergoing a period of transition from a solid (tangible) modernity to liquid (intangible) modernity, as described by Zygmunt Bauman (2000); as Joan Subirats (2006) points out, we are going through a period of accelerated and global change. Certainly, nation states are experiencing times of uncertainty and asymmetrical interdependence with implications for the construction of sovereignty. As detailed by Charles Tilly (1992), this is a reflection of the history of collective violence that ultimately crystallized as the nation state. Nonetheless, it is worth underscoring that today, in the midst of the passage through the post-global period, Europe continues to be an object of study as a space of democracy and welfare under construction, consolidated in the stable democracies that are referential for today's cosmopolitan world.

When we focus on the great global changes, we can see that the features of today's world display the logics of expulsion (Sassen 2014). Meanwhile, the citizenry enjoys enormous technological advances (Goldin 2013), well described as a 'smartification' of the relations and efficient productivity of contemporary capitalism (Rifkin 2014), once perceptively defined as 'creative destruction' (Schumpeter

1947). Today, standardization of European Community systems, bureaucracies and models of multi-governance means that each nation state makes and rethinks its own strategic dynamic of stability within the EU framework. This in turn produces a rethinking and molding of the perceptions and habits of the citizenry of each nation state, who must also rearticulate their forms of welfare, relations and life, now inserted into a reflexive and post-industrial post-materialism. The citizenry channels its demands for more sovereign stability and democratic governance into their corresponding organizations, demanding democratic legitimacy from political parties as well as non-governmental organizations and social movements. In some European states, including Spain, we also find a reemergence of historical 'nationalities'. These are facilitated in part by the non-crystallization of a unitary nation state project, or the unfinished nature of nation state-building, and in part by the failed management of peripheral nationalist projects by the state. The non-closure of contentions such as the Basque dispute ultimately highlights the need to resolve new demands and articulations in some manner, in the European context as well as the larger global framework.

Theoretical reflections

Without question, our analytical proposal is based on a somewhat complex theoretical framework. The issue of sovereignty is closely tied to concepts like people, nation, democracy, territory and the state. At the same time, these concepts, with some exceptions, always operate from two perspectives: the objective and the subjective. As a result, it is obligatory to establish a relational process that defines these concepts, and to do so from both of the two perspectives.

People and nation

The relation between *demos* (people) and nation is the starting point for elucidating our complex relational model. There is a 'people' when a community perceives and defines itself as a democratic community, and puts that definition into practice. The key lies in the decision-making process. A 'people' is affirmed and constituted in democratic practice, and maintains the popular democratic status through its social practices and institutions. What is relevant in that consciousness of being a 'people' is not so much the content that is collectively asserted as the repetition of defining oneself in the popular condition, through continuous and enduring decision-making processes.

As a 'people', the community that is materially defined by living in a particular territory shares the conviction of being the bearer of the right to justice, of the right not to be relegated from the common welfare, of the demand for the reestablishment of justice when it is violated, and for the reparation of affronts when these occur. Above all, what it shares is the fact of being a community that characterizes and defines itself through the exercising of democracy, in the definition of needs and priorities, in the choice of its leaders and in the demand that the latter should fulfil their promises and commitments. In the final instance, this happens through the conviction of the community that it has the legitimate right, and is prepared, to democratically decide on its future.

The final democratic conviction already expresses the existence of a national will. Arising from the demos, the conviction of being a nation, of being a unitary political subject, implies the certainty that there is a historical process of communitarian differentiation; that the democratic community also constitutes a differentiated community and that the differential factor that makes the nationalist discourse plausible is based on objective features like language, shared history, etc. Without doubt as well, the process of affirmation, recognition and defense of that difference is nourished from everyday practice. It is increasingly indisputable that both the construction and the corresponding affirmation of the nation rest not only on objective data, but on life experiences that are experienced as different and as one's own. This ranges from the construction of difference on the basis of the nuances of everyday life – the cultures of leisure, work, shared management of common affairs – to the culture of assertion and protest.

The affirmation of being a community with democratic capacity, with the full capacity for deciding on its political future without any limitation, constitutes a distinctive feature that we could say *closes* the construction of the national imaginary. This is also reflected in academic theorization on the construction of the national as imaginary. Benedict Anderson's idea of the 'imagined community' establishes the community as a construction rather than a preexisting object (Anderson 2006). An inadequate (but quite common) interpretation of this idea posits the community as *nothing but* imaginary. What is worth noting is that the 'imagined community' is not *only* imaginary, which would appear to be almost delusional or crazy, or without meaning. In other words, to imagine that we share something with others is not an imaginary in the sense of a foolish delusion. On the contrary, this imaginary is something that ultimately builds reality socially and gives meaning to the life of the community. Following Ernesto Laclau (2005), we could say that the collective imaginary discourse circumscribes the idea of a life in common, or shared sense of community.

The process of nation-building, which is not so much based on the demos but takes place alongside it, is a simultaneous process of mutual feedback between the one and the other. One – the people – contributes the lived experience and demand for democracy. The other – the nation – the existence of a 'complete' political subject. The 'people' becomes national, acquiring consciousness of its unity arising from shared difference and taking up a historical project of self-government. The nation becomes democratic and it uses the democratic argument of the right to decide that emerges, amongst other sources, from its practice as a people.

This confluent dynamic between people and nation makes it practically impossible for exclusive differences to be established between the two. There can be a 'people' that does not reach the category of nation. That is, there can be a 'people' that does not assume that its category as a collective subject *requires* that it demand the unrestricted right to rule itself. But there are also many nations that define themselves according to 'popular' features, above all (but not exclusively) nations whose citizens share the collective will to live in justice, welfare and liberty, and above all to decide on their political self-government for strictly democratic reasons. And there are also 'more national' nations, whose conception and political demands are identified more (but not exclusively) with a series of collective differentiating features involving identity.

It is also possible to assign with a provisional character greater subjectivity to the concept of people and greater objectivity to the nation. But its supposedly objective features are really measurable data. It is a nation because it shares collective difference, because certain cultural, linguistic, historical and other features are shared, to which, additionally, special relevance and meaning are given. Those are the features that make up the nation. Thus the nation exists because a particular group of persons has decided to choose particular cultural and historical features and use these to form a shared vision and narrative. That is where collective difference is found: it exists, but it is constituted for national use.

Sovereignty

The concept, experience and demand for sovereignty 'sail along', appear or are sometimes only latent in these processes of confluence of popular and national imaginaries.

For the purpose of our work, we set out from a limited conception of sovereignty – a conception that is distanced from the classic state version. Indeed, we are not referring to that sovereign state which supposedly exercises in fullness, without limits or exterior controls, its normative capacity, its full and unrestricted capacity for imposing its political will. We are now referring to the status of sovereignty in communities, peoples, nations that do not have their own state. In nations – latent or active – that in the final instance aspire to have a political power of their own.

On this terrain, sovereignty is perceived as a lived experience and, at the same time, as a demand. To feel and demand sovereignty emerges as a consequence of that conversion of the people into the nation and, at the same time, of the popularization, the democratization, of the nation on inserting its discourse, its symbols and its differential practices into the popular community.

As a lived experience, sovereignty appears rarely in an express form – and even more rarely verbalized as an obvious routine of a community that takes decisions. Its social demands are heard and even in part resolved by the leaders it has elected. Social criticisms are borne with greater or less enthusiasm by those elected leaders, and these latter tend to be answerable for their activity and to incorporate claims and criticisms into their decision-making processes. The exercise of democracy therefore has consequences for decision-making. That community also takes decisions about its forms of collective life. About leisure, about its culture, about its organization of work, about resolving particular collective problems and grievances, about how to demand changes in society and in politics.

On our terrain of stateless nations, sovereignty is also a political demand. At heart, sovereignty implies achieving a status of plenitude for that diffuse lived experience. An activation of that collective decision-making potential that is only felt, only perceived, in particular spaces, and activating it in its political dimension. That is, affirming that a specific community, or people, is a nation and therefore has the capacity and legitimacy to decide for itself about what its political future and its level of self-government should be.

With respect to our relational model, we shall see at the appropriate point how the demand for political sovereignty is articulated and driven by different variables, depending on what factor or culture has played a leading role in that confluent and enriching relation between people and nation. If the popular dimension has been more influential, the democratic discourse and the demands for a welfare state will be the decisive factor, and if it is the nation that has been more influential, then contexts, discourses and convictions of a more cultural character will be decisive.

The model: relational processes

In the framework of the processes of confluence of popular and national imaginaries and their consequences for the lived experiences and demands of sovereignty, our analysis starts by observing how, from a determinate community, a sense of the perception of shared difference is built collectively. We consider what factors of experience and culture cause the emergence of that perception. Different languages, different traditions, different histories, different forms of economic and political life. This collective self-perception of difference enters a process in which it is agitated, orientated and driven by different actors, and it is framed in determinate institutional spaces led by political actors who, in their turn, confront other political actors from other higher communities.

It is in this dynamic process that the existence of a collective national identity emerges and is made explicit, affirming the existence of the nation. At the same time, simultaneously or successively and not always in an ascendant lineal form, the conviction emerges within that national conception that the community constitutes a sovereign entity. That set of individuals who occupy a determinate territory and who have given a status of objectivity to their perception and construction of collective difference demands to decide on the management and future of their community in all its dimensions, including the political dimension. Perception and affirmation that they form part of a sovereign nation that has the full right to decide on the general interest, on how conflicts should be managed, and on how to establish a series of principles of justice, equality and liberty. And, at the same time, it and only it must decide and choose who are to be its governors.

Sovereignty, imagined sovereignty, is something that is evidently constructed from society. But also, as we have just noted, the dynamic in the construction of that sovereignty – of what is in the final instance an affirmation and at the same time a demand – varies according to a series of circumstances and variables. Thus, the economic and cultural context, the role of political parties, the role of social mobilizations and of the 'enemy' state, have an influence and are determinate to a degree that will be seen. And of course in the Basque case, there is the function of political violence. On the other hand, different confluences of these variables and contexts shape and propose different types of nation; more or less inclusive, more or less civic, etc. Differences which, in their turn, determine different pro-sovereignty strategies: the ethnic strategy, the strategy of resistance and the democratic one, etc.

There is an interactive relation amongst all of these contexts, variable conjunctures and processes. In their pro-sovereignty proposals the political actors do not confine themselves to reproducing the level of collective consciousness on this question found in the population. We can say that those political and institutional actors formalize, rationalize, generalize and politicize that sense of belonging that is perceived and felt by the social majorities – that collective emotion, established in symbols and complicities, that makes them live and feel themselves to be participants of a sovereign imagined community. And on the other hand, the ideological and strategic claims of the political actors must be adapted to the specific and concrete form in which the population feels the differential collective fact and sovereign capacity.

Here we reiterate something that was said before. Usually the concept of sovereignty is employed to define a central feature of states. It is said that what characterizes a state is its sovereignty, its unlimited and non-dependent capacity of taking political decisions. This is not where our reflection is situated. We are speaking of communities, even if they are perceived diffusely, that are able in practice to take certain collective decisions, and at the same time convinced that they want to fully exercise their sovereignty through a state that they want, but do not have. That is, we are talking of territorial communities that assert themselves as a nation, and that therefore have the right to decide as a nation how they wish to govern themselves, and up to which point they wish to do so. In our case, then, sovereignty is indistinguishable from the sovereign capacity of deciding to exercise political power. This is the terrain in which our case is situated, as it is a determinate community that is asserting itself as a nation.

The historical process: towards new networks

We fully agree with Lecours (2007: 24) when he states that 'Basque nationalism is totally exceptional among cases of sub-state nationalism in the West. This is true if one focuses uniquely on ETA, but appears more problematic if the Basque case is considered more broadly'. If we widen our analytical gaze, not only focusing on the exceptional character of ETA, the Basque case bears much more resemblance to the Scottish or Catalan cases. The collective will of these 'imagined communities' in this type of case is determinant and expresses itself in a democratic collective act; that collectively expressed national will have as a reference, as a support, the existence of objective elements. This has nothing to do with the defence of a pre-existing, eternal and unnegotiable objective nation (Ibarra Güell 2008; Ibarretxe 2010; Goikoetxea 2013). We are interested in those emergent demands for more sovereignty that have as their 'target' obtaining more self-government power for their corresponding demos and how these will be articulated. For this reason, the theoretical framework of European multi-governance leads us to situate our research on at last five levels in a hierarchic and asymmetrical form: the global, the communitarian, the state, the regional and the local levels, framed and anchored in the two hegemonic discursive frameworks/spaces of global capitalism and Western European democracy.

Historical antecedents: until the start of the civil war (1936)

The historical evolution of the concept of sovereignty in the particular Basque case takes us back to distant periods of history. It should be recalled that the Basques had their own state, territory, sovereign authority and rights (constituted under the Kingdom of Navarre until 1512). Subsequently, the competition between the two great imperial states of Europe (the French and Spanish states) over the Basque country is rooted in different politico-military conflicts: in the loss of sovereignty and its rearticulation/constitution and consensus or imposition over the course of civil wars. It also passes transversally through both civil and local-regional conquests to form part of alliances in world wars, and the competition is today situated and problematized within the greatest global financial crisis ever experienced in the institutionalized Western democracies. Consequently, the different crystallizations of each nation-state have provided the differentiated communities with different possibilities with different actors and conflicts. The territories of Hegoalde (the Basque country in Spain) kept their *fueros* (old laws), while in Iparralde (the Basque country in France) the native institutions were suppressed following the French Revolution, and the Basque regions were integrated into the *département* of the Lower Pyrenees. In the Spanish state there was a flowering of the national spirit of the Basque homeland as a community differentiated from the rest of Spain, while in the French state this was avoided due to its strong crystallization as a nation state.

At the end of the nineteenth century, new ideologies and new political movements appear – socialism and Basque nationalism – together with trade unionism. Basque nationalism was founded by Sabino Arana, and socialism was introduced into Bizkaia by Facundo Perezagua. In the mid-nineteenth century the first process of industrialization and capitalist development occurred. The most important area of industrial activity was around the Bilbao estuary, which attracted considerable immigration from Spain. By 1900, 27.8 per cent of the population of Bizkaia and twelve per cent of the population of Gipuzkoa were of immigrant origin. From the mid-nineteenth century onwards, there was also an intense emigration from Navarre to Euskadi and other areas. Sabino Arana created a discourse of those from 'here' and the 'maquetos' from abroad (Basque national identity was at first articulated as Basque nationalism around the idea of race, a shared common ethnicity). It has its corresponding iconography and symbolism (Basque flags, musical instruments, dances, popular songs), and a Basque folklore emerged that both served to differentiate and to bind together a well-founded community that was closed to the outside world. The whole social system changed with the industrialization in the late nineteenth century which produced a high, middle and petit bourgeoisie, professional classes, farmers and fishermen and a wage-earning working class.

The created discourse of the hermetic cultural identitarian community was to endure as an argument in contexts ranging from neighborhood and tavern discussions to the work of renowned academics – both Basque and Spanish or international experts – as a central question for understanding the Basque case. However, the great power of historians to further differentiate what is different, and to underscore racial ethnic difference, has in many cases led to the Basque problem being understood in a way that focuses solely on the ethnic aspect, leaving aside aspects referring to the question of sovereignty.

The Spanish Restoration ended in a *coup d'etat* that installed the dictatorship of Miguel Primo de Rivera (1923–30). In 1931, however, the Second Republic was proclaimed, forcing King Alfonso XIII into exile. The Second Republic brought great political activity, followed by the military rebellion of Francisco Franco and a long civil war (1936–39). The demand for the recovery of self-rule was made from Euskadi, but the Autonomy Statute was not approved by the Republican Parliament until October 1936, at the height of the civil war. The first Basque government was then created, with José Antonio Aguirre as President. This Executive was formed of five Basque nationalists, three socialists, one communist and one member of each of the republican parties. It had significant powers due to the special situation of the time, but was only able to control the territories of Bizkaia and Gipuzkoa, as Araba and Navarra were in the hands of the Francoist army from the outset. All of the Basque country was taken by the Francoist army in July 1937, which forced the Basque government to move first to Cataluña and then into exile in April 1939.

It is now worth emphasizing from the foregoing those cultural and political contexts, together with the discourses and strategies of parties, that shape the affirmation and demand for Basque sovereignty. Throughout the twentieth century and until the civil war, the Basque Nationalist Party (Partido Nacionalista Vasco, PNV) extended the reach of its national discourse to sectors of the Basque population who perceived themselves to be members of a differentiated community. Without any doubt, this perception – based above all on the Basque language, on symbols and traditions, on certain communitarian economic experiences and on practices of institutional self-government – did not in itself lead to the affirmation of being a nation, and even less of being a sovereign nation with everything that is implied by that. It is the nationalist discourse and the social and political action of the first nationalist movement that give political meaning to that perception and collective consciousness of shared difference.

The nationalist discourse is adopted by broad sectors of the population insofar as they themselves see their traditions, their language and their pre-national collective identity placed in danger because of the liberal policies of the central government, the industrialization proceeding from competitive capitalism and, in the final instance, because of modernization. Thus, this first nationalism, this first understanding and collective affirmation of being a sovereign community, appears closely linked to what we could call an identity of resistance. The demand of sovereignty for the Basque nation appears necessary so as to resist the drive of external cultural and political forces that place that differential identity, which is experienced as something positive, in danger.

On the other hand, in the imagined Basque nation which was constructed in that period, in the interactive relation between the population and the Basque nationalists in PNV, ethnic features hold a special relevance. Let us recall where they emerged from, namely the lived experiences of differentiating objective realities – language, tradition, etc. – understood to constitute the untouchable body of the community. The definition of the national community also tended to be exclusive, directly or indirectly affirming that the Basque nation is formed solely by those who share and defend the objective identity features.

Historical antecedents: the Francoist dictatorship (1939–77)

Euskera (the Basque language) and Basque culture in general were persecuted, all political and trade union activity was banned and there was an immense repression (imprisonment, exile, executions), especially in the first stage. Any hope that international powers would help overthrow the Francoist regime disappeared in the early 1950s, when the United States and the Vatican reached agreements with Franco. The definitive step came in 1953, when on 27 August the Regime signed the Concordat with the Vatican, which resolved relations between Church and State. This was, moreover, an international endorsement of Francoism. The situation was settled one month later with the signing of the so-called Pact of Madrid, by which Spain and the United States reconfirmed their relations. On 14 December 1955, the General Assembly of the United Nations admitted sixteen new countries, including Spain (as number sixty-five, alphabetically ordered at the time of its admittance). It would take another twenty years for the country to be restored to democracy.

In the late 1950s and during the 1960s, there was a second industrialization, which produced significant economic and social changes in the Basque provinces and a new wave of immigration of workers from other Spanish provinces. The resistance to the dictatorship from the left and from nationalism was very active, especially from the late 1960s onwards. There was a rebirth of interest in Euskera and Basque culture. The workers' movement grew in strength. The ETA organization was created in 1959. This had a nationalist and left-wing ideology and began an armed struggle during the 1960s. In the 1970s, Francoism entered into crisis. There was a growth in political and labor strikes, ETA increased its armed actions and the Basque church adopted critical positions towards the regime. All of this brought even stronger repression, with court martial, states of exception, thousands of arrests and imprisonments, some executions (a.o. Puig Antich, Txiki, and Otaegi), deaths during demonstrations (San Sebastián, Vitoria-Gasteiz in 1976, and Pamplona in 1978) and in police stations, and an erosion of support for the regime. In 1973, a bomb planted by ETA killed the Spanish Prime Minister, Luis Carrero Blanco, who was designated to succeed Franco.

Isolation, nostalgia, agony and resistance are the four sensations, attitudes and experiences of the population that are closest – in traditional narratives – to the national collective imaginary. The groups and social sectors related to or influenced by the Basque Nationalist Party (PNV) shared with it an attitude of a certain resigned passivity. And the survival of the Basque nation beyond the nostalgia for past times, in which there was a sensation of belonging to a community that also exercised a certain political power, seemed far removed given the existing repression. The PNV envisaged the future of that nation in the establishment of democracy in Spain. On that line, it maintained its alliances with Western European and North American allies, without these alliances attaining their objectives. This was a feeling and discourse that would wait for the dictatorship to end, so as to begin the recovery and affirmation of the experience of the national community in a democratic situation. These were times when the desire for the fullness of a sovereign national community appeared to be far off on the horizon. The nation was only experienced as the collective project of being able in the future to appear and express oneself as a member of a different community.

The feeling of national belonging was experienced in a restricted way, given its limited diffusion amongst those minority sectors of the population who in principle found self-affirmation in collective difference. At the same time, they experienced this in an agonizing form: agony as a feeling of the loss of something close, which leads to the radicalization of action. Along this line, a different kind of discourse and national experience emerged from the armed option of ETA. ETA's national proposal was different and radical. It was different insofar as its message coincided with a type of social perceptions and experiences that were different from the ethnic/traditional perceptions proceeding from the nationalism of the PNV. For this reason, access to its community of reference was not only achieved through ethnic belonging, but also due to the idea of sharing attitudes of confrontation with the dictatorship, due to sharing radical democratic attitudes. From this perspective, the conception of the nation was broadened. In principle, all of those who, while giving special importance to certain identity questions such as the Basque language, took part in the democratic will to reject the Francoist dictatorship could and should form part of the nation.

Nonetheless, the option of armed struggle and its practice marked both the discourse and the social perception of those who accepted and upheld it in society. Indeed, opting for violence was justified as the answer to a state of necessity, which arose from defining the situation of the Basque nation as being on the point of death. This is a situation that generates the belief that the nation – or more exactly the feeling of national belonging – is going to disappear buried beneath the repression, due to fear and due to forgetting. This is a situation that requires, according to its discourse, radical, violent measures that, while being traumatic, are the only way to stop the process of disappearance.

This practical and discursive radicalism in a certain way deactivates that more-inclusive conception of the nation that was noted above. Although in theory the latter is open to all those who struggle for democracy, in practice it is defended, and also defined, as something acceded to by those who effectively struggle to attain the full independence of the Basque nation. It is from this perspective of radicalization that one must understand the non-appearance within social perception of a political 'feeling' corresponding to sovereignty. The Basque national community linked to the violent proposal experienced the nation as something that must be saved in an absolute, radical form, without intermediate processes. This implied a leap, which is also radical, towards independence. The choice, apparently, was between the death of the nation and full national independence. Sovereignty conceived as the step of affirming the capacity to decide – and that such a decision could lead to eventual independence – was perceived as an unnecessary and dangerous process.

Historical antecedents: from the democratic transition to the end of ETA

With Franco's death in 1975, the transition to democracy began without any break with the dictatorship. Those responsible for the crimes of Francoism were never punished. Following a referendum that approved a series of reforms, the first legislative elections were held in June 1977, and the Spanish Constitution was approved in December 1978. The Constitution, which did not include the right of the Basques to decide on their future (the right to self-determination), only received the approval of one-third of eligible voters in Euskadi, and half of those in Navarre. The Statute of Autonomy was approved in a referendum in 1979, and Araba, Bizkaia and Gipuzkoa formed the Autonomous Community of the Basque Country, or Euskadi, with 53.96 per cent of the votes of the census. In Navarre the Organic Law of Reintegration and Improvement of the Foral Regime of Navarre was approved without a referendum in 1982. Conversely, Iparralde did not have any degree of autonomy.

While ETA continued to be active during these years, and its activism dragged behind it and contaminated the national proposals of the Basque nationalist left, moderate Basque nationalism led by the PNV dedicated itself to institutional management. It is from its leadership in the autonomous institutions of Euskadi that it has been building the sense of belonging to a different country with a certain political power.

Basque citizens, through the use of a series of public services like education, health, security and infrastructures and through the practice of the welfare state, begin to feel themselves members of a community that in some way already exercises that sovereignty – of a community that through its institutions decides by itself and for itself what is most beneficial for its citizens: what is in the general Basque interest.

In this respect we could talk of a quotidian pro-sovereignty experience, the experience of being and forming part of a national community, insofar as it decides for itself on collective public aspects. We could talk of a pro-sovereignty benefit. The citizens perceive that exercise in making their own decisions takes them comparatively closer to higher levels of welfare. As a result they tend to interiorize the benefit of developing that decision-making capacity to the maximum.

A context of sovereignty or semi-sovereignty is perceived but not formalized. Only at the start of 2001 was a proposal formulated by the Basque Nationalist

Party. This was the Ibarretxe Plan, which proposed a new status for the Basque Country assuming the existence of a sovereign nation with the right to decide. The proposal was rejected by the Spanish Parliament.

A pro-sovereignty proposal was also formulated within the radical nationalist left. The concept of self-determination as the exercise of that sovereignty had already emerged in the late 1990s within the left-wing nationalist movement. The appearance of pro-sovereignty discourse within a constituted sovereign state, whether the Spanish or French state, places whoever claims sovereignty under suspicion, especially if they do so under the form of a 'national liberation guerrilla war'. The victims resulting from its development and the collateral damages and impacts on civil society left the democrats representing that people in a position of discursive illegitimacy. From 1968 onwards, about 1,000 people died as a result of political violence; 800 of these deaths were caused by ETA. Especially following the transition to democracy, ETA carried out extremely bloody attacks and socially painful actions – attacks such as those at Hipercord and Vallecas, murders of democratically elected politicians, the kidnapping of Ortega Lara . . . Nonetheless, the state was not exemplary. There were para-police murders and deaths under torture in police stations, as well as limitations on political rights, *incommunicado* arrests, the closure of newspapers, etc.

In this period, in a more pronounced way than in the previous one, two senses of national belonging coexisted and competed, with their corresponding political and social discourses. With respect to the moderate nationalism of the Partido Nacionalista Vasco, throughout the period it opened up its conception of the Basque nation, introducing its characterization of a sovereign nation with the capacity and the right to decide. This opening up, this inclusive process, is due to the aim of adapting its discourse to changes and readjustments that are taking place in what we could call the national collective consciousness. Especially that belonging to the sectors of the population that, while defending nationalist positions, find themselves increasingly distanced from – if not in direct confrontation with – the radical nationalism defended by political violence. In this way civic readjustments appear. The national community continues to be perceived as that space where differentiated conditions of life and relationship are shared. But the national will also appears as a constitutive element of the nation. The existence of a nation is thus affirmed because its citizens, or a large part of them, consider it to be so, believe it to be so and want it to be so. The democratic discourse, fed by the practices and democratic culture of the period, conceptually shapes that feeling of belonging to a national community. And utilitarian readjustments emerge.

In the radical nationalist discourse and the national consciousness of the ensemble of citizens who support it, some fissures appear with respect to the previous period. But there is no substantial change while the violent activity of ETA continues. The permanent and hard demands of defending the armed option do not permit support communities that are excessively plural, excessively diffuse and that have a low level of commitment. On the contrary, that unconditional defense requires a committed community and one that is thus inevitably exclusive, a resistance community that although not identified with the nation is presented as that part of the population that really represents its essence.

However, it is also true that the contamination this radical community undergoes from quotidian nationalism, from the experience of large sectors of the population that are in some way a community with a reasonable level of self-government (from which the perception of the risk of imminent national death has disappeared), introduces a more evolutionary and gradual strategy. It is no longer necessary to take quasi-impossible but necessary leaps from the nation to independence. It is possible and even desirable to establish the pro-sovereignty process. That is, to advance towards that capacity of deciding and eventually to finalize the decision-making process with independence.

The present situation: a new and renovated political context

The analysis of the current situation has relied on extensive interviews in the Basque country to which we refer in the title of this book. In the final chapter of this book, we will detail the responses of these interviews, and ultimately we will confirm the main features that we have outlined.

The violence practiced for fifty years by ETA has finally come to a definitive end. The nationalist left can participate in the elections and, moreover, has representation as a major political force in the Autonomous Community of the Basque Country. The prominent *abertzale* left politician Arnaldo Otegi was released from prison in March 2016, cutting short a ten-year sentence from 2011 for attempting to rebuild the banned political party Batasuna. Despite Spanish inertia on penitentiary policy regarding ETA prisoners the Basque country is advancing on the path of peace and democracy. The Basque government has stability agreements for its budgets with the ruling party in Spain, it has formulated a plan for truth and reconciliation together with the former founder of Elkarri and Baketik, and it has introduced a new dialogue on Basque self-government and its status in the Basque Parliament.

The new context of peace makes it necessary to consider the contemporary reorientation of Basque perspectives on sovereignty. New reflections on the past and democratic demands are central components in the reconsideration of the sovereignty issue. In the process of defining a people's sovereignty, apart from culture and language, a people that aspires to have sovereignty and become a 'demos' must compete with regard to social rights, security and economic powers. This differs from the earlier focus, which has too often been placed on a concrete aspect, either on the cultural aspect or on terrorism/ violence.

Both are important 'fields', but without any doubt they are insufficient for explaining the Basque community's current trajectory towards sovereignty. The democratic debate is being incorporated into the different positions on sovereignty and into its different alternatives or formulations.

After more than thirty years of the state of the autonomous communities, with a quasi-federal system of parliamentary monarchy, the Spanish state has not fully crystallized as a 'standard' nation-state. Within it there are broad regional majorities grouped into autonomous communities with strong demands for sovereignty, even for secession in the Basque and Catalan cases. In the Spanish case it is foreseeable that we could be facing the opening up and readjustment of the constitutional architecture (a constitutional reform that has not been carried out since its creation). In the supranational sphere, the Basque case encounters 'transnational self-determination'. This involves an accelerated articulation that corresponds to cluster city-regions within a variable economic geometry, where 'the Basque case' is ranked amongst the successes by the OECD. And, at the same time, it encounters supranational institutions like the Strasbourg courts that on issues of justice and human rights provide protection to its citizens for their legitimate demands within the European framework.

In earlier historical phases, we established that nation-building and sovereignty proposals emerged from two social spaces and were also shaped differently. In very recent years we have been able to observe a tendency towards confluence. The perception and discourse proceeding from the community linked to radical nationalism has clearly entered a phase of opening up. With the disappearance of political violence, the need to construct a closed, exclusive community in defense of instrumental political violence disappears.

In the mainly institutional political struggle – and in any pacific case in favor of the liberation of the Basque nation – everyone can be present. No special commitment is needed. The features of identification of – and with – the national community become more flexible, more accessible:

- A certain recognition of 'objective' differences, with special reference to the language.
- Identifying democracy with the Basque nation by affirming that the demand to exercise national sovereignty is a democratic claim.
- Constitutive subjectivism: the decision of belonging to a national community by simply affirming its existence.

The political leaderships, and their corresponding national collective consciences proceeding from this field, are spreading this new inclusive discourse. To that end, and now from a more political perspective, the political parties with a more radical origin that lead this space are carrying out a set of mobilizations and forming social and political alliances that are also certainly widening their influence within the social demand for the exercise of national sovereignty.

The other nationalism, influenced by the Basque Nationalist Party (Partido Nacionalista Vasco), is re-orientating its perception of the nation and the corresponding demand for sovereignty on a similar line. The rigidly ethnic, essentialist features are being deactivated while the Basque language is maintained as the pillar of differentiality, making substantial use of the democratic argument in the affirmation of sovereignty and its political decision-making capacity. National consciousness is thus impressed with the need to develop sovereignty to the maximum in order to guarantee the limited but effective self-government that exists today, and to consolidate and widen the level of social welfare achieved to date. It seems that these more utilitarian arguments and perceptions have not yet been fully adopted in the discourse proceeding from the left-wing nationalism.

One of the factors which, as we noted at the beginning of the text, has had a significant influence on the configuration and development of these perceptions, discourses and strategies, has without doubt been the national policy of the central state – the Spanish state – with respect to the national and pro-sovereignty claims proceeding from the Basque country.

During the stage of the Francoist dictatorship the unconditional and permanent repression of the state facing national indications generated, in the first phase, a closure that involved a restrictive passivity. But it is clear that subsequently, above all from the 1960s onwards, this repression exacerbated, radicalized and spread national consciousness and its corresponding national claims.

Following the democratic transition, the actions and reactions arising from the always conflictive, confrontational relation between the central Spanish state and the national political movements and Basque political institutions opened up to more complex situations, whose consequences in terms of identity and discourse are more difficult to trace.

In any case, in recent years it has become evident that a clearly recent policy is now being put into effect by the Spanish state. It is of course no longer a question of widening powers in favor of the autonomous communities. On the contrary, it is a question of recovering powers that were in their day transferred to these autonomous communities, amongst them the Autonomous Community of the Basque Country. As a consequence of this regressive process of retrocession, it can be said that the pro-sovereignty discourse is acquiring even greater confidence. Such affronts are perceived as a provocation that requires more forceful answers, and at the same time the value of the democratic discourse makes even more sense in this new scenario.

Towards a democratic sovereignty

We find ourselves facing a novel form of articulating the pro-sovereignty strategy based on initiating civic ties in a democratic and pacific democratic form while moving towards a scenario where all political options are possible. We are facing a new dynamic of new attitudes, with new people mobilizing at the grass-roots level. But at the same time, we can see that in this case the institutions are also under way, working on the status of Basque self-government in the Basque Parliament. Success will depend on how the politic sphere (demand for the right to decide), political materialization (agreement amongst the different political parties) and a democratic, social mobilization are articulated.

At the structural level, we are living through a constituent process initiated by the citizenry and fed and strengthened by global and particular criticisms of the political system in general and of political mediatization in particular. We could say that the fields of decision-making have become distanced from, or privatized with respect to, ordinary citizens.

The evolution of the Basque dispute since 2004 with the proposal of a new political status initiated a novel course, starting on a path of political sovereignty in a discursive, civil and democratic mode, using exclusively pacific channels. This legacy, involving the Basque citizenry's right to decide democratically, has crystalized – or is crystalizing – little by little. Starting from popular grass-roots and with the confluence of the formalized demand and the popular demand, it is advancing with the institutional level thanks to the creative will of the Basque people and its capacities developed through practical experiences of successes and setbacks.

The recent mobilization organized by the Gure Esku Dago group succeeded in mobilizing over 150,000 people to form a human chain from Durango (Bizkaia) to Pamplona (Navarre), symbolizing and demanding the right to decide. These practices are examples of how the Basque citizenry has been the protagonist, helping to create networks of trust and repair broken bridges, starting from the grass-roots of politics: people. These broken bridges, found within political families that favor the right to decide, are starting to be rebuilt in a process leading towards a democratic scenario where the right to decide resides in the Basque citizenry.

It seems that this new scenario has, metaphorically speaking, stripped the collective actors bare with respect to relations, making possible a new, more relaxed and less hurried capacity to develop a new identity, without so much pressure from 'others': an identity that is not so much cultural as democratic. A reflection of this is the bill on the status of the Basque government.

The hybridization of the institutional, the organizational and the popular makes a scenario possible where the a priori issue is creating as a collective, with the tools at hand or creating new ones for that universal task. We define this trajectory as a trajectory towards the democracy of the Basque people, given that its majority – parliamentary, social, trade union, political – expresses it as such. This is a novel dynamic in which different actors come together and in which the discourse on the right to decide lies solely in the democratic decision of the Basque citizens. That self-fulfilled, imagined sovereignty puts into question earlier scenarios where the only dynamic lay in imitating the state.

Previously with ETA, in the political context, some shook the tree and others collected the fallen fruit. But it appears that dialectic has ended with the cessation of strategic fields of warlike action. It is also clear that the dynamic is unresolved, and that the political question will remain unresolved for the time being. That lack of resolution of the political question enables new articulations as well as new practices where political sovereignty is put into question and, at the same time, a new democratic and relational field is sought. The logic of the past led to a certain 'habitus' in Bourdieu's terms (1990), or in the terms of Fligstein and McAdam (2011, 2012), to a strategic line of action that was simply action-reaction-action.

What was sought in the lack of communication was, on the one hand (what ETA wanted), interlocution for an orderly finish, and on the other hand (what the Spanish state wanted), a final defeat of the Other, the enemy framed as the principal problem. Meanwhile, the citizenry did not advance in its desire for more status, with all that existed being its referential (reproductive) site: Basque self-government and its autonomy statute.

Both globalization and Spain's incorporation into a representative democratic scenario have strengthened the democratic dimensions in both the definition of the nation and its sovereign character from the decision-making perspective. The previous factors, together with the crisis of ideologies plus migratory flows, and a generalized increase of levels of welfare, have transformed the perception defining the nation, with growing civic features as against previous ethnic features.

The disappearance of the political violence led by ETA is producing a conception of the Basque nation that is more inclusive, more open, more civic, and is at the same time strengthening, from the affirmation of sovereignty, the legitimacy of the democratic demand to exercise the right to decide against the earlier radicalism of immediate independence.

References

Anderson, B. 2006. *Imagined Communities: Reflections on the Origin and Spread of Nationalism*. London: Verso Books.

Bauman, Z. 2000. *Liquid Modernity*. Cambridge, MA: Polity Press.

Bourdieu, P. 1990. *The Logic of Practice*. Cambridge, MA: Polity Press.

Fligstein, N., and McAdam, D. 2011. 'Toward a General Theory of Strategic Action Fields', *Sociological Theory*, 29(1): 1–26.

———. 2012. *A Theory of Fields*. Oxford: Oxford University Press.

Goikoetxea, J. 2013. 'Emancipatory Nationalism and Catalonia', *Ethnopolitics*, 12(4): 394–397.

Goldin, I. 2013. *Divided Nations: Why Global Governance Is Failing, and What We Can Do About It*. Oxford: Oxford University Press.

Ibarra Güell, P. 2008. *Relational Democracy* (William A. Douglass Distinguished Scholar Series). Reno, NV: Center for Basque Studies, University of Nevada, Reno.

Ibarretxe, J. J. 2010. 'Principio ético, principio democrático y desarrollo humano sostenible: Fundamentos para un modelo democrático' [Ethical Principles, Democratic Principles and Sustainable Human Development: Foundations for a Democratic Model]. Doctoral thesis submitted to Euskal Herriko Unibertsitatea-Universidad del País Vasco (EHU- UPV).

Laclau, E. 2005. *On Populist Reason*. London: Verso.

Lecours, A. 2007. *Basque Nationalism and the Spanish State*. Reno, NV: Center for Basque Studies, University of Nevada, Reno.

Rifkin, J. 2014. *The Zero Marginal Cost Society: The Internet of Things, the Collaborative Commons, and the Eclipse of Capitalism*. New York: Macmillan.

Sassen, S. 2014. *Expulsions: Brutality and Complexity in the Global Economy*. Cambridge, MA: Harvard University Press.

Schumpeter, J. A. 1947. 'The Creative Response in Economic History', *The Journal of Economic History*, 7(2): 149–159.

Subirats, J. 2006. 'Multi-Level Governance and Multi-Level Discontent: The Triumph and Tensions of the Spanish Model', in S. L. Greer, ed., *Territory, Democracy and Justice: Regionalism and Federalism in Western Democracies*. New York: Palgrave- Macmillan, pp. 175–200.

Tilly, C. 1992. *Coercion, Capital, and European States, AD 990–1992*. Oxford: Blackwell.

3 Sovereignty and contention

The evolution of Basque nationalism in Spain

Mario Zubiaga

The historical formation of the concept of sovereignty is inextricably linked to conflict. The concept's modern origins can be found in the state-building process that began in Europe with the crisis of the feudal legal and political model. For authors such as Hobbes and Bodin, sovereignty emerges as internal to statehood. In other words, sovereignty is a quality of a state's political power when it sets out to hold ultimate and supreme political authority in a particular territorial community, at odds with the jurisdictions of the medieval manors and the Church (Hinsley 1986). Later on, the concept of sovereignty was used in different ways, as legal-international sovereignty, Westphalian sovereignty and inter-dependent sovereignty (Krasner 1999). These conceptual modes are indeed connected with the achievement of mutual recognition between sovereign entities, the ability to exclude other state powers, and attempts to control flows of capital, information and people within the sphere of the territory's own borders. They are also linked to conflict dynamics wherein state agents and non-state actors interact in a contentious way.

Without losing sight of the external dimension of sovereignty, this chapter will focus on internal sovereignty, and contentions and discussions about the supreme and original authority of a state power over a territory and its citizens. The tension between the authoritarian principle and the popular principle is a key aspect of the debate on the legitimacy of political power. In the medieval cosmological view (C. De Cabo 1997), the divine origins of regal sovereignty were contrasted with the foundational character of the political community as the ultimate source of all political power. The categories that highlighted such tension were those of 'absolute sovereignty', 'limited sovereignty' and 'dual sovereignty'.

Once the threshold of modernity had been crossed, the historical process of state-building based on strengthening the state's institutional capacity correlated with progress in the ability of an ever-growing body of citizens to define public policies and elect representatives who would implement them. Thus, sovereign power, which at the outset was a mere quality of an authoritarian state power, steadily reinforced the connection with its political community, in a process that was later defined as democratization (Tilly 1984).

Within the framework of this historical survey, the conceptual category 'sovereignty' steadily evolves towards strengthening the idea that the original entitlement to political power rests with the political community. In the first instance, 'national sovereignty' (as a corollary of nation-building) replaced the symbolic source of political power characteristic of the monarchy with 'the nation', understood as a community with a sense of belonging that perceives itself as sovereign. In this sense the nation became the reference collective subject of supreme and original political power. Later on, the ideal community identified more and more with the body of citizens of the state – the *demos* –, whose collective will progressively determined institutional decision-making capacity, while at the same time the exercise of that institutional capacity steadily shaped the *demos'* own collective will (Goikoetxea 2014).

From that shift onwards, as a conceptual category, sovereignty became 'popular and democratic'. However, the actual transition from national sovereignty to popular sovereignty, in so far as it involved an expansion of the body of citizens that broke with the status quo, was conflictive, as we can see from European history over the past two centuries (Tilly 2004; Letamendia 1997). Moreover, even though national sovereignty (the nation) and popular sovereignty (the *demos*) are conceptually fused together in contemporary democratic states, in the second instance there emerges another question that enlivens the controversy: not all nations eventually become state *demoi* and not all state *demoi* have as a reference a single national community.

The conflictive character of the concept of sovereignty is intrinsic. It is no accident that a political community that defines itself as the supreme and original seat of political power wishes to express the desire for unfettered self-government via the sovereign state – the sole instrument that holds out such a possibility in the contemporary world, at least from a formal viewpoint. Nor is it an accident that such a political community will necessarily vie with other communities with the same aim.

To summarize, historical state-, nation- and democracy-building processes constitute the framework within which the concept of 'sovereignty' evolves over time, and these processes have been anything but peaceful. The theoretical debate has always been accompanied by ideological battles and, inevitably, social and political struggles. (Sassen 2006, 2007)

Thus, it is nationalism that is summarized in the demand for sovereignty, or the highest level of self-government, usually with the aim of acquiring or using the 'state' form which in turn changes a social group into a 'nation' (Brubaker 1996; Haas 1986). This constructivist outlook, connecting the emergence of the nation with political mobilization, enables us to apply to conflict over sovereignty – or national conflict – the analytical categories used for studying social movements (Maiz 2008; Guibernau 1999; Hastings 2000).

Contentious sovereignty-related processes and mechanisms

Some authors have applied the variables of the classic agenda of social movements to the nationalist struggle over sovereignty (Maiz 2008; Hroch 1993), and have analyzed the structure of political opportunity that favours the emergence of nationalism, nationalist speeches and organizations, and their mobilization repertoires. However, in so far as nationalism is a kind of political struggle within which can be detected similar processes and mechanisms as are present in other forms of struggle, we have opted in this paper for the theoretical framework provided by McAdam, Tarrow and Tilly (McAdam et al. 2001). Its overarching view is suitable for understanding the features of the contemporary Basque cycle of protest, in as much as that cycle is a confluence of various contentious episodes such as nationalism itself, democratization and even a few features proper to revolutionary episodes (Tarrow 2011; Diani 1996; Zubiaga 2008). The nationalist political struggle hence comes down to 'who has the right to control which territories, and who has the right to be a spokesperson for which community'. In such a struggle it becomes clear who enjoys sovereign political power, from whence that power comes and over which territory, and which population, that sovereignty is exercised.

Following this, there has been a longstanding Basque nationalist contention between 'the efforts of those members who identify themselves as the [Basque] nation, which does not control its own state, to acquire an independent state' and 'the efforts of the [Spanish and French] governing organs to ensure that their definitions of national culture and interest prevail within their own territories' (McAdam et al. 2001). One of the features of this mobilization cycle is that the Basque nationalist demand has gained a certain amount of institutional recognition, even though fragmented, in part of the territory that it proclaims as its own. The democratization episode which was opened up in Spain following Franco's death brought with it the decentralization of the state and the constitution of two autonomous territorial governments in the Spanish Basque territories. The government of the Autonomous Community of the Basque County (ACBC) has traditionally been run by moderate Basque nationalist forces – in contrast with what happened in the Chartered Community of Navarre, where the historical pact of the pro-Spanish forces closed the door to Basque nationalism.[1] At the same time, over the past few decades, a leftist nationalist force has advocated an insurgent alternative supported by the activity of the armed organization ETA.

The interaction between Spanish (and French) institutions, Basque institutions, Basque nationalist actors – institutional and insurgent – and Spanish political actors has defined a complex, transgressive and contained contentious episode, which calls for sophisticated analytical instruments. In a deep sense, a process of re-composition of sovereignty and integration or disintegration of states has been opened up in these nationalist mobilization cycles. This requires an analysis of dynamic mechanisms and processes as suggested by McAdam, Tarrow and Tilly in their work 'Dynamics of Contention' (McAdam et al. 2001), which gives special importance to what the authors call 'solid processes': the constitution of new actors and entities, polarization, and change of scale (McAdam et al. 2001: 315). Obviously, in the wide range of episodes in which a demand for sovereignty is in play, all three of these processes are generally present. Here I focus particularly on the first two, which are closely linked in nationalist episodes. The change of scale and diffusion process is on the fringe of the analysis, having less to do with the core of the episode than with the conditions under which it is extended.

The demand for sovereignty, to the extent that it goes hand in hand with the possibility of creating new political entities – whether sovereign state structural entities or merely decentralized ones – develops as a contentious episode through two great processes that are indispensable for the purpose: the constitution of new identities and actors – a new collective identity called 'Basque sovereignist'[2] – and the necessary polarization so as to enable that creation to be produced. That is, 'the enlargement of the political and social space between the claimants present in a contentious episode and gravitation toward one, the other, or both ends by certain formerly uncommitted or moderate actors'. In this case, polarization occurs along the axis of 'Basque sovereignty' vs. 'Spanish/French sovereignty'.

Processes of polarization and the emergence of new identities trigger various mechanisms – environmental, relational and cognitive. This tripartite classification (McAdam et al. 2001: 26) is somewhat arbitrary, in so far as only events that are beyond the control of the actors may be understood, in an extreme reading, as environmental mechanisms. In addition, cognitive and relational aspects may be difficult to separate. However, the expanded schema proposed here positions 'the opportunity spiral' tendentially as an environmental mechanism and defines 'competition', 'brokerage', 'social appropriation' and 'certification' as relational mechanisms. Finally, 'category formation', 'attribution of opportunity and threat' and 'tactical innovation in repertoires of action' are all regarded as cognitive mechanisms.

This map of explanatory mechanisms expands on the list suggested by McAdam et al. (2001), giving greater importance to processes of polarization and changing identity linked to defection. The new *map of secession mechanisms and processes* is put forward as an analytical model that should be useful for comparative studies (see for instance R. Riera and Zubiaga 2014). In the new model, to the extent that a connection between two processes is proposed, the separate mechanisms suggested by McAdam et al. (2001) come together. In this coming together, 'category formation', an essential cognitive mechanism both in change and the emergence of new identities, and in polarization, acquires special importance. Bearing in mind that we are analyzing the evolution of 'imagined sovereignty' in the Basque country, I will focus in this paper specifically on analyzing that 'category formation' and other mechanisms connected with it, particularly 'attribution of opportunity and threat'.

McAdam et al. (2001) defines 'category formation' thus: 'A social category consists of a set of sites that share a boundary distinguishing all of them from and relating all of them to at least one set of sites visibly excluded by the boundary.' As such, category formation defines a new boundary, or a new way of categorizing a concept, a demand, and a social and political site. At the same time, that boundary is incomprehensible unless reference is made to interaction with the space that lies outside of it. To paraphrase Laclau (2005), we would say that the imagined exterior is constitutive of imagined sovereignty.

The constitution of a discursive/symbolic boundary, and the resulting polarization, is at once a social pre-condition and result of the collective mobilization in which the political field is made clear. This is the point where processes of polarization and constitution of identities, activated in unison, express antagonism by way of an element substantially similar to the political.[3] This is the theoretical bridge that we wish to build between the analysis of contention proposed by McAdam et al. (2001, 2008) and the critical theory of discourse as presented by Ernesto Laclau and, more fully, by the so-called Essex school (Howarth and Stavrakakis 2000; Fairclough 1995; Chouliaraki and Fairclough 1999; Jørgensen and Phillips 2002).

In recent years, studies based on Marxist, post-structuralist and psychoanalytical theories have responded to the emergence of new collective imaginations and identities in which the question of sovereignty has become fundamental. Every discourse is *political* in the most intrinsic sense, in so far as it radically institutes a reality that defines an antagonism: a 'without' and a 'within' (outside and inside). At the same time, this is an act of *power* because it always involves the exclusion of certain possibilities and the articulation of various argumentative *topoi* (Ducrot 1988) and social agents. Finally, all discourse is *historical* and is subject

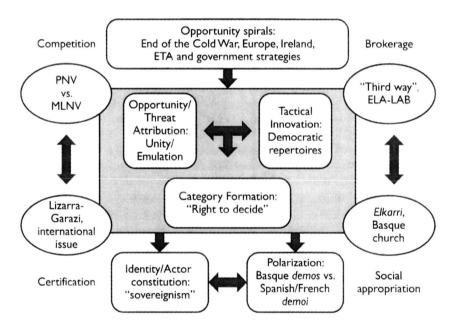

Figure 3.1 Nationalist contentious episodes: mechanisms and processes.

EAJ-PNV: Eusko Alberdi Jeltzalea-Partido Nacionalista Vasco (Basque Nationalist Party)

ELA: Euskal Langileen Alkartasuna (Basque Workers' Solidarity)

ETA: Euskadi 'ta Askatasuna (Basque Homeland and Freedom)

LAB: Langile Abertzaleen Batzordeak (Patriotic Workers' Committee)

BNLM: Movimiento de Liberación Nacional Vasco (Basque National Liberation Movement)

to contingent struggles and to the dislocations that defy the agents' attempts to control them. (Howarth et al. 2000; Torfing 2005: 14). All these theoretical features of discursive formation can be applied to the analysis of nationalism or the national demand, and of the place of the statement of 'sovereignty'. Importantly, this is among the few cases in which the contingent political dimensions of power are present in such an obvious form.

The statement of 'sovereignty' is more than the textual discourse which contains that term (Foucault 1985). It is located in a discursive formation – Basque nationalism, in our case – which determines what can and cannot be said from a certain standpoint in a certain time and place. This is the discursive formation in which the principle of exclusion or admittance (which excludes or includes certain statements) is configured (Goikoetxea 2009). Thus, in the nationalist discursive formation not everything can be said in relation to sovereignty, by any subject and at any time.

I am speaking here of a 'formation' as an uninterrupted process of discursive (re)production, or an exercise in sustained and dynamic collective 'imagining'. Secondly, that discursive formation includes the argumentative *topoi* or contingent common places that emerge in connection with the statement of 'sovereignty' at different times in history – in our case, as an expression of the mechanism for 'attributing opportunities and threats'. Thirdly, this is inseparable from the social praxes that emerge in connection with sovereignty, in our terminology as a mechanism of 'innovation in the repertoires of social mobilization and protest' (McAdam et al. 2001).

As Laclau and Mouffe (1985) point out, the conditions for the possibility of discursive formations are contingent consequences of a continuous struggle for hegemony, the result of which is measured by the success of discursive praxis – the attribution of opportunities or threats, category formation, etc. – which obviously include social mobilization. What can be said about sovereignty in each moment by each subject is always determined by his or her hegemonic position.

In this connection, what in recent years was 'able to be said' with regard to sovereignty is the result of a dual hegemonic contest within Basque society. The conflict sets Basque nationalist stances against Spanish (and French) ones, and the hegemonic operations of each of the *abertzale* families or branches – the moderate one clustered around the BNP, and the more radical one articulated by the *abertzale* left – against each other (Ibarra Güell and Irujo 2011). The conditions for discourse to be possible depend on the connections that it establishes between diverse demands or stances that arise, in turn, out of mixed dislocations. Identities are dislocated as they can never be fully constituted. Instead, they form a system that is impossible to close up, which always depends 'upon an outside which both denies that identity and provides its condition of possibility at one and the same time' (Laclau 1994).

These dislocations – always contingent – arise in all spheres where it is possible to constitute an identity, whether cultural, political or socio-economic. Demand discourses express the constitutive lack derived from dislocation. Thus, the various political plans that aim to reach a hegemonic position 'will attempt to weave together different strands of discourse in an effort to dominate or organise a field of meaning so as to fix the identities of objects and practices in a particular way' (Howarth et al. 2000: 3). The degree of amplitude and strength of these articulatory practices is, in the end, the measure of the degree of hegemony achieved by a discursive formation.

The category formation to which I refer in what follows is the crystallization of a complex discursive articulation in which the hegemonic contest between moderate and radical nationalism is lessened by the constitution of a new identity: that of the sovereignist. At the same time, such a category of identification defines in a new way the polarization between 'Basque *demos*' and 'Spanish *demos*'. This is one of the chapter's main hypotheses.

The evolution of 'sovereignty' in the nationalist press

The end of ETA's armed activity gave rise to an evolution in repertoires of action, and the emergence of new forms of mobilization that have led to a higher degree of grassroots involvement. These innovations in mobilization and methods of protest act as opportunities, and this may be the object of attribution and feedback in the evolution of the discursive formation. While this is not the object of study here, it is relevant to the dynamic that has progressively adopted the statement of 'sovereignty' in the Basque country (Letamendia 2015).

My first objective here is to study the evolution of the concept of 'sovereignty' and the discursive *topoi* connected with it, within the discursive formation 'Basque nationalism' following on from the approval of the 1979 Statute of Autonomy. The premise is that, effectively, the nationalist discursive formation has varied over time, through various discursive *topoi* connected with the term 'sovereignty', in other words common places that would enable us to connect or articulate discourses and subject positions (Jäger 2001; Billig 1995). The second, and necessarily less ambitious, objective of this chapter is to offer a tentative explanation concerning the mechanisms that have encouraged or determined the discursive evolution in recent years. This refers to two main mechanisms. The main environmental mechanism – the spiral of internal and external opportunities – relates to the context, both internal and external, to which Basque nationalism has had to adapt its discourse over the course of these years. This adaptation is summed up by a second cognitive mechanism through which certain events, situations or characteristics are framed as opportunities or threats: the attribution of opportunity and threat that discursively frames the above-mentioned context (McAdam et al. 2001: 43).

The main hypothesis is that the dynamic has reinforced democratic discursive *topoi*. That is to say, 'imagined Basque sovereignty', understood as a statement in the 'nationalist discursive formation', has progressively reinforced its attunement with a democratic master frame (Snow and Benford 1992; Klenn 2001).

At the same time, the discursive evolution has gradually (re)defined a new 'sovereignist' identity that has articulated a renewed 'us' which brings together nationalist and non-nationalist actors who were formerly unconnected and/or immobilized. In this connection, we should say that the activation of the 'category formation' mechanism expressed in '(Basque citizens') right to decide' is connected with the constitution of a new 'sovereignist' political identity. This identification process is open at all times (Laclau 1996), as we shall see.

In so far as I am trying to identify a change in the public space and, ideally, in Basque public opinion, the empirical work specifically linked with this hypothesis consists not so much of analysing the discourses of Basque nationalist political actors on sovereignty as of detecting that statement's evolution in the media, the instrument that the two great families of Basque nationalism use to (re)produce the public opinion which identifies with that statement.

As Bourdieu points out, the political field is where 'political products' are formed, through the competition between political agents in creating political ideas, programmes and concepts. The existence of the political field limits the 'universe of political discourse, and thereby the universe of what is politically thinkable'. The political field is to a large extent defined in the media, since the distribution of opinions in a given population depends on the state of the instruments of perception and expression available, and on the access that different groups have to these instruments (Bourdieu 1991; Crettenand 2014).

In a conflictive scenario such as the Basque case, the mass media are open to a range of mobilized citizens. Discourse takes place in society, not only in the minds of individuals. In order to understand the social production of this discourse it is useful to analyse the mass media (Wodak and Meyer 2001; Van Dijk 1985). Accordingly, media content will be analysed in this study to investigate the evolution of Basque sovereignty demands. For this purpose, I analyse the editorials of three newspapers: the daily *Deia* (in Euskera, 'The Call') affiliated with the Basque Nationalist Party, Partido Nacionalista Vasco (PNV); and *Egin* and *Gara*, both close to the *abertzale* left.

Deia was founded in 1977, and together with its publishing house it was created by PNV with moderate Basque nationalists as its intended audience. *Egin* ('Doing' in Euskera) was a Basque news and general information daily with a leftist and *abertzale* (patriotic) ideology, and a bilingual nature (including articles in Euskera as well as Spanish). It was published in Hernani by Orain S. A., a company that also managed the radio station Egin Irratia. For years, *Egin* was accused of being 'in the service of the terrorist organization ETA'. The company was temporarily suspended in 1998 on the orders of Judge Baltasar Garzón, and its executives were given heavy prison sentences. In 2009, the decision on its unlawfulness was overturned. However, due to the long suspension it was impossible to restart publishing and broadcasting activities. The newspaper that currently targets *Egin*'s former readership is the daily *Gara*.[4]

The analysis in this chapter includes these newspapers' editorials in copies featuring Aberri Eguna, the Basque Patriot Day. Aberri Eguna always coincides with Easter Sunday, or Resurrection Sunday in the Catholic liturgy. It is a festive celebration of Basque nationalism, celebrated throughout Euskal Herria and in Basque diaspora communities all over the world.[5] Historically, the sample begins in 1979, the year the Statute of Autonomy of the Autonomous Community of the

Basque Country (ACBC) was approved. The sample ends in 2014. In most cases, the sample includes both the edition published on Resurrection Day itself and that of the following day. One needs to bear in mind that throughout the first ten years, these newspapers lacked proper editorials. The sample thus includes news articles that cover the celebration of Aberri Eguna.

The discursive formations from which sovereignty is spoken will be analysed both synchronically and diachronically (Weaver 2005). This makes it possible to compare each chosen print medium's discourse, corresponding to each of the Basque nationalist ideological branches respectively. The focus is on the actor and the cognitive mechanisms. Diachronic analysis enables us to trace the discursive evolution, and entails addressing the relationship between structure and agents – considering environmental and relational mechanisms that simultaneously determine, and are determined by, the actors. This leads us to the study's second step, which involves elucidating elements that have influenced how the statement of 'sovereignty' has evolved.

With regard to the first step, the operationalization of the category formation, opportunity attribution and threat attribution mechanisms are carried out in accordance with the frame analysis model. Both mechanisms are analysed using problematization frames: defining the problem, the person responsible and the proposed solution (Benford and Snow 2000). Although the classic tripartite classification is not used systematically, I have taken it into account when codifying discourse that attributes opportunities and threats, and describes the demand for sovereignty and the means of obtaining it, and the *topoi* connected with that demand (Stobaugh and Snow 2010). This has enabled me to synthesize a broad textual panorama and make various discourse maps of an interpretative nature (Weaver 2005; Krippendorf 2004; Johnston 2002)), presented in figures 4 and 5 below.

Some obvious limitations of this set-up should be noted. Firstly, my sample contains only two or three editions per year. This limits the study to the detection of general lines of discursive evolution. More in-depth research would be necessary to find key moments of that evolution, along with its scope and depth. Secondly, the sample is limited to the main *abertzale* (patriotic) media, and the study thus ignores the possible impact of discursive evolution in other media. This means that it abstracts one of our theoretical premises – the premise related to the 'constitutive exterior' that makes 'identification' possible (Laclau 1996). This is especially relevant when it comes to the 'sovereignist' identification, which is constituted primarily from the outside – by adversaries of the 'sovereignist'. Notably, it could also be considered a methodological limitation that the target audience of *Deia* consists of moderate (or less radical) nationalists, which means that its editorial line might try to avoid the topic of 'sovereignism'.

Threat and opportunity attribution mechanisms in relation to 'sovereignty'

In measuring opportunity and threat attribution mechanisms I have applied the classic model, distinguishing between opportunities defined within the framework of the relationship between political actors, those relating to the internal institutional framework and international sphere, and discourse that seeks to activate motivation as a collective psychological opportunity. In the case of threat attribution, the analysis is centred on aggressive acts by the Spanish state, internal obstacles and relationship between actors, and more general contextual factors that might turn into threats.

The table below (Table 3.1) presents findings on opportunity attribution in the coverage of Aberri Eguna in the sampled newspapers *Egin/Gara* and *Deia* during the years 1979–2014. They are listed according to four different frames: relational, institutional, international and motivational, and the years are provided in parentheses. As we can see, the most relevant opportunity attribution in the relational sphere relates to the idea of 'unity', especially as presented by *Egin* and *Gara*, the newspapers close to the *abertzale* left. Unitarian dynamics and patriots working together are defined as an opportunity throughout the period under study. However, in recent years the references to plurality of sentiments and non-uniformity appear to become stronger. The discourse one might expect on the celebration of the day of the *patria* – nationalist unity – is no longer referring to an 'idealized communion' but rather begins to be understood in more complex ways. This shift can be observed in all the sampled newspapers.

Table 3.1 Opportunity attribution on Aberri Eguna in *Egin/Gara* and *Deia*, 1979–2014

	EGIN/GARA	DEIA
Relational frame	unity ('79, '93, '99, '00, '02, '07, '09, '14), reciprocal respect ('79), unitarian dynamic in Iparralde ('94, '98), trade-union unity ('03), working together possible ('97, '98, '03), new undertakings ('05), convergences, common strategy ('06, '10), combining of nationalist forces ('08, '10), different sentiments, non-uniformity ('08, '09), confluence of leftist sovereignists ('12)	nationalist democratic majority ('79), nationalist recomposition and vigour ('89), ties of national loyalty ('95), union-unity of action, joining of forces ('99, '03, '07), plurality ('14)
Institutional frame	failure of Autonomous Community ('89), alternative forums; *udalbiltza* ('00, '02, '03, '04), discussion forum ('08), *Gure Esku Dago* ('14)	self-government achievements ('79, '82), legal/official Aberri Eguna ('82), renewed statute, democratic normality ('87, '88), Ibarretxe's proposal (consultation on new statute) ('08), institutional nationalism ('09)

(Continued)

Table 3.1 (Continued)

	EGIN/GARA	DEIA
International frame	internationalization ('87), European stateless nations ('91), new European context ('91), Ireland ('98)	Europe, government evolution ('89), direct dialogue with Brussels ('90), resurgence of nationalism in Europe ('91), international solidarity ('96), Irish gradualism ('98)
Motivational frame	mobilization ('80), democratic firmness ('81), struggle ('82), demands ('83, '84, '88), commitment and combat ('84), festivity ('84), combativeness, dignity, sacrifice ('85), friendliness ('87), heroic sacrifice ('96), peace ('99), popular will, mass participation ('00, '01), hope ('08, '12) popular wave ('10), self-criticism ('10), organized multitude ('11), determination of youth ('12)	Labour ('81), festivity ('83), joy, hope and faith ('84, '99, '03, '06, '11), living people ('92), capacity ('93), history, PNV leadership ('97, '01), thousands of people ('00), serenity ('01), urgency ('08), peace ('11, '14), detachment from politics ('13)

When we look at opportunity attribution within the institutional framework, this is where we find the discourses expressed in the two *abertzale* media most clearly opposed to one another. The anti-system option expressed by the dailies *Egin* and *Gara* insistently refer to para-institutions or alternative forums (*udalbiltza*), defending them as opportunities for achieving sovereignty. As the medium for expressing moderate nationalism, *Deia* insists on the virtues of the institutional route and emphasizes existing self-government achievements. The competition mechanism is clearly activated in this question, through the opposition between the statutory Autonomous Community route and alternative routes. The divergence is maintained throughout the period under analysis. Only at the end of the period does it appear to lessen.

As for the international framework, no great differences are observed between the print media analyzed here. In both cases, opportunities provided by the international context are generally seen in a positive light. In any event, the difference is diachronic – occurring throughout the period. The emergence of new European states in the early 1990s and the Irish example towards the end of the same decade appear as opportunities for progressing the demand for sovereignty. In the latest phase, Scottish and Catalan protagonism is presented as a political 'opportunity' by providing an example for Basque patriots.

Finally, in the discourse contained within the motivational framework we can see some common elements proper to a national demand discourse, often using terms such as 'hope', 'faith', 'will' and 'participation'. However, we can observe differences between the two media. *Egin* and *Gara* emphasize the value of combativeness and sacrifice as motivations, using terms like 'commitment', 'combat' and 'dignity'. *Deia*, meanwhile, brings out the Basques' own leadership capacity (PNV leadership) and values related to 'peace', 'serenity' and 'joy'. This divergence is explainable in so far as the first newspapers are vehicles for an anti-system struggle led by the *abertzale* left, while the second speaks for more moderate 'patriots'.

Threat and opportunity attributions both require a context of uncertainty (McAdam et al. 2001: 95). Nonetheless, threat attribution tends to use more simplistic discourse in which enemies and obstacles are characterized more clearly than opportunities that are inevitably broader and more diffuse. Threat attribution in the sampled dailies is in fact simpler, and less diverse in some respects (as presented in Figure 3.2 below). As regards the threat from the Spanish state, discourse referring to 'state repression' ('police persecution', 'the dirty war', etc.) can be found in all of the sampled newspapers, although it is much more pronounced and constant in the dailies *Egin* and *Gara*. However, discourse related to 'attacks on Basque self-government' show up only in the daily *Deia*. Moreover, threats linked to the more general context, such as economic recession, unemployment, modernisation challenges and globalization are constructed discursively in

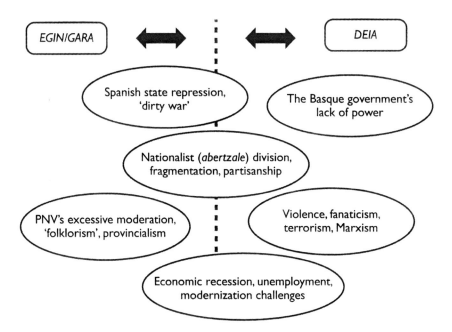

Figure 3.2 Threat attribution in *Egin/Gara* and *Deia*, 1979–2014.

a fairly common way, although they occupy a more significant place in *Deia*. Thirdly, the discursive construction as a threat of 'nationalist division or fragmentation', linked to epithets such as 'partisanism' or 'electoralism', occupies a practically equal and central place in all the sampled dailies. Thus, *abertzale* unity and division are at the centre of the mechanism for the attribution of opportunity and threat respectively. Finally, the attribution, as a threat, of either excessive moderation (expressed as folklorism or provincialism) or extreme radicalism (violence, fanaticism, terrorism or Marxism) emerges as the expression of inter-*abertzale* competition.

Category formation in relation to 'sovereignty'

The mechanisms described above merely frame a context discursively, to make possible category formation related to the statement of 'sovereignty'. In some ways, the evolution of opportunity and threat attribution determines the very evolution of the conceptualization of sovereignty.

In order to present the findings of this study related to category formation, I have opted to make discursive maps that distinguish (for operationalization purposes) between three levels of analysis. These are firstly, the key terms that express most directly the demand for sovereignty; secondly, the terms related to suitable instruments or procedures for meeting these demands; and thirdly, other discursive *topoi* that emerge in connection with sovereignty demands. For reasons of space, the discursive maps for each of the different print media are presented in two separate figures. Figure 3.3 (below) covers the dailies *Egin* and *Gara*, while

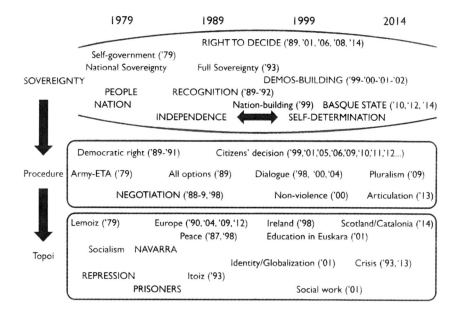

Figure 3.3 Category formation in the newspaper *Egin/Gara*, 1979–2014.

Figure 3.4 covers *Deia*. The analysis presented in these maps is both synchronic and diachronic, to facilitate the testing of the main hypothesis of this study. To reiterate, the figures illustrate three levels of analysis. The use of key terminology is presented in the upper sections of each figure, the political processes involved are presented in the middle sections and the related *topoi* are presented in the lower sections. The years at the top convey the timeline.

As shown in the discursive map of the dailies *Egin* and *Gara*, the expressions of the *abertzale* left, we find a constant tension between the demand for self-determination and the demand for independence. Terms related to this tension crop up contemporaneously or successively, and with greater or lesser intensity depending on the political situation. At no time is the pairing permanently broken, although sometimes the term 'self-determination' appears as the suitable means to an end: 'independence'. Something similar happens with the terms 'Basque people' and 'Basque nation'. The boundaries of the political subject are not clearly defined and, normally, 'people' and 'nation' are used as synonyms.

In the daily *Deia*, however, no significant presence of the term 'independence' can be found, save for the term 'original freedom'. Nevertheless, the term 'self-determination' is fairly constant up until the early 2000s. Similarly, practically throughout the whole period the discourse on sovereignty emerges in connection with 'self-government' and day-to-day management (or the 'everyday nation').

In the case of *Egin* and *Gara*, we find a rapid and intense strengthening of discourse based on the democratic principle – 'demos-building' – to the detriment of discourse related to nation-building. However, in the moderate nationalist discourse expressed in *Deia*, the use of an identity-based definition of the Basque

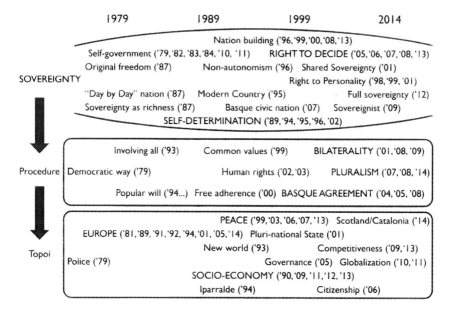

Figure 3.4 Category formation in the newspaper *Deia*, 1979–2014.

nation is more constant and emerges in connection with the demand for recognition for the Basque 'character', as well as 'self-identification' and nation-building. In *Deia*, discourse based on the 'nation' continues to predominate over the 'people', although 'civic' and 'modern' definitions are also found. Although less clearly, in this case too we find a significant strengthening during the later years of the period of terms such as 'citizens' (as a collective) and 'Basque society', framed within the code of 'demos-building'.

In the same vein, although in *Egin* and *Gara*'s discourse the first references to the 'right to decide' are old (1989), from 2001 onwards this becomes a term that defines a new meaning for the concept of sovereignty. There is a progression from a rhetoric of 'recognition' towards one centred on 'own decision-making', which is palpable from the Lizarra-Garazi Agreement (1998–1999) onwards. This is the time when the term 'sovereignist' emerged as an expression of a new identification: 'sovereignist forces', especially by the PNV. Likewise, in this medium from 2010 onwards reference to the 'Basque state' as a concrete expression of sovereignty starts to become stronger. Hence we could affirm that in the case of *Egin* and *Gara*'s discourse, the activation of this category formation mechanism causes sovereignty to become defined as 'being able to decide to be a Basque state'. This is found in the years 2010, 2012 and 2014).

In parallel, the 'right to decide' also has a very intense presence in *Deia*'s editorial line from the mid-2000s onwards. In this case, the influence of the period begins with the 'Proposal for a New Statute' implemented by Lehendakari (President) Ibarretxe in 2004 and ends with the 'law on consultation of the people' approved by the Basque Parliament (2008). Both regulatory instruments are expressions of the 'right to decide', and they are located within the framework of the new 'sovereignist' identity that grew up in that period. These two proposals for political change, which came out of the Basque Parliament, were turned down by the Spanish authorities.

In *Deia*'s editorial line of later years, references to 'shared sovereignty' or 'subsidiarity' (2001) are combined with citations of 'full sovereignty' (2012). Unlike *Gara*, the term 'sovereignist' appears late in *Deia*'s editorial line (2009). Furthermore, it appears not in order to self-identify the political line that is defended in this medium, but in order to refer to other political actors. However, the defining of those adversaries as 'pretend-sovereignists' – referring to the collective clustered around the EH Bildu coalition – clearly shows up the competition mechanism in relation to that identification.

In direct connection with the earlier evolution, the discourse on the procedures whereby Basque sovereignty would be achieved has progressively become adapted to the democratic principle. Nevertheless, references to democratic processes are present in all periods. In the case of *Egin* and *Gara*, the initial reference to ETA's armed route (1979) is supplemented later on, although without giving up the political-military paradigm, by the discourse related to 'negotiation' (Ibarra Güell 1987). This coincided particularly with the Algiers negotiations between ETA and the Spanish state (1988–89) and the discussions that led to the Lizarra-Garazi agreement (1998–99), each linked to a truce on ETA's part. Later on (2000), still under the influence of the *abertzale* Lizarra-Garazi agreement, *Gara*'s editorial line shows a discourse related to the alternative Basque institutionalization (*udalbiltza*) route. From that time (2001) onwards, the 'decision by Basque citizens' became the main leitmotif, in direct connection with the 'right to decide'.

On its part, the daily *Deia* kept up a discourse demanding the 'democratic route' as opposed to ETA's violence, ever since the beginning of the period under study (Arregi 2001). In the initial period references to 'human rights' and 'common values' crop up regularly. Later on, there are three dominant discursive elements: the 'plurality' of Basque society; the 'internal agreement amongst Basques'; and 'bilaterality', or the dialogue with the Spanish state. In this case too, the 'right to decide' becomes important at the later stage.

As for the discursive *topoi* that crop up in relation to the demand for sovereignty, we find a relative plurality suited to the historical context, along with other topics that are more persistent in time. In general, political sovereignty is never an abstract *desideratum*, but rather linked to specific content, primarily cultural and socio-economic. Europe, in its various senses ('European Union', 'Europe of the Peoples', etc.) is a mainstream discursive element in the editorials analyzed, especially in *Deia*. In specific situations, references crop up in all the media to European countries that are regarded as interesting models to follow, especially Ireland, Scotland and Cataluña. The discourse related to the territorial unity of Euskal Herria (references to Navarre, principally) is very present in *Egin* and *Gara*, though less so in *Deia*. The anti-repressive discourse – 'Basque prisoners' rights', 'amnesty' – is constant in the *abertzale* left's reference daily, but is not found in *Deia*. The demand for peace is also present, especially in *Deia*.

Socio-economic discursive topics, which are present in all the sampled dailies, show appreciable differences. In *Egin* and *Gara* we find references to environmental conflicts (especially the cases of Lemoiz and Itoiz). These are not mentioned in *Deia*. Terms such as 'labour', 'working' and 'socialism', which crop up in the media close to the *abertzale* left in the 1980s, are later replaced by more moderate references, such as 'the Basque labour-relations sphere'. The economic and industrial recession, and sovereignty as a solution to it, is a subject that comes up in delicate economic situations (early 1990s, and recent years). In *Deia*'s case, overcoming the recession is connected with competitiveness and wellbeing, whilst in *Egin* and *Gara* the latter reference predominates, along with 'workers' rights'. Finally, aspects related to cultural identity ('Euskera', 'education', 'Basque public television') are more present in *Egin* and *Gara*. In all the media studied, these issues crop up in relation to the challenges of globalization.

Conclusions

Without discussing in detail the discursive *topoi* just described, we are in a position to present an initial indicative conclusion in the light of the opinions published by the reference media of the two *abertzale* branches, on the evolution since 1979 in topics related to the demand for 'sovereignty'. Particularly since the late 1990s, the emergence of categories such as that of the 'right to decide' is relevant in so far as that category has functioned as a nodal point which has made it possible to reinforce the connection of 'sovereignty' with democratic *topoi*.

In Laclau and Mouffe's (1985) conception, 'articulatory practice consists, precisely, of constructing node-points that partially fix meaning'. Thus, the new 'right to decide' category functions as an empty signifier that becomes an articulating nodal point for various discourses in relation to sovereignty, whether they are 'patriotic' (*abertzale*) or not. This nodal point is essential for explaining the constitution of a new 'sovereignist' identity, still in the process of being formed, and constantly changing.

Correlatively, the routes for attaining Basque sovereignty also converge around 'Basque citizens' democratic will'. Likewise, the definition of the decision-making subject increasingly revolves around a Basque *demos*, or civic nation, far removed from essentialist views. In the final analysis, the connected discursive *topoi* may vary, although, during the later years, issues relating to the socio-economic sphere seem to be getting stronger.

In point of fact, the discursive convergence that can be observed in the two media under analysis enables us to identify some statements about sovereignty that appear to be connected to contemporary Basque nationalist discourse formation: the will of the Basque *demos*, plurality and wellbeing (social policies). As we stated at the beginning of the chapter, there are statements that today 'can be said' only with difficulty within that discursive formation. We are referring, for example, to three enunciations that, while they might have been present in the Basque nationalist discursive formation over the last few decades, have been getting weaker, or have even totally disappeared in recent times. These are the ethnic definition of the Basque political subject, the discourses that legitimized the use of violence for attaining sovereignty, and the clear defence of neo-liberal socio-economic models.

However, it is too early yet for determining the nature of the discursive articulation that will become hegemonic within the new identity and, later on, in Basque society. Indeed, one has to note that the 'sovereignist' identification is far from closed, as has been emphasized in the theoretical section. As a matter of fact, its emergence and gathering of strength is highly dependent on other relational and contextual mechanisms, which we shall refer to in what follows.

As for the second hypothesis, corroborating it will call for more of a narrative input. One of the weaknesses of the dynamics of contention (Oliver 2003; Koopmans 2003; Demetriou 2009; Taylor 2003) is precisely that. This is because, while the activation of the mechanisms proposed by McAdam et al. (2001) can, with some difficulty, be empirically measurable, confirming the causality or connection between those mechanisms and more complex processes is even more hypothetical (Elster 2007; Earl 2008; Lichbach 2008; Mayntz 2004; Rucht 2003). For us it would be a case of connecting the mechanisms that underlie the evolution of the nationalist discursive formation and the statement of 'sovereignty' (category formation, opportunity and threat attribution, and tactical innovation) with other mechanisms that, by explaining that formation, give us a basis for more far-reaching processes such as the constitution of identities and polarization (Falleti and Lynch 2008).

Since we are aware of this difficulty, I will not deny narration's explicative function (McAdam et al. 2008). Many of the discourses analyzed here as attributions of opportunity and threat are precisely a good means of testing other contextual or interactive mechanisms that can explain in part the discursive evolution analyzed in this chapter. The evolution of the nationalist discursive formation from the statement of 'sovereignty' can be determined by various environmental mechanisms which, obviously, do not function as elements wholly outside the actors' cognitive processes and those of Basque society in general. The 'opportunity spiral', understood as an environmental mechanism, is perhaps most peripheral of the actors' strategies. From the 1980s onwards, the Europe-building process, the evolution in national conflict-management in democratic contexts, the end of the Cold War and changes to European borders, and the political action paradigm shift within the anti-system left, amongst other factors, activated a spiral of opportunities for stateless nations to demand sovereignty. The examples of this are growing in number: Quebec, Northern Ireland and, more recently, Kosovo, Scotland and Cataluña. These 'external' opportunities have, in turn, created or reinforced 'internal opportunities' which, in a spiral feedback process, have altered non-state nationalist actors' opportunity structures. Decentralization in Spain and the Autonomous Community structures in the Basque Country, despite the cutting back of competences, have strengthened the Basque democratization process (Goikoetxea 2014). The actors' discursive attribution of those opportunities has already been described in this chapter.

The process of Autonomous Community institutionalization and the ensuing democratization can thus be understood as an internal opportunity that favors, and is at the same time strengthened by, the evolution in the statement 'sovereignty'. From a viewpoint closer to the actors' strategies, we have to take into account the influence that the avatars of violent political conflict have had on the evolution of the discourse about sovereignty. We have seen that the changes and the forward and backward steps in that evolution are closely linked to negotiating processes and changes of strategy by the State and Autonomous Community governments, and by ETA. Obviously, the end of ETA's armed activity is an important factor in the discursive evolution of the later period, although it only strengthens a process that could already be detected in the mid-1990s. In this connection, the final end of ETA, decreed by the organization itself on 20 October 2011, should be understood not as a cause, but as a consequence of the discursive evolution that analyzed here.

Moreover – and now I am entering the sphere of relational mechanisms – the various degrees and points in time of the competition mechanism's activation amongst the two *abertzale* ideological branches, in as much as that competition was being produced in a shared democratic discursive and institutional framework, has influenced the democratization of the idea of sovereignty. The two *abertzale* branches have certified one another as legitimate dialoguers – at the

Lizarra-Garazi talks in 1998 and on other occasions. The demand for Basque sovereignty in its various manifestations (all conflictive to some degree) has also been certified internationally. Basque sovereignty, as a question to be reflected upon, is an internationally certified topic. Hence, the conditions for dealing with these questions have also influenced the progressively democratic character of the statement of 'sovereignty'.

Nonetheless, as we have seen, the intra-*abertzale* competition, despite the fact that it favours discursive convergence around a 'democratic sovereignty', also keeps open the identification process that I have called 'sovereignism'. In the early 2000s, sovereignism enabled the articulation of the more moderate sectors of the *abertzale* left and the more radical ones of the PNV, through brokerage by third-party actors. Following the legalization of the *abertzale* left and the formation of the EH Bildu coalition, there was a relative re-activation of the competition between a 'leftist sovereignist cluster' and a more moderate 'sovereignism', represented by the current leadership of the PNV. The new brokerage that made it possible to re-articulate a less competitive identification around 'sovereignism' came about through civil society initiatives such as *Gure Esku Dago* (It's in Our Hands), involved in hugely popular mobilization for the 'right to decide'.

Brokerage is fundamental to the category- and identity-building process, and it is easy to see why. The formation of a new category – 'the right to decide' – functions as an articulating node for discursive *topoi*, and the creation of a social cluster or identity – 'sovereignism' – has depended to a large extent on the existence of brokers who, by using their political imagination, have facilitated the transversal circulation of ideas and the connecting of hitherto unconnected or unmobilized places – that is, brokerage. Within that group of brokers, the *abertzale* trade unions played a prominent role from 1995 onwards (Elorrieta 2012). For that mission of brokerage, the mechanism of organizational appropriation has also been activated, inasmuch as organizations that in principle had no direct connection with the demand for sovereignty or with the conflictive consequences of the fact that it was not being met, came to function as agents directly involved in those issues. Examples of this mechanism are the appropriation of the ecologists' organization Lurraldea, whereby it changed into the pacifist actor Elkarri (later Lokarri), and its efforts to lead the demand for sovereignty through dialogue, as well as the role that the Basque church took on as a mediator.

These relational and contextual mechanisms, interacting with the cognitive ones directly present in the discursive formation, can explain the great processes of the constitution of actors and identities – that is, of identifications (Laclau 1994) – and those of polarization and antagonism, in Laclauian terms, which open up for social and political change. The evolution of the concept of sovereignty is closely linked with the process of social and political change: change that is perceived on a global scale, although Euskal Herria may be a prime site for studying it.

Notes

1 In both cases there have been short-lived exceptions, namely the Basque Government presided over by Patxi López, with the support of the PSE-EE (Partido Socialista de

Euskadi-Euskadiko Ezkerra; Basque Socialist Party-Basque Left) and PP (Partido Popular; People's Party), in an exceptional situation due to the illegalization of the *abertzale* (patriotic) left (2009–12); and the very short-lived government of Javier Otano in Navarre (1995–96).

2 This paper will not discuss the theoretical formation of the concept of 'sovereignist' or 'sovereignism'. Taking the Québécois experience as their starting-point, authors such as Ollora (1996) and Zallo (1997), and later among others Zubiaga (1999, 2002), have worked on this topic.

3 When Marchart speaks of the Schmittian – or dissociative of the political – moment, as opposed to the Arendtian associative moment, he reminds us that 'what operates as a political principle of a given community is a dissociative operation: antagonism' (Marchart 2009: 64). Mouffe, on her part, emphasizes the ontological nature of antagonism, which cannot be eliminated. Democratization is engendered in the tension between an eradicable antagonism and the institutionalization that attempts to domesticate it (Mouffe 2000).

4 See http://es.wikipedia.org/wiki/Gara and http://www.naiz.eus/hemeroteca/gara

5 See Auñamendi Encyclopaedia, online at: www.euskomedia.org/aunamendi/6047

References

Arregi, J. 2001. *La Nación Vasca Posible*. Barcelona: Crítica.

Benford, R. D., and Snow, D. A. 2000. 'Framing Processes and Social Movements', *Annual Review of Sociology*, 26: 611–639.

Billig, M. 1995. *Banal Nationalism*. London: Sage.

Brubaker, R. 1996. *Nationalism Reframed*. Cambridge, MA: Cambridge University Press.

Bourdieu, P. 1991. *Language and Symbolic Power* (G. Raymond & M. Adamson, Trans.). Cambridge, MA: Harvard University Press.

Cabo Martin, C. de, 1997. *Contra el Consenso. Estudios Sobre el Estado Constitucional y el Constitucionalismo del Estado Social*. Mexcio: Unam.

Chouliaraki, L., and Fairclough, N. 1999. *Discourse in Late Modernity: Rethinking Critical Discourse Analysis*. Edinburgh: Edinburgh University Press.

Crettenand, M. 2014. *Le Rôle De La Presse Dans La Construction De La Paix: Le Cas Du Conflit Basque*. Paris: L'Harmattan.

Demetriou, C. 2009. 'The Realist Approach to Explanatory Mechanisms in Social Science: More Than a Heuristic?' Philosophy of Social Science, 39: 440–464.

Diani, M. 1996. 'Linking Mobilization Frames and Political Opportunities: Insights From Regional Populism in Italy', *American Sociological Review*, 61(6): 1053–1069.

Ducrot, O. 1988. 'Argumentación y Topoi Argumentativos', *Lenguaje en Contexto*, 1: 63–84.

Earl, J. 2008. 'An Admirable Call to Improve, But Not Fundamentally Change, Our Collective Methodological Practices', *Qualitative Sociology*, 31(4): 355–359.

Elorrieta, J. 2012. Renovación Sindical: Una Aproximación a la Trayectoria de Eta. Tafalla: Txalaparta.

Elster, J. 2007. *Explaining Social Behavior: More Nuts and Bolts for the Social Sciences*. Cambridge, MA: Cambridge University Press.

Fairclough, N. 1995. Critical Discourse Analysis. London: Longman.

Falleti, T. G., and Lynch, J. 2008. 'From Process to Mechanism: Varieties of Disaggregation', *Qualitative Sociology*, 31(4): 333–339.

Foucault, M. 1985. *The Archaeology of Knowledge*. London: Tavistock.

Goikoetxea, J. 2009. 'La Práctica de la Incomunicación o el Conflicto Discursivo'. Doctoral Thesis. Leioa: University of the Basque Country.

———. 2014. 'Nation and Democracy Building in Contemporary Europe: The Reproduction of the Basque Demos', *Nationalities Papers*, 42(1): 145–164.

Guibernau, M. 1999. *Nacions Sense Estat*. Barcelona: Columna.

Haas, E. B. 1986. 'What Is Nationalism and Why Should We Study It?', *International Organization*, 40: 707–744.

Hastings, A. 2000. *La Construcción de las Nacionalidades*. Madrid: Akal.

Hinsley, F. H. 1986. *Sovereignty*. Cambridge, MA: Cambridge University Press.

Howarth, D., Norval, A. J., and Stavrakakis, Y. 2000. *Discourse Theory and Political Analysis: Identities, Hegemonies and Social Change*. New York: Columbia University Press.

Hroch, M. 1993. 'From National Movement to the Fully-formed Nation', *New Left Review*, 1(198).

Ibarra Güell, P. 1987. *La Evolución Estratégica de Eta: De la 'Guerra Revolucionaria' (1963) a la Negociación (1987)*. Donostia: Kriselu.

Ibarra Güell, P., and Irujo, X. 2011. *Basque Political Systems*. Reno, NV: University of Nevada Press.

Ibarretxe, J. J. 2010. 'Principio Ético, Principio Democrático y Desarrollo Humano Sostenible: Fundamentos Para Un Modelo Democrático'. Doctoral Thesis. Leioa: University of the Basque Country.

Jäger, S. 2001. 'Discourse and Knowledge: Theoretical and Methodological Aspects of a Critical Discourse and Dispositive Analysis', in R. Wodak and M. Meyer, eds, *Methods of Critical Discourse Analysis*. London: Sage, pp. 32–62.

Johnston, H. 2002. 'Verification and Proof in Frame Discourse Analysis', in B. Klandermans and S. Staggenborg, eds, *Methods of Social Movement Research*. Ann Arbor, MI: University of Michigan Press.

Jørgensen, M. W., and Phillips, L. J. 2002. *Discourse Analysis as Theory and Method*. London: Sage.

Klenn, J. 2001. *Framing Democracy: Civil Society and Civic Movements in Eastern Europe*. Palo Alto, CA: Stanford University Press.

Koopmans, R. 2003. 'A Failed Revolution – But a Worthy Cause'. *Mobilization San Diego*, 8(1): 116–118.

Krasner, S. D. 1999. *Sovereignty. Organized Hypocrisy*. Princeton, NJ: Princeton University Press.

Krippendorf, K. 2004. *Content Analysis: An Introduction to Its Methodology*. London: Sage.

Laclau, E. ed., 1994. *The Making of Political Identities*. London: Verso.

———. 1996. *Emancipation(S)*. London: Verso.

———. 2005. *On Populist Reason*. Verso. London.

Letamendía, A. 2015. *La forma social de la protesta*. Leioa, Bizkaia: UPV-EHU.

Letamendía, F. 1997. *Juego de Espejos*. Valladolid: Trotta.

Lichbach, M. I. 2008. 'Modeling Mechanisms of Contention: Mctt's Positivist Constructivism', *Qualitative Sociology*, 31(4): 345–354.

Máiz, R. 2008. *La Frontera Interior*. Murcia: Tres Fronteras.

Marchart, O. 2009. *El Pensamiento Político Posfundacional. La Diferencia Política en Nancy, Lefort, Badiou y Laclau*. Buenos Aires: FCE.

Mayntz, R. 2004. 'Mechanisms in the Analysis of Social Macro-Phenomena', *Philosophy of the Social Sciences*, 34(2): 237–259.

McAdam, D., Tarrow, S., and Tilly, C. 2001. *Dynamics of Contention*. Cambridge Studies in Contentious Politics. Cambridge, MA: Cambridge University Press.

————. 2008. 'Methods for Measuring Mechanisms of Contention', *Qualitative Sociology*, 31(4): 307–331.

Mouffe, C. 2000. *The Democratic Paradox*. New York: Verso.

Mouffe, C., and Laclau, E. 1985. Hegemony and Socialist Strategy. New York: Verso.

Oliver, P. 2003. 'Mechanisms of Contention', *Mobilization*, 8: 119–122.

Ollora, J. M. 1996. *Una Vía hacia la Paz*. Donostia: Erein.

Riera, M., and Zubiaga, M. 2014. *Nation and State Building as Collective Action: A Comparative Analysis of Mechanisms and Processes in Catalonia and the Basque Country*. Barcelona: Anuari del Coflicte Social. UAB.

Rucht, D. 2003. 'Overcoming the "Classical Model?" ', *Mobilization*, 8: 112–116.

Sassen, S. 2006. Territory, Authority, Rights: From Medieval To Global Assemblages. Princeton, NJ: Princeton University Press.

————. 2007. Elements for a Sociology of Globalization [Or a Sociology of Globalization]. New York: W.W. Norton.

Snow, D. A., and Benford, R. D. 1992. *Frontiers in Social Movement Theory*. New Haven, CT: Yale University Press.

Stobaugh, J. E., and Snow, D. A. 2010. 'Temporality and Frame Diffusion: The Case of the Creationist/Intelligent Design and Evolutionist Movements from 1925 to 2005', in R. Kolins Givan, K. M. Roberts and S. Soule, eds, *The Diffusion of Social Movements: Actors, Mechanisms and Political Effects*. New York: Columbia University Press.

Tarrow, S. 2011. *Power in Movement: Social Movements and Contentious Politics*. Cambridge, MA: Cambridge University Press.

Taylor, V. 2003. 'Plus Ça Change, Plus C'est La Même Chose', *Mobilization*, 8: 122–126.

Tilly, C. 1984. 'Social Movements and National Politics', in C. Bright and S. Harding, eds, *State Making and Social Movements: Essays in History and Theory*. Ann Arbor, MI: University of Michigan Press.

————. 2004. *Contention and Democracy in Europe, 1650–2000*. New York: Columbia University Press.

Torfing, J. 2005. 'Discourse Theory: Achievements, Arguments, and Challenges', in D. Howarth and J. Torfing, eds, *Discourse Theory in European Politics. Identity, Policy and Governance*. New York: Palgrave Macmillan.

Van Dijk, T. A., ed. 1985. *Handbook of Discourse Analysis*. New York: Academic Press.

Weaver, O. 2005. 'European Integration and Security: Analysing French and German Discourses on State, Nation, and Europe', in D. Howarth and J. Torfing, eds, *Discourse Theory in European Politics: Identity, Policy and Governance*. New York: Palgrave Macmillan.

Wodak, R., and Meyer, M. 2001. *Methods of Critical Discourse Analysis*. London: Sage.

Zallo, R. 1997. *Euskadi o la Segunda Transición*. Donostia: Erein.

Zubiaga, M. 1999. 'La Autodeterminación Como Cambio Político', in M. Gomez Uranga, I. Lasagabaster, F. Letamendía and R. Zallo, eds, *Propuestas Para Un Nuevo Escenario. Democracia, Cultura Y Cohesión Social En Euskal Herria*. Bilbao: Manu Robles- Arangiz Institutua.

————. 2002. *Hacia Una Consulta Popular Soberanista*. Bilbao: Manu Robles- Arangiz Institutua.

————. 2008. 'Boteretik Eraginera: Mekanismoak Eta Prozesuak Leitzarango Eta Urbina-Maltzagako Liskarretan'. Doctoral Thesis. Leioa: University of the Basque Country.

Zubiaga, M., Lasagabaster, I., and Gomez Uranga, M. 2003. *Por un Proceso Soberanista Civil y Democrático*. Bilbao: Manu Robles-Arangiz Institutua.

4 The contested transnational mirror of the Basque country

Playing homeland politics with the diaspora

Pedro J. Oiarzabal

Today, if we are a nation, to a large degree it is thanks to you as well – that's to say, the Basques who live far away from the Basque Country – because you are, without any doubt, the mirror of the true Basque Country. Although so many have tried to destroy the true image using the unacceptable violence of ETA in a rotten and evil organized spider's web.

Joseba Azkarraga, former Minister of Justice of the Basque government,
in a speech delivered at the Basque Cultural Center, San Francisco,
California, February 2004.

Diaspora politics and political diasporas

Within the fields of international relations and diaspora studies, the study of diaspora politics has given rise to a substantial body of literature. Political science inquiry tends mainly to interpret the diaspora as non-state actors, while emphasizing the socioeconomic and political capital they represent for their homeland at the macro level (e.g., Albert et al. 2001; Baylis and Smith 1997; Sheffer 1986a; Tölölyan 2012). Diverse authors highlight the politicization of the diaspora and their ability to influence both homeland and host governments, through efforts such as lobbying and attracting diaspora investment and remittances (e.g., Connor 1993; Esman 1986; Guarnizo et al. 2003; Koinova 2010; Panossian 1998; Safran 1991; Shain 1999; Shain and Barth 2003; Sheffer 1986b, 2003; Tölölyan 1996).[1]

As this chapter will show, relationships between diaspora populations and their homelands, especially non-state or sub-state homelands such as the Basque country, should be understood as socio-politically multifaceted and multi-directional. The Basque country is a sub-state homeland where various actors are engaged in ongoing nation-building efforts, and this is of vital importance to the politicization and political engagement of its diaspora (see Douglass and Bilbao 1975; Molina Aparicio and Oiarzabal 2009). Whereas Basques may claim French or Spanish citizenship as well as citizenship in their host country, the government of the Autonomous Community of the Basque Country (ACBC government; hereafter the Basque government) claims to be the sole representative of all Basques living abroad, regardless of their origins. This complicates issues of loyalty and involvement in the diaspora-homeland relationship. Indeed, the Basque government has undeniably provided the main homeland institutional reference for the Basque diaspora over the past decades, just as it did during the period of Basque government-in-exile (1937–1978).

Following Shain and Barth (2003, see also Shain 1999), the Basque case facilitates the exploration of power relations in diaspora-homeland relations, i.e., the balance of power between an administratively fragmented homeland and its various diaspora communities. It also provides grounds for analyzing the notion of cultural contestation among diasporas and homelands in the context of asymmetrical power relations. Though the concept of cultural contestation is usually used to interpret colonial encounters 'where disparate cultures meet, clash, and grapple with each other' (Pratt 1992: 4–6), it can also be useful to examine the social spaces where homeland and diaspora Basques meet and unequal power relations are displayed. Contemporary Basque diaspora-homeland interactions have only recently been subjected to scholarly analysis (e.g., Totoricagüena 2005; Oiarzabal 2007, 2012a). However, this is a critical dimension of the recent socio-political history of the Basque country and its diaspora. Its further exploration can also shed light on the contemporary contestation of sovereignty in the diaspora, and in diaspora-homeland political relations.

The Basque case illustrates the complex interactions between a diaspora and its non-state homeland from a transnational and comparative approach (Glick-Schiller et al. 1992; Vertovec 1999). In analyzing this case, I investigate how the homeland government influences the diaspora's social organizations and the implications of these influences. The main questions that guided this research were as follows: What is the socio-political relationship between Basque diaspora organizations and the Basque government as the institutional representative of a non-state homeland? In other words, what roles do Basque diaspora organizations play in a highly contentious homeland politics, and why? What influences does a sub-state government assert on diaspora organizations and communities? Finally, what is the balance of power between Basque diaspora organizations and the Basque government?

The organized Basque diaspora

Diasporas (or ethno-national diasporas, Sheffer 1986a, 1986b, 2003), including the Basque, are composed of migrants who share homeland identities and have either been forced by structural, socioeconomic or political conditions, or have chosen to leave their land of origin to settle in other countries. There, migrants and their descendants collectively maintain and develop cultural, religious and political expressions of their identities, which are distinct from those of the dominant host culture(s). They create organizations and transnational networks that maintain explicit and implicit personal and institutional cultural, social, economic, political and business ties with the homeland and other Basque diaspora communities (Oiarzabal and Oiarzabal 2005).

In the Basque case, the diaspora population is nearly impossible to estimate, as it depends on the operational definition of 'being Basque' as well as on a complete statistical database. For instance, according to the 2011 United States census, more than 58,000 people in the USA self-identified as 'Basque'. However, Basque organizations in the USA only had around 6,000 members. In Argentina, diaspora organizations such as the Buenos Aires-based Juan de Garay Foundation claim that more than ten per cent of the population is of Basque ancestry, comprising approximately four million people. However, only 18,000 people are members of Basque associations. In 1996, the Basque government estimated that there were 4.5 million people of Basque ancestry abroad, while Basque diaspora associations worldwide reported less than 18,000 members (Gobierno Vasco 1996: 47, 2000). If these estimates are correct, only 0.4 per cent of Basques living abroad are members of diaspora institutions, which raises questions about the representativeness of such associations as legitimate interlocutors between their communities and the homeland, as well as the host societies at large (see Veredas Muñoz 2003).

My research identifies a worldwide institutional network that includes more than 200 formal organizations – some over a century old – in twenty-five countries (Andorra, Argentina, Australia, Belgium, Brazil, Canada, Chile, China, Colombia, Cuba, El Salvador, France, Germany, Italy, Mexico, Paraguay, Peru, Puerto Rico, Spain, Switzerland, the Dominican Republic, the United Kingdom, the USA, Uruguay and Venezuela). Among the key organizations, the Federation of Basque-Argentine Entities (Federación de Entidades Vasco-Argentinas or FEVA, its Spanish acronym) was established as early as 1955. North American Basque Organizations (NABO) was founded in 1973, and the Federation of Basque Centers of Venezuela in 1975. The Federation of Centers of Euskal Herria was set up in 1985 in Spain, and the Federation of Basque-Uruguayan Institutions was founded in 1998.

Diaspora associations that self-identify as Basque are generally non-partisan and apolitical, with strong group self-awareness that has been sustained over a considerable period (Douglass and Bilbao 1975; Molina Aparicio and Oiarzabal 2009). These groups rely nearly exclusively on volunteers. They are characterized by low human capital and funding recourses, low levels of generational diversity, minimal youth membership and leadership, and failure to reach new members. The Basque diaspora institutions are also characterized by aging members. A decade ago, sixty-four per cent of members were over forty-six years old, and the migrant generation was slowly disappearing, as eighty-three per cent of the members were then born outside the homeland (Gobierno Vasco 2000: 27–32).

The establishment of diaspora federations in Argentina, the USA, Venezuela, Spain, and Uruguay, long-distance transportation and new technologies such as the Internet (Oiarzabal 2012b) have facilitated communication among Basque diaspora individuals and associations. Since the 1980s, international diaspora congresses – mostly organized, funded and hosted by the Basque government – have become venues for diaspora organizational leaders to meet face-to-face and create institutional declarations and action plans, as well as cultivate personal and institutional relationships. Nevertheless, the diaspora organizations are characterized by low levels of internal cohesiveness and do not provide a unified voice for influencing home and host country policies. Despite some attempts (of which the most recent was in 2009), neither have these organizations established a confederation that successfully represents the diverse interests of the various entities (Oiarzabal 2013).

Basque diaspora communities may well be described as ideologically ambivalent and fractured, ranging from strong supporters of Basque independence to adherents of political neutrality. While diaspora voters exhibit similar voting patterns as their counterparts in the homeland, their participation rate is typically low. As of the 2009 ACBC elections, the number of registered diaspora voters was over 43,500. Only sixteen per cent of these individuals voted. Since the restoration of democracy in Spain, the Basque Nationalist Party (EAJ-PNV, Eusko Alberdi Jeltzalea-Partido Nacionalista Vasco, or simply PNV) has received the most support from both diaspora and homeland voters. PNV was also the main party of the government-in-exile, and has been responsible for diaspora policy and management. Since the transition to democracy and until March 2009, and again after October 2012, nationalist parties and coalitions have dominated the Basque government. During these periods, the departments responsible for foreign policy and diaspora affairs have also been controlled by the PNV.

Diaspora organizational leaders often exhibit ambivalence and mercurial attitudes towards involvement in homeland affairs. Over the years, the diaspora has been asked by the Basque government to play the main role in promoting a positive and peaceful image of the Basques in their respective country of residence. This role has been taken to heart by some diaspora organizational leaders as a commitment to the homeland (Oiarzabal 2013). In fact, the engagement of the diaspora in homeland domestic politics is nearly non-existent, having been reduced to testimonial and celebratory declarations and public displays of support for the self-determination of the Basque people and the resolution of the Basque political conflict through negotiations (Oiarzabal 2012a).

Methodology

According to Tölölyan, 'As scholars of diaspora studies we need to foreground, to remind ourselves, and others of the amazing complexity of everyday life of local diaspora communities while also attending to the demands of engagement with other diasporas and the homeland' (2012: 13). This chapter presents findings from an interdisciplinary study, which is part of a larger longitudinal research project that began in 2002. This study combines qualitative, quantitative and comparative approaches and relies on a range of research and data-collection methods, including in-depth, semi-guided interviews with Basque government policy makers and diaspora organization leaders, and multi-sited ethnographic research including participant observation in diaspora community events and activities for over a decade.

In 1994, the government established a registry of Basque clubs 'abroad' (i.e., beyond ACBC administrative limits) under Public Law 8/94, May 27. This law defines the current legal institutional relationship between the ACBC and diaspora to 'preserve and reinforce links between Basque Communities and Centers on the one hand, and the Basque Country on the other hand' (Gobierno Vasco 1994). Under this law, Basque associations abroad must be registered with the Basque government to receive financial assistance. The project initially analyzed and compared discourse on identity, nationhood and homeland generated by Basque diaspora organizations worldwide, and those generated by the Basque government since the 1980s (Oiarzabal 2007).[2]

The initial research was complemented by an examination of diaspora-homeland mobilization episodes, addressing conflicting views about Basque nationhood and the Basque homeland produced in daily diaspora practices (Oiarzabal 2012a, 2013). This understands the Basque diaspora community as an active participant in the construction of the idea of the Basque nation in its everyday practices. An analysis of the data yields insights into the role of sub-state actors such as the Basque government in international politics, foreign policy and para-diplomacy, as well as insights into the mobilization of the Basque diaspora in maintaining an institutional presence in international and domestic political arenas (Oiarzabal 2013).

Basque government officials and politicians usually visit diaspora communities a few times a year, often for annual communal and institutional celebrations. Within this ethnographic frame, I selected four diaspora community cases – Córdoba and Rosario in Argentina, and Boise and New York in the USA – that strongly represent and clearly reveal the implications of contentious and disrupting face-to-face encounters between the homeland and diaspora, producing spaces of cultural contestation or resistance among actors. Social relationships are about power relations, and power, in its simplest form, is the ability to influence or control the behavior of people. The selected cases provide evidence of structural problems and unbalanced power in the homeland-diaspora relationship, articulated through the diaspora organizations and Basque government, and evident in the imbalance of power between them.[3]

Emigrant Basques carved out new lives in diverse contexts where labor demand was high, especially in the Americas during the nineteenth and twentieth centuries, incorporating additional migration waves following the Spanish Civil War, post-war repression and socio-economic crisis. In Argentina and the USA, Basque migrant associations emerged rapidly, including Zazpirak Bat and Euzko-Etxea, which were established in 1912 in Rosario and in 1913 in New York, respectively. Zazpirak Bat, established with a clear Basque nationalist perspective (see Tápiz Fernández 2000), currently has approximately 370 members, while the New York club has approximately 100 members. The Euzkaldunak Basque Center was established in 1949 in Boise and has approximately 800 members, while the Gure Txokoa was created a decade later in Córdoba and has more than 110 members.

In the following I present an analysis of four encounters, which all took place at the beginning of the twenty-first century, that exemplify homeland-diaspora politics and related construction and reconstruction of Basque identity, nationhood and homeland, as well as the conflicting views embedded in everyday diaspora practices.

Córdoba and Rosario: contesting PNV dominance

Within the diaspora, the Argentinian cities of Córdoba and Rosario were among the earliest battlefields of Basque cultural hegemony, in Gramsci's (1971) terms. The political context was one of rivalry in the homeland between the two main Basque nationalist parties, the time-honored Partido Nacionalista Vasco (PNV) and the newcomer Batasuna, created in 2001 to revive the historical Herri Batasuna, which was established in 1978. In March 2003, Batasuna was outlawed by the Spanish Supreme Court for its association with ETA, allegedly being ETA's political arm. This was the first time since the democratic transition that a political party was banned and its politicians prevented from running for elections.[4]

PNV has extraterritorial assemblies in Argentina, Chile, Mexico, Spain (Barcelona and Madrid), Uruguay, and Venezuela. Some of these assemblies were established over sixty years ago, during the massive exile that resulted from the Spanish Civil War. Basque organizations in Argentina have a longstanding and close relationship with PNV. However, with support from the Basque pro-independence leftist movement (also known as *ezker abertzalea*, or the patriotic left), Basque-Argentinean groups started to challenge PNV's cultural hegemony in the Basque diaspora community in Argentina. These groups organized the first street demonstrations against visiting homeland authorities, challenging the image of Basque diaspora organizations as folkloric entities frozen in time, and the official non-partisan stand of the organizations, which masked their alignment with the PNV and its doctrine. The direct confrontations not only brought public attention to the protestors' concerns, but also helped construct an alternative and counter-hegemonic space and ideological discourse that opposed the dominance of PNV and the diaspora organizations.

Throughout the years, a small number of political, humanitarian, or advocacy groups within the diaspora have defended the rights of ETA prisoners and refugees, fought against the extradition of Basques to Spain, and denounced human rights violations in the Basque conflict such as the closure of the only Basque-language newspaper, *Egunkaria*, and the ban of Batasuna. These political groups are pro-Basque independence, similar to the *ezker abertzalea* and its subsequent coalition parties.[5] Some associations were formed in response to the failure of diaspora organizations to allow political participation or political discussion within their clubhouses. Consequently, these groups have created their own offline and online spaces in which they can voice their views and construct an alternative discourse to that constructed by the 'official' diaspora organizations. These groups are eager to convey the message that there is another, less visible and less promoted diaspora community, that is, a political diaspora 'committed to its country' and 'to the struggles in Euskal Herria' (*Semanario* 2005).

Of these groups, the Basque Diaspora Association in Argentina, Asociación Diáspora Vasca (ADV), occupies a central role. ADV is a self-defined virtual community for diaspora Basques and their descendants, created in 1997 under the motto 'independence, peace, and democracy'. The organization claims to have members in twenty countries. It articulates its mission through a website, a mailing list distributed in five different languages, and two electronic newsletters. ADV argues that 'the pro-independence movement has to create its own space in the diaspora, so that the collectivity will not become a manipulated object of partisan politics [. . .] all the spilt blood of the gudaris [soldiers of the Basque Army during the Spanish Civil War and/or ETA members] will not have been wasted [and] all the dreams of the grandparents will not have been betrayed. In every town, in every Basque center, the sleeping or silenced sentiment must awake!' (*Berriak* 2005a).

ADV not only blames the diaspora for its disengagement with Basque politics but also accuses the Basque government of obscuring the true Basque country. According to Daniel Bilbao, ADV's founder, 'Members of the Basque Autonomous Community Government arrived at the diaspora to talk only about a fantastic Disneyland where there are no tortured people, nor dead prisoners' relatives on the road, nor an average of 100 workers dead every year in working accidents . . .' (*Berriak* 2005b). That is, the diaspora political associations and Basque government project present competing images of the true Euskal Herria to Basques abroad.

Basque National Week is an annual celebration organized by FEVA, which has been hosted by one of its member clubs since 1972. During the Basque National Week in Córdoba (23–29 October 2006), ADV sympathizers and representatives of the homeland pro-independence organization Udalbiltza-Kursaal held a street demonstration with the slogan 'Another Diaspora is Possible: Progressive and Committed'.[6] The demonstration ended at the steps of the lodgings of the visiting homeland delegation, which included the then-president or *lehendakari* of the Basque government, Juan José Ibarretxe (1998–2009). As a result of that demonstration, the Extraterritorial Assembly of PNV in Argentina issued a public call directed at the Basque-Argentinean community, 'to leave aside partisan political activity within [the Basque clubs . . . and] 'unify the Basque clubs in Argentina, and to reaffirm their fraternal cohabitation from an *abertzale* [patriotic] perspective' (Junta Extraterritorial de Argentina del PNV December 2006). The Argentinean PNV argued, 'We have become aware that Basque political cannibalism has arrived in Argentina, and it is manifested in the Basque [National] Weeks, on Internet sites, and finally in the Basque clubs [. . .] threatening the cohabitation and harmony developed throughout the years thanks to the work of Basque nationalism [. . .] Now, there have appeared those who proclaim that a new diaspora is possible, as if nothing built previously had ever existed or had any value' (ibid., December 2006).

The PNV defended the hegemonic nationalist discourse projected to the diaspora community and exhorted the Basque-Argentinean community to avoid partisan politics. The PNV response was discussed and the statement signed in the library of the Basque club, Denak Bat, in Mar del Plata, where PNV representatives met regularly. Ironically, according to Denak Bat statutes, political activity is not allowed within the club. This very statute was wielded by the Denak Bat board of directors against representatives of Udalbiltza-Kursaal who wanted to hold a public meeting in the clubhouse (see Bilbao, 5 December 2006).

Similarly, in 2007, the Basque National Week of Rosario (1–7 October 2007) was characterized by bitter protests and tension between the local host club, Zazpirak Bat, and elements of its membership and homeland guests. The club's board of directors announced the cancellation of a talk by the *ezker abertzalea* representative, Josetxo Ibazeta, which was scheduled to take place at the Zazpirak Bat clubhouse at the same time that President Ibarretxe was scheduled to deliver a speech to nearly 1,000 people at a local theater. Ibarretxe was on an official trip to Argentina, Chile, and Colombia at the time. Ibazeta was the political opponent of Ibarretxe, and, by extension, *ezker abertzalea* represented a challenge to PNV hegemony.

Sympathizers of the *ezker abertzalea*, including a Basque-Argentinean youth group from Rosario, JO TA KE, decided to protest the cancellation by demonstrating in front of the theater. The occupation of the space was their immediate response. In addition, the Zazpirak Bat dancers refused to perform the following day. Inside the theater, Ibarretxe presented a new political proposal to end the Basque conflict.[7] Outside, the protesters carried banners condemning the lack of freedom of expression within Basque organizations and waved Euskal Presoak[8] (Basque Prisoner) flags. Ibarretxe meanwhile defended inclusive dialogue, referring to the banned political coalition, Batasuna, and stating that 'Illegalizing ideas is not the way' (*EuskalKultura*, 9 October 2007).

JO TA KE and Ibazeta publicly accused the Basque government and its foreign affairs secretariat for requesting that the Zazpirak Bat board of directors cancel Ibazeta's talk. According to Ibazeta, 'The PNV's goal has always been to avoid any political discussion at the Basque clubs' (*Gara* 2007a; Ibazeta 2007; JO TA KE 2007). However, the then-secretary of the club, the late Felipe Eyheraguibel,[9] refuted allegations of censorship and government interference, emphatically stating that 'We are not an appendix of the Basque government' (*Gara* 2007b).

Boise and New York: the (re)appropriation of the diaspora

In the homeland-diaspora encounters described in this section, the diaspora organizations played quite different roles. The New York Basque association was at the center of an incident that created many layers of conflicts between itself and the government, and between *ezker abertzalea* and the Basque Nationalist Party (PNV). In Boise, the Basque migrant organization had a quarrel between the then-governing Socialist Party of Euskadi (Partido Socialista de Euskadi-Euskadiko Ezkerra, PSE-EE) and PNV, raising a number of issues including the homeland identity model in the diaspora. At the core of both episodes is the PNV defense of its ideological position towards the diaspora communities, its institutional network, and its cultural hegemony within the diaspora.

In the March 2009 elections in the ACBC, the PNV failed to win enough parliamentary seats to form a government, by itself or in a coalition, and Ibarretxe was unable to renew his cabinet. For the first time, the Basque pro-independence left movement was prohibited from taking part in the elections, which damaged the legitimacy of the elections while affecting the balance of power between Basque nationalists and Spanish nationalists in the new parliament. Against the background of acute global financial crisis and a rapidly deteriorating Spanish economy, the People's Party (Partido Popular, PP) led a relentless political opposition, together with the Spanish Socialist Workers' Party (Partido Socialista Obrero Español, PSOE), which had been in government since 2004. The PSE (the PSOE chapter in the ACBC) formed a minority government with the explicit support of the PP in May 2009. The goals of normalizing and democratizing Basque society were at the core of their agreement (see PSE and PP 2009). Patxi López thus became the first non-nationalist *lehendakari* in Basque history.

For the first time since the restoration of democracy, the PNV was not included in the government and, consequently, not responsible for diaspora politics. As the leading opposition party, the PNV, through its highest political institutional figure in power – the General Deputy of the Provincial Council of Bizkaia, José Luis Bilbao – took its political antagonism towards the PSE and the new government to the diaspora playing field. The re-appropriation of the symbolic patrimony of the diaspora reached its apex during the sixth International Basque Cultural Festival, Jaialdi, in Boise (28 July–1 August 2010).[10] President López led an institutional delegation that toured Nevada, California and Idaho, which included the Jaialdi. This would be his first visit to a diaspora community, and an attempt to 'renew the emotional and cultural ties between the Basque descendants that emigrated to the American West and the Basque Country' (Barriuso 2010a).[11]

By early June 2010, the Basque government became aware that Bilbao was leading his own institutional delegation to the festival to present an award to Pete Cenarrusa, a former secretary of the state of Idaho whose parents had migrated from Bizkaia. The government, PSE, and allied media condemned such disloyalty towards the Basque government and the *lehendakari* as the highest institutional representative of all the Basques. In the newspaper *El Correo* (3 June 2010) they argued that 'the presence' of Bilbao at the event would prevent the PSE from 'monopolizing it' (*El Correo* 2010a). In *El País* (8 June 2010), the conflict was called the 'Duelo en Boise Corral' [Duel in Boise Corral], reminiscent of the famous 1881 'Gunfight at the O.K. Corral' in Tombstone (Uriarte 2010). The PSE accused the PNV of claiming the Basque diaspora as its own patrimony, its own territory with the goal of homogenizing and politicizing perceptions of Basque identity, while acknowledging that PSE contacts with Basques abroad had been 'scarce, although not nonexistent' (*El Correo* 2010a). 'To a great extent the legitimation of the nationalist strategy for self-determination is sustained abroad . . . with the inestimable support of the Basque collectivities abroad,' *El País* added (8 June 2010). However, the predicted perfect political storm never materialized in Boise. Continuing the western film imagery, Barriuso (2010b) stated that 'López and Bilbao buried the hatchets of war in Boise' (*El Correo*, 31 July 2010).

After the delegations returned from their trips and the Basque festival had ended, the echoes of the event were heard as the homeland media and two main political forces, PNV and PSE, attempted to claim victory in winning the diaspora over to their respective causes. An editorial in *El Correo* (2 August 2010), 'Sumar para Integrar' [Inclusion for integration], summarizes López's political discourse in Boise, maintaining that Jaialdi 'exemplifies the people's capacity to coexist, without the need to renounce, but rather to encourage inclusion by integrating differences in an enriching result' (El Correo 2010b). That is, Boise is an example of integration, the 'fusion of Basque-Americans', the coexistence of diverse identities that the Basque government is promoting by leaving politics aside (Barriuso 2010c in *El Correo*, 1 August 2010). During the festival, Basque Americans embraced, as they normally would, powerful American political symbols such as the national anthem ('The Star-Spangled Banner'), which was sung at the opening ceremony, and the United States flag, which was displayed at all times. If this was unproblematic, then why was it a problem to do the same with Spanish national symbols in the homeland? According to López: 'The Ikurriña [Basque flag] and the spangled [United States] flag, hoisted here, are the clearest evidence of the type of coexistence that I am talking about' (Barriuso 2010b). This discourse resembles Jürgen Habermas' constitutional patriotism, which was embraced by much of the Spanish political spectrum (right and left) at the time.

On the other hand, an editorial in *Deia* (2 August 2010) entitled 'The diaspora, expression of the Basque nation', defined Jaialdi as 'the collective evidence of the identity markers of the Basques who feel as members of a nation called the Basque Country.' In other words, the existence of an enduring Basque diaspora is hard evidence of a perennial, authentic, unique, and autochthonous nation. In addition, the newspaper criticized López' 'assimilationist discourse' by highlighting that his 'sum of identities, Basque and American' was 'an attempt to assimilate the Basque into the Spanish' (2 August 2010). The Basque diaspora in Boise and elsewhere in the USA remained aloof and did not take a political stand, waiting for the next duel, if any, to unfold at the subsequent Jaialdi.

In November 2011, the PP won in the Spanish parliamentary elections, ousting the PSOE from government and forming a majority government. In an eleven-page statement, López dedicated three lines to foreign policy without mentioning the diaspora or its institutional networks. 'We have radically reformed the government's foreign action,' he said, 'in order to serve our companies and our economy, and not to serve a particular ideology' (Presidencia 2012). In August 2012, President López called for early elections after the PP ended its agreement with the PSE in May that year. The parliamentary elections took place on 21 October 2012, the first anniversary of the ETA declaration of the definitive end of its armed activity. On this occasion, the *ezker abertzalea* politicians were allowed to participate in the elections under the banner of Euskal Herria Bildu (EH Bildu), forming a coalition with Sortu, Eusko Alkartasuna (EA), Aralar and Alternatiba.[12]

The PNV won twenty-seven parliament seats of seventy-five, followed by EH Bildu with twenty-one seats. The two parties would not cooperate to form a majority government. Consequently, PNV formed a government through a simple majority, allowing its members to elect Iñigo Urkullu as president of the Basque government. Governing as a minority would force Urkullu to establish agreements with various parliamentary forces to succeed. His image as a skillful negotiator would require producing a consensus among the parties. 'To reach agreements' would be the unofficial leitmotif of his government. EH Bildu, PNV's main political rival, hence became the largest opposition party in the Basque parliament.

Regarding the government's foreign affairs objectives, Urkullu stated, one of the goals was 'to strengthen our ties with the Basque community around the world [. . .] The Basque diaspora is part of this nation [the Basque Country]. The Basque diaspora is one of the main players in making Euskadi so well-known all over the world [. . .] The diaspora has worked to make [Euskadi] known all over the world for years, and we definitely have to carry on protecting that treasure by working together' (Bieter 2013).

President Urkullu's first official diaspora visit was to the USA. The reason for the trip was the centennial celebration of the Euzko-Etxea Basque club of New York City, which took place from October 7 to 14, 2013. A major controversy was sparked by what appeared in the eyes of most observers to be an insignificant protocol incident. Once again, this illustrates the consequences of playing homeland politics with the diaspora. The board of directors of the Basque club intended to play an innocuous one-minute congratulatory video (in the Basque language) from the Mayor of Donostia-San Sebastián, Juan Karlos Izaguirre, at the closing of the Centennial Gala on October 13, which was directly opposed by the Urkullu delegation (see Izaguirre 2013). Izaguirre became mayor in June 2011 as a representative of the coalition Bildu, which included Sortu, EA, and Alternatiba. The video did not mention Izaguirre's political affiliation.

The club informed the presidential delegation of their decision to screen the video at the ceremony because this altered the previously agreed-upon event program and was a breach of protocol. Confronted with stubborn opposition from the delegation, negotiations between both parties began. The delegation delivered an ultimatum: Urkullu would not attend the 13th of October Gala with the video on the program. The club, defending its institutional autonomy and independent decision-making process, proposed playing the video message during the first minute that the Gala doors opened, without any journalists or Urkullu present. The idea was rejected. 'More than one hour after the Gala started and considering the great anticipation that the scheduled visit by the Basque Premier had generated among guests, the directorate decided to stand down and agree to the terms of the Basque Government's delegation', the club stated in an open letter released to the public on the 16th of October (Euzko-Etxea of New York 2013a). Furthermore, President Urkullu was not greeted formally by the Basque club president, Aitzol Azurtza,[13] as he entered the room with his team due to the delay caused by the negotiations. A representative of the Basque club referred to the fact that Urkullu was not announced to the floor as an 'unintended error'. Most of the 300 guests were unaware of the breech of protocol. During the closing ceremony, Azurtza claimed that the New York Basque club represented 'the plurality of the Basque people' (*Deia*, 14 October 2013). The club uploaded the video to its You-Tube channel on the 15th of October, followed by the aforementioned open letter to the public the next day.

The Basque government accused the Basque club of a lack of institutional respect, particularly because 'the event is partially subsidized' by the government. As in the controversy between López and Bilbao three years earlier in Boise, the government argued that the *lehendakari* is the highest institutional representative of Basque society and institutions. Therefore, there is no need for another institutional representative. Again, Izaguirre's (virtual) contestation was considered a threat to the hegemonic power of the government and the PNV, as it could potentially overshadow the supposedly hegemonic figure of the *lehendakari* and his monopoly of public space. However, the government argued that the screening of a single video, produced by an institutional representative of the Basque Country, 'did not guarantee the necessary plurality of institutional representation that an event like this must have' (Barriuso in *El Correo*, 15 October 2013; *El Correo*, 16 October 2013; Guadilla 2010; Santarén 2013).

Azurtza noted that the Gala 'was not about honoring the *lehendakari*, but it was our centennial celebration to which we invited the *lehendakari*, the president of Navarre, and other authorities . . . It was our celebration, the Euzko Etxea's, and we invite whomever we want, and we organize it however we want' (cited by Guadilla 2010). However, EH Bildu requested President Urkullu's presence at parliament to explain the reasons for vetoing the Izaguirre video. Urkullu, the coalition argued, 'does not accept the Basque political reality, the institutional reality of Gipuzkoa', which was in the hands of EH Bildu (*El Correo*, 16 October 2013; Iriondo 2013).

As in the Boise episode, homeland media played a central role in the reinterpretation of the protocol incident in New York, which sparked a vivid offline and online media discussion that lasted fourteen consecutive days, especially in the Basque American blogosphere.[14] The news also made its way into the Spanish mainstream media, leading to multiple discussions and further politicizing of the scenario.

On the 18th of October, Azurtza announced his resignation due to personal reasons, stating that his decision was unrelated to the Gala controversy. The next day, *El Correo* (19 October 2013) published a report about Azurtza's private life, including his sexual orientation and past involvement with the adult film industry (Reviriego and Guadilla 2013). The news was widely reproduced by major right-wing Spanish newspapers, including *ABC*, *El Mundo*, and *La Razón*. In addition, the papers accused PNV of being behind the disclosure of Azurtza's personal life, a point that was bluntly rejected by the nationalist party (Mediavilla 2013). A choir of distorting political media voices that added little to the dialogue between the diaspora and homeland, and, indeed, damaged dialogue, ended in personal attacks against Azurtza. As a result, the Basque club's general assembly issued a letter condemning 'the invasion of privacy promoted by part of the press in an effort to discredit our member Aitzol Azurtza', and 'to express its solidarity with Aitzol, to whom we acknowledge the huge personal sacrifice incurred in order to defend the independence of Euzko-Etxea' (Euzko-Etxea of New York 2013b). NABO President Valerie Arrechea also released a public message supporting Azurtza and the New York Basque club stating, 'We fully support our member organizations' activities and decisions. We know just how much hard work and passion it takes to keep our culture vital in our daily lives, and appreciate all those who work to perpetuate that culture in our communities. No member or volunteer deserves to have their personal life publicly scrutinized' (Arrechea 2013).[15]

By the end of this unethical public lynching, everybody forgot about the successful celebration of the oldest Basque club in North America, which was overshadowed by negative publicity. The news faded in time, but for the Basque American diaspora, and particularly for the Basque community in New York, it would take time to digest the ordeal. The image of the club and, by extension, of the diaspora in the USA had been negatively affected, as were the image of President Urkullu and his government, certain homeland media outlets, and homeland politics in general.

The incident raised three main issues that have implications for the diaspora community in the USA in the near future. First, the Basque government referred to its funding of the NY Basque club, which may have increased the mistrust of government involvement in its affairs and highlighted ulterior motives for doing so.[16] This suspicion is not new for some NABO member clubs. For instance, some clubs have not registered with the government to protect the privacy of their members, while others are reluctant to request public funding. Second, the event revealed the potentially destabilizing effect of government interference in the Basque club's autonomy as an independent apolitical and non-partisan organization. The incident highlighted the weakness of the diaspora's institutional structure. For instance, the NY Basque club lacked the tools to predict the consequences of their decision to play the video. Finally, once again, the diaspora also witnessed the brutality of homeland politics (described as 'political cannibalism' by the Argentinean PNV) in presumed retaliation for publicly disagreeing with the Basque government, which ruined a person's private life. The diaspora organization was ill prepared to stand on its own in homeland politics, and the political estrangement of diaspora from its homeland political establishment worsened because of the incident.

Conclusions

The chapter illuminates the influence of a non-state homeland government on diaspora social organizations and the destabilizing consequences that homeland political parties introduce to diaspora communities by attempting to (re)construct their cultural hegemony. The diaspora becomes a desired lost object from which to validate even contradictory homeland ideologies.

Four cases of diaspora-homeland political relationships are examined at a micro level, which is rarely addressed in research, providing a new empirical insight into homeland politics from the perspective of the diaspora. The homeland-diaspora encounters reveal spaces of cultural contestation with the goal of resisting and/ or changing the dominant socio-political structure. This complexity enriches and redefines the relationship of non-state homelands, such the Basque Country, to its diaspora in political, cultural, and territorial identities, nationhood and homeland in daily practice. We observe that previous reinterpretations of these interconnected concepts frequently conflict with the interpretation formulated in the homeland as part of a contested nation-state building process.

The existence of a few political groups within the Basque diaspora – mostly supporting Basque independence – suggests that the majority of individuals are politically disenfranchised from the homeland. Groups such as the ADV take on the intellectual mission of awakening a presumed dormant national conscience within diaspora Basques by alerting them that Basque identity is endangered by Spanish and French oppression, idle ACBC government politics, and conservative diaspora associations. These groups believe that the apolitical stance of diaspora organizations, particularly in countries such as Argentina, masks alliance to the PNV, which is eager to maintain the bureaucratic and administrative status quo of the Basque Country as an autonomous community within Spain.

Furthermore, the data collected indicate that the diaspora provides the opportunity for a political performance in which homeland political parties display their real and symbolic hegemonic power. This is particularly true when the diaspora is, in Lacanian terms, the homeland's contested '*object petite a*' – a lost and therefore desired object – whose (re)appropriation by various homeland ideologies is still necessary to validate the existence of a nation, which occurs in the case of Basque nationalism, or the co-existence of different (political) identities within an overarching political integration model with the idea of constructing an encompassing civic citizenship, which occurs in the case of the Basque socialism. This finding raises an important argument. The Basque diaspora, understood as an ethno-national diaspora in Sheffer's terminology, is not only utilized by the Basque nationalist movement at large but its conceptual amplitude, hybridity, and malleability (Hall 1993: 259–262) also helps fuel other ideologies, including socialism, within homeland identity discourse.

Regardless of the composition of the Basque Autonomous Community government, diaspora organizations seem unprepared to address the volatility and virulence of homeland politics in a ritualistic struggle for power among actors. Within the diaspora, homeland politics are decontextualized from its frame of reference. Consequently, the diaspora experiences difficulties fully comprehending the political reality of the homeland because it lacks the tools to decode its meanings. Diaspora communities can be mere spectators, involuntarily involved, or participants in politics. Similarly, the homeland interprets the diaspora according to its frame of reference, which prevents its understanding. This situation represents a two-way estrangement.

Consequently, harmless incidents are perceived as major affronts to the legitimacy of the highest institutional representative of Basque society because they challenge both the balance of power between the homeland and diaspora as well as the cultural hegemony of the PNV within diaspora communities. The government is then obliged to maintain the status quo by reminding the diaspora that they are in charge. The reduction or suppression of subsidies is the most effective (and visible) coercive tool the government uses to convey such a message. The government interferes in the internal affairs of diaspora organizations by constraining the organizations' autonomy as private entities. Unlike other diaspora communities whose financial contribution to their countries of origin is paramount, the Basque government has become a critical financial asset to the diaspora, particularly in South America, and its main institutions, including FEVA. Moreover, within this complex situation, the media in the homeland is a major actor with a strong ideology and interests in greatly inflated tension between the diaspora and homeland.

The consequences of politicizing diaspora organizations and communities should be carefully considered by the responsible homeland political and institutional actors. Playing homeland politics within the diaspora benefits homeland institutions to the detriment of the diaspora and its interests. Paraphrasing Shain and Barth (2003), the weaker the diaspora (in terms of dependence on homeland assets and leadership, permeability to homeland pressures – problematic politicization of the diaspora – and fragmentation, that is, lacking a supra-structure to provide an organized influence on homeland policies), the greater the influence of homeland on the diaspora. In other words, if the strength relations (balance of power) between the homeland and diaspora favor the former, then the homeland will be better able to influence the diaspora. In this regard, encounters, understood in terms of power relations, between the homeland and diaspora are unequal and subject to constant change. The balance of power between the diaspora and homeland clearly favors the homeland and harms the future of the relationship.

Notes

1 I would like to thank Joseba Zulaika of the University of Nevada, Reno, Sónia Pereira of the University of Lisbon, and Xabier Landabidea of the University of Deusto for reviewing previous drafts of this chapter.
2 Most of these organizations are in Argentina and the USA, which currently have about sixty-five per cent of Basque diaspora organizations worldwide. According to the Basque government's official registry, as of May 2014 there were 187 associations abroad, of which eighty-four were in Argentina and thirty-seven were in the USA.
3 Interviews with representatives of groups and active participants in these events were conducted in person, via telephone, and/or via e-mail within days of their occurrence. Respondents are not identified to protect their anonymity and guarantee confidentiality.
4 Consequently, new coalitions were formed to preserve the leftist Basque pro-independence ideology in elections. However, judges again barred their participation in the Basque parliamentary elections in March 2009, again citing links with ETA and Batasuna. The banned parties then called for null or blank votes, and relatively successfully, tens of thousands of blank votes were cast in protest.
5 The associations include the London Basque Campaign (United Kingdom), 6 de México (6 from Mexico), Josu Askatu (Argentina), Asociación Venezolana de Amigos de Euskal Herria (Venezuelan Association of Friends of the Basque Country), and the International Basque Organization for Human Rights (USA). As of the time of writing, most of these associations had ceased their activities and dissolved (see Oiarzabal 2013).
6 Udalbiltza-Kursaal was an assembly of Batasuna-elected town councilors.
7 The Ibarretxe Plan was first presented in the *lehendakari*'s address to the Basque Parliament on 28 September 2007 (Gobierno Vasco 2007). It proposed a political agreement with the Spanish government and elections to be held following a plebiscite in the ACBC on 25 October 2008.

8 '*Euskal Presoak Euskal Herrira*' (Basque Prisoners to the Basque Country) is a slogan for relocating ETA members imprisoned in Spanish and French jails to Basque jails, which is a demand supported by both the ACBC government and parliament.

9 Eyheraguibel was the secretary of FEVA in 2006 and 2007, president of FEVA from March 2008 to March 2010, and president of the Argentinean PNV from 2010 until he passed away in 2014.

10 The first Jaialdi festival was celebrated in 1985, and since then it has been celebrated every five years.

11 In fact, López's first diaspora encounter occurred just a few months after he was sworn into office. On 21 September 2009, Eyheraguibel, then-president of FEVA, sent a letter to López regarding the nationalist sentiment of the Basque-Argentinian community and the inalienable Basque right to self-determination. This provided a clear signal to the Basque socialist administration that they were not welcome. López never visited Argentina while in office.

12 Sortu, established in February 2011, is the new Basque pro-independence leftist party. Its statutes explicitly reject all political violence.

13 Azurtza was born in Venezuela, where his family was exiled during the Franco dictatorship. His father and uncle were among the promoters of the famous Basque government-in-exile clandestine radio station, Radio Euzkadi, in Caracas (1965–1977). Azurtza was raised in Donostia-San Sebastián. After moving to New York, he became an active member of the NY Basque club, where he was the Basque language instructor. Paradoxically, he became a member of the PNV in October 2013 (Interview, 8 July 2014, New York).

14 See for instance, 'A Basque in Boise' (www.blogseitb.us/basqueboise/) and 'Hella Basque' (http://hellabasque.com/). An analysis of the Basque American online discourse of the incident is beyond the scope of this chapter.

15 Basque American bloggers such as Hella Basque also defended Azurtza from the media's scrutiny into his private life. In addition, the only homeland media specializing in the Basque diaspora, EuskalKultura.com, published an editorial defending Azurtza (Etxarri 2013).

16 The issue of Basque government subsidies to diaspora institutions as a way to influence them was broached earlier during President López's term. During the annual FEVA meeting at the 2010 Basque National Week (Mar del Plata, Argentina), the then Basque government diaspora affairs representative, Julián Celaya, implied that a person who provided money could dictate its use. This unfortunate statement infuriated FEVA delegates (see EuskalKultura 12 November 2010; Ezkerro, Deia 20 November 2011). As of 2011, the Basque government provides approximately seventy-eight per cent of FEVA's annual fixed costs but only seventeen per cent of NABO's annual income (Oiarzabal 2013: 65).

References

Albert, M., Jacobson, D., and Lapid, Y., eds. 2001. *Identities, Borders, Orders: Rethinking International Relations Theory*. Minneapolis, MN: University of Minnesota Press.

Arrechea, V. 2013. 'Message From NABO President Valerie Arrechea on NY Eusko Etxea's Centennial Celebrations', North American Basque Organizations (NABO), 24 October. www.nabasque.org/new_nabo_test/astero_a8_43.html

Baylis, J., and Smith, S., eds. 1997. The Globalization of World Politics: An Introduction to International Relations. Oxford: Oxford University Press.

Barriuso, O. 2010a. 'López Estrecha Lazos con la Diáspora', *El Correo*, 25 July.

———. 2010b. 'López y Bilbao Entierran el Hacha de Guerra en Boise', *El Correo*, 31 July.

————. 2010c. 'López rompe Prejuicios', *El Correo*, 1 August.

————. 2013. 'Tensión y Desaires en la Gala del Centenario,' *El Correo*, 15 October.

Berriak. 2005a. Editorial, *Berriak*, 10 August.

————. 2005b. Editorial, *Berriak*, 2 August.

Bieter, M. 2013. 'A Conversation With the Basque President'. http://bieterblog.com/2013/05/07/a-conversation-with-the-basque-president.aspx

Bilbao, D. C. 2006. 'Exhorto Antidemocrático del PNV en Argentina', *Berriak*, 5 December.

Connor, W. 1993. 'Diasporas and the Formation of Foreign Policy: The United States in Comparative Perspective', in D. Constas and A. Platias, eds, *Diasporas in World Politics: The Greeks in Comparative Perspective*. London: Macmillan.

Deia. 2010. 'La Diáspora, Expresión de la Nación Vasca', Editorial, *Deia*, 2 August.

————. 2013. 'Fiesta Vasca por el Centenario de la Euzko Etxea de Nueva York', Editorial, *Deia*, 14 October.

Douglass, W. A., and Bilbao, J. 1975. *Amerikanuak: Basques in the New World*. Reno, NV: University of Nevada Press.

El Correo. 2010a. 'El Diputado General de Bizkaia llevará su Rivalidad con el Lehendakari López al Jaialdi de Julio en Boise, EEUU', Editorial, *El Correo*, 3 June.

————. 2010b. 'Sumar Para Integrar', Editorial, *El Correo*, 2 August.

————. 2013. 'El Gobierno Vasco Puntualiza que el Vídeo "No Preservaba" la "Necesaria Pluralidad"', Editorial, *El Correo*, 16 October.

Esman, M. J. 1986. 'Diasporas and International Relations', in G. Sheffer, ed., *Modern Diasporas in International Politics*. New York: St. Martin's Press.

Etxarri, J. 2013. 'En Defensa de Aitzol Azurtza, en Defensa de la Diáspora', *EuskalKultura. com – Boletín de Cultura y Diáspora Vasca*, 21 October.

EuskalKultura.com – Boletín de Cultura y Diáspora Vasca. 2007. 'Repaso mediante un Reportaje Fotográfico (I) de la recién concluida Semana Nacional Vasco Argentina de Rosario', 9 October.

————. 2010. 'Semana Nacional Vasca Argentina 2010: Reunión de Delegados de FEVA y XII Encuentro de Bibliotecas (VI)', 12 November.

Euzko-Etxea of New York. 2013a. 'An Official Letter Released by the Euzko-Etxea of New York Regarding the Events That Occurred During the Centennial Gala Celebration', 16 October.

————. 2013b. 'A Letter to Our Members and Friends Following the Assembly Meeting of October 20th', 20 October.

Ezkerro, M. 2011. 'La Teta que da la Leche', *Deia*, 20 November.

Gara. 2007a. 'Denuncian la Censura de Lakua a un Acto en Argentina', *Gara*, 8 October.

————. 2007b. 'Niegan que Lakua censurara la Charla de Ibazeta en la Euskal Etxea de Rosario', *Gara*, 23 October.

Glick-Schiller, N., Basch, L., and Blanc Szanton, C. 1992. 'Transnationalism: A New Analysis Framework for Understanding Migration', *Annals of the New York Academy of Sciences*, 645: 1–24.

Gobierno Vasco. 1994. *Law of Relations With Basque Communities Outside the Autonomous Community of the Basque Country*. Vitoria-Gasteiz: Servicio Editorial de Publicaciones del Gobierno Vasco.

————. 1996. *Euskaldunak Munduan, Building the Future*. Vitoria-Gasteiz: Servicio Editorial de Publicaciones del Gobierno Vasco.

————. 2000. *World Congress on Basque Communities, 1999*. Vitoria-Gasteiz, 26–29 October 1999. Vitoria-Gasteiz: Servicio Central de Publicaciones del Gobierno Vasco.

———. 2007. *A Political Initiative Aimed at Resolving the Basque Conflict*. Vitoria-Gasteiz: Servicio Editorial de Publicaciones del Gobierno Vasco.

Gramsci, A. 1971. *Selections for the Prison Notebooks of Antonio Gramsci*. New York: International Publishers.

Guadilla, D. 2010. 'La Eusko Etxea de Nueva York se Queja de que Urkullu Impidió un Vídeo de Izagirre', *El Diario Vasco*, 16 October.

Guarnizo, L. E., Portes, A., and Haller, W. 2003. 'Assimilation and Transnationalism: Determinants of Transnational Political Action Among Contemporary Migrants', *American Journal of Sociology*, 108(6): 1211–1248.

Hall, S. 1993. 'Culture, Community, Nation', *Cultural Studies*, 7(3) (October): 349–363.

Hella Basque. 2013. 'In Defense of Aitzol Azurtza', 20 October, San Francisco, CA.

Ibazeta, J. 2007. '¡Aguante Euskal Herria!', *Gara*, 24 October.

Iriondo, I. 2013. 'Urkullu veta en Nueva York un Minuto de Saludo de Izagirre', *Gara*, 17 October.

Izaguirre, J. K. 2013. 'Donostiako Alkatearen Zorion Mezua NYeko Euskal Etxeari', Euskal Etxea New York YouTube channel, 15 October. www.youtube.com/watch?v=-qGFS320yhs

JO TA KE. 2007. 'Comunicado de Prensa', Rosario, Argentina, 7 November.

Junta Extraterritorial de Argentina del PNV. 2006. 'A la Colectividad Vasco Argentina', Mar del Plata, Argentina, December.

Koinova, M. 2010. 'Diasporas and International Politics: Utilising the Universalistic Creed of Liberalism for Particularistic and Nationalist Purposes', in R. Bauböck and T. Faist, eds, *Diaspora and Transnationalism: Concepts, Theories and Methods*. IMISCOE Research. Amsterdam: Amsterdam University Press.

Mediavilla, K. 2013. 'El Límite de lo Privado', 22 October. http://koldomediavilla.blogspot.com.es/2013/10/el-limite-de-lo-privado.html

Molina Aparicio, F., and Oiarzabal, P. J. 2009. 'Basque-Atlantic Shores: "Ethnicity, the Nation-State, and the Diaspora in Europe and America (1808–1898)"', *Ethnic and Racial Studies*, 32(4): 698–715.

Oiarzabal, A. M., and Oiarzabal, P. J. 2005. *Identidad Vasca en el Mundo: Narrativas Más Allá de Fronteras*. Bilbao: Erroteta.

Oiarzabal, P. J. 2007. 'We Love You: The Basque Government's Post-Franco Discourses on the Basque Diaspora', *Revista Sancho el Sabio*, 26: 95–132.

———. 2012a. 'Una Verdadera Imagen de Paz: Los Congresos Mundiales de la Diáspora Vasca', in M. Acillona, ed., *Marcos Interpretativos de la Realidad Social Contemporánea*. Bilbao: Universidad de Deusto.

———. 2012b. 'Diaspora Basques and Online Social Networks: An Analysis of Users of Basque Institutional Diaspora Groups on Facebook', *Journal of Ethnic and Migration Studies*, 38(9): 1469–1485.

———. 2013. *The Basque Diaspora Webscape: Identity, Nation and Homeland, 1990s–2010s*. Reno, NV: Center for Basque Studies, University of Nevada.

Panossian, R. 1998. 'Between Ambivalence and Intrusion: Politics and Identity in Armenia-Diaspora Relations', *Diaspora*, 7(2): 149–196.

Partido Socialista de Euskadi (PSE) and Partido Popular (PP). 2009. 'Bases para el Cambio Democrático al Servicio de la Sociedad Vasca', March.

Pratt, M. L. 1992. Imperial Eyes: Travel Writing and Transculturation. London: Routledge.

Presidencia. 2012. 'Primer Consejo de Gobierno. Intervención del Lehendakari', 21 October. Vitoria-Gasteiz: Presidencia. Secretaría General de Comunicación.

Reviriego, J. M., and Guadilla, D. 2013. 'Azurtza en la Eusko Etxea de Nueva York, Harri en el Porno', *El Correo*, 19 October.

Safran, W. 1991. 'Diasporas in Modern Societies: Myths of Homeland and Return', *Diaspora*, 1(1): 83–99.

Santarén, E. 2013. 'Nueva York', *Deia*, 21 October.

Semanario. 2005. 'Asociación Diáspora Vasca'. 1(1), June. Santa Rosa, Argentina.

Shain, Y. 1999. Markcting the American Creed Abroad: Diasporas in the U.S. and Their Homelands. Cambridge: Cambridge University Press.

Shain, Y., and Barth, A. 2003. 'Diasporas and International Relations Theory', *International Organization*, 57(3) (Summer): 449–479.

Sheffer, G., ed. 1986a. *Modern Diasporas in International Politics*. New York: St. Martin's Press.

———. 1986b. 'A New Field of Study: Modern Diasporas in International Politics', in G. Sheffer, ed., *Modern Diasporas in International Politics*. New York: St. Martin's Press.

———. 2003. *Diaspora Politics: At Home Abroad*. Cambridge, MA: Cambridge University Press.

Tápiz Fernández, J. M. 2000. 'La Actividad Política de los Emigrantes: El Caso Vasco (1903–1936)', in Ó. Á. Gila and A. A. Morales, eds, *Las Migraciones Vascas en Perspectiva Histórica (Siglos XVI–XX)*. Bilbao: Servicio Editorial de la Universidad del País Vasco.

Tölölyan, K. 1996. 'Rethinking Diaspora(s): Stateless Power in the Transnational Moment', *Diaspora*, 5(1): 3–36.

———. 2012. 'Diaspora Studies: Past, Present and Promise.' *IMI Working Paper*, 55: 1–14. www.migration.ox.ac.uk/odp/pdfs/WP55%20Diaspora%20studies.pdf

Totoricagüena, G. 2005. 'Diasporas as Non-Central Government Actors in Foreign Policy: The Trajectory of Basque Paradiplomacy', *Nationalism and Ethnic Politics*, 11(2): 265–287.

Uriarte, E. 2010. 'Duelo en Boise Corral', *El País*, 8 June.

Veredas Muñoz, S. 2003. 'Las Asociaciones de Inmigrantes en España. Práctica Clientelar y Cooptación Política', *Revista Internacional de Sociología*, 36: 207–225.

Vertovec, S. 1999. 'Conceiving and Researching Transnationalism', *Ethnic and Racial Studies*, 22(2): 447–462.

5 Multiple sovereignties?

Civil society and territorial construction in Iparralde

Xabier Itçaina

The literature on peripheral nationalisms presents the French Basque country (Iparralde) as a classic case of a 'failure' of nationalism in contrast to the 'success' of its southern equivalent (Linz 1986). In 2006, a cross-border survey on territorial identities reiterated this view when noting that eleven per cent of the French Basque defined themselves as 'only Basque', against forty per cent in the Basque Autonomous Community (Baxok et al. 2006: 49). This conclusion, I argue, is valid only insofar as (a) the intrinsic value of quantitative surveys measuring self-identification is overstated (Itçaina 2010), and (b) identity-based movements are reduced to their *formal* political dimensions (i.e. their degree of institutional autonomy, the impact of peripheral nationalism on electoral contests and the party system, and the intensity of political violence). The conclusion would be less straightforward if one looks instead at civil society mobilizations that are no less political, although seemingly further removed from the formal institutional sphere.

Since the 1970s, mobilizations in Iparralde concerning Basque language and culture, peasant agriculture and social economy have played a special role in generating social capital and legitimizing the idea of a shared territorial destiny. These mobilizations are not expressed in terms of a single ideological matrix, and they should not be regarded as mere cultural or socio-economic expressions of Basque nationalism. Each of the sectors mentioned above is subject to various scales of regulation, from the local to the global, generating distinct experiences of sovereignty. Thus, the strengthening of territorial autonomy for the Basque country would not have similar effects on linguistic mobilizations as, for example, on milk producers operating under European constraints. In other words, we shall emphasize here the multiplicity of conceptions of sovereignty in the everyday life of French Basques.[1]

This chapter addresses the relationship between three research questions: (a) what imaginary, in terms of sovereignties, has been conveyed by the mobilization of French Basque civil society, particularly as regards cultural and economic matters? (b) in what way has the new model of territorial governance experienced by the French Basque since the early 1990s helped channel, institutionalize or radicalize 'sovereignist' claims? and (c) in what ways have sector-based regulatory constraints influenced the unification or (on the contrary) the proliferation of diverse 'imagined sovereignties' (cultural, socio-economic, territorial or food sovereignties) contending with each other?

This study is located at the intersection of three theoretical debates. The first concerns the literature on ethnic and territorial identities. While the literature on social movements has largely addressed the procedural dimensions of identity construction (Hunt and Benford 2008), we will focus here on the phenomena of superposed identities (ethnic, social or professional identities) which character- ize the 'new' social movements. Mobilizations of Basque small farmers, in par- ticular, will be re-interpreted as featuring simultaneously a *professional* identity in crisis, a deeply-rooted *territorial* identity and a transnational *militant* identity. These superimposed identities are not necessarily congruent with each other. Fol- lowing Brubaker (2001) and Avanza and Laferté (2005), we will adopt here an institutional-constructivist approach to identity mobilizations. The second debate concerns the role of identities, cultures and 'imagined sovereignties' in territorial development (Keating 2008). Iparralde is a case of a 'culture of dissent' (*cul- ture réfractaire*) (Berthet and Palard 1997), where territorial identity in its cogni- tive, emotional and instrumental dimensions (Keating, Loughlin and Deschouwer 2003) has had a direct effect on the conception of territorial development. The third debate concerns the role played by civil society in the construction of territo- rial development and identity as a political issue. Given the participatory model of governance set up in the 1990s, Iparralde offers an ideal case study for dia- logue between proximity economists (Leloup et al. 2005), approaches to territo- rial regimes (Itçaina et al. 2007) and territorial institutionalism (Carter and Smith 2008; Jullien and Smith 2008). The French Basque case has been specifically addressed by work on territorial governance (Chaussier 1996; Hourcade 2007; Etcheverry 2008; Urteaga and Ahedo 2004), Basque nationalism (Jacob 1994; Ahedo 2005, 2008, 2014; Izquierdo 2004), cross-border relations and European integration (Bray and Keating 2013; Bray 2004; Harguindéguy 2007; Letamen- dia 1997), youth mobilizations (Bray 2006) and linguistic mobilizations (Laborde 1999; Harguindéguy and Itçaina 2012; Heidemann 2014; Pierre 2013). Drawing on this research, we intend to pursue questions at the intersection between ter- ritorial and sectorial approaches, in order to better understand the plural nature of civil society mobilization. Besides these studies, we shall use original data col- lected between 2004 and 2014 by several surveys on French Basque cultural and socio-economic mobilizations.[2]

This chapter will take the form of a sequentially-ordered historical presenta- tion. The first part will review the emergence of civil society mobilizations in the years 1970–1980, a period when conceptions of territorial sovereignty portrayed by political, cultural and economic activists were unified and weakly institution- alized. The second part will review the effects that the emerging institutionaliza- tion of the French Basque country has had on mobilizations of civil society from the 1990s onwards. How were those in charge of the new territorial governance able (or unable) to enlist actors within civil society in this process of institution- alization? The final part will discuss the proliferation of civil society mobiliza- tions between 2000 and 2010, and thus the increase in 'imagined sovereignties', whether these mobilizations should be regarded as within or outside the formal (public) model of territorial governance.

1970s–1980s: sovereignty in dispute

The first historical sequence corresponds to the 1970s-1980s and is character-ized by the emergence of a new generation of social movements in Iparralde. Expressed in diverse ways within each sector, these mobilizations, originating in civil society, had in common a 'sovereignist' discourse. This not only aspired to institutional recognition of Basque identity in its various expressions, but also had a self-management dimension, producing much of the exemplary nature of bottom-up grassroots initiatives with their origins in local communities and peer groups.

If we adopt the approach taken by Jullien and Smith (2008) to the construction of public problems, we should emphasize that French Basque social movements initially thought of local development as a *collective problem* which emerges 'whenever their definition is shared by an inter-organizational grouping of actors who can claim to be representative of their industry and/or their profession' (Jul-lien and Smith 2008: 20). Gradually, however, these collective problems were to become *public problems*, developing 'when the process of definition widens to include politicians and civil servants, who, at least in theory, are supposed to work for the public interest' (ibid.). While actors would initially mobilize in favor of the structuring of the movement, they would increasingly seek more involve-ment from politicians and public administration. This dynamic was part of a joint politicization of territorial development *and* Basque identity, meaning that eco-nomic and cultural issues were reinterpreted as 'value choices' by belief groups (Hassenteufel 2008).[3]

Socio-economic and cultural mobilisations thus appeared as the counterpart of an *abertzale* ('patriotic' or Basque nationalist) political movement which was itself in the process of change. This movement developed in the late 1960s, from an autonomist movement tinged with Christian democracy and social Catholi-cism, to become a firmly left-wing and secularised pro-independence movement. The appearance of an ethno-political movement and founding of Enbata in 1960 reflected a change in the ideological development of Basque nationalism in the direction of a 'nationalitarian' (Seiler 1994), federalist and self-government move-ment (Jacob 1994). In addition to this change in the political movement, a new generation of collective action appeared in cultural and socio-economic domains.

Collective action in favour of Basque language and culture made itself felt in three areas. On the one hand, the first Basque language immersion schools (*ikastolak*) were set up as associations in the French Basque country from 1969. The *ikastolak* were to develop following a model subject to a range of influences including the southern Basque *ikastola* movement (at that time in the process of becoming institutionalized during the democratic transition), alternative pedago-gies and self-management governance models. The second dynamic relates to the networking of associations aspiring to unite the various cultural and linguistic initiatives. A division of labour took place between those operators aspiring to structure the cultural networks and to increase Basque-language education (Ikas, since 1959) and those more oriented towards the public authorities (Euskal Konfederazioa, since 1995) (Oronos 2002). Finally, this period was also marked by the development of associative cultural initiatives in areas as diverse as theatre, music, dance and the media. This cultural revival took place at the same time as similar movements involving other regional languages of France, but here it was above all the social change taking place in the Spanish or southern Basque country that was a decisive inspiration.

The relationship between the public authorities and this first wave of cultural mobilization was at first tinged with distrust. Faced with a hostile attitude on the part of the French state and its representatives, the cultural movement's initial tactics were cautious and defensive, in order to ensure the legal viability of its social organizations, especially the *ikastolak*. These were also guaranteed at first by logistical support from a sector of the Church. Enbata was banned as a political party by a government decree in 1974, and there were real threats to the Basque movement as a whole. It was not until the late 1980s that French Basque cultural actors moved from a defensive strategy to one of negotiating with the state, influenced by developments south of the border (Oronos 2002).

This period was also marked by a process whereby local development became politicized. The economy, like culture, became a political object, in the sense of a field of struggles between values, representations and interests. This politicization was relatively new in the economic sector as one of the new priorities of the *abertzale* movement. Local development was constructed as a public problem, and the idea of *endogenous* development gained ground. This discourse had been anticipated during the 1950s and 1960s by sectors within social Catholicism favourable to an economic 'third way'. It was then to be taken up especially by teachers and by the *abertzale* (Enbata) and Christian Democrat (Herria) press. This inspiration took concrete form through agricultural and social economy initiatives.

Within agriculture, institutional change and the politicization of local development took two complementary forms. On the one hand, the structure of the trade unions changed. The monopolistic position of the agricultural union FDSEA[4] was first contested within the Movement of Rural Christian Youth (MRJC),[5] a traditional breeding-ground for professional and trade-union elites. In the late 1960s, a new generation of MRJC youth activists challenged from within both the organization's network dynamics, judged to be too much in the sway of the Church for a lay movement, and the patterns of professional elite recruitment resulting from the MRJC mode of government. Young MRJC protesters then began to question the productivist orientation espoused by the FDSEA monopoly of labour representation. Close to the peasant-worker movement in the 1970s, these activists brought about a split in 1982 with the formation of the Union of Basque Country Peasants, Euskal Herriko Laborarien Batasuna (ELB), which became the Basque branch of the left-wing French union Confédération Paysanne (Confederation of Small Farmers) in 1987. Union action, already geared to institutional issues, was coupled with action to redefine the productive model in a bottom-up fashion. From the 1970s, initiatives emerged to promote a 'peasant, and sustainable' agriculture,[6] seen as an alternative to productivism and agro-business. As an alternative, these initiatives were intended to favour local farm production, that is to say, to produce territorial *specificity* (Gumuchian and Pecquer 2007). This included initiatives such as moves to adopt labelling of product origin (AOC, Appellations d'Origine Contrôlée, or 'Controlled Designation of Origin'), and those that came together in 1991 in the Arrapitz ('Rebirth') federation. Associated with these were bodies advocating a quality-based approach (the Idoki Charter), associations promoting organic farming (BLE, Biharko lurraren Elkartea, the Association for the Land of Tomorrow), Association des bergers transhumants (the Association of Transhumant Shepherds) and organizations supporting young farmer entrepreneurship such as Lur Hats ('Breath of the Earth') and acquisition of land for agricultural purposes such as the Mutual Agricultural Land Grouping, Groupement Foncier Agricole Mutuel (GFAM) known as Lurra ('Land').[7]

This model of collective action, an innovation in agricultural communities, had two key features. On the one hand, the customary peasant model remained a central reference point, whether centered around the small family farm (*etxea*, literally the 'house-farm') or the transhumant shepherds. At the same time, however, these mobilizations distanced themselves from the traditional model. Support for young farmers setting themselves up in business outside the family framework enabled, for example, a resumption of operations by neo-rural operators from outside the customary circuit of transmission. Similarly, the call for public subscriptions to enable the acquisition of land for agricultural use (GFAM Lurra) removed the agricultural issue from its merely sectorial dimension, in order to construct it as a public and political problem which concerned the territory *as a whole* (Lascoumes and Le Gales 2007). Given the crisis of the customary model and the critical response to the productivist model, the collective action model advocated by peasant and sustainable initiatives offered a viable alternative.

Politicization also involved the promotion of the social economy outside the agricultural sector, and in particular workers' cooperatives, as an organizational response to the deficiencies of local development. Starting in the 1950s and 1960s, the Spanish Basque Mondragón cooperative was seen as a virtuous model representing an integrated cooperative movement bringing together the system of industrial production, banking, consumption and education. Attempts to set up a comprehensive cooperative movement in rural areas, such as the Zuñiga experiment in Navarre,[8] were also followed with interest on the French side of the border. In the 1970s, the inspiration of social Catholicism unraveled in favor of greater influence from the French and international cooperative movement. The cooperative business was now perceived as an alternative based on certain political principles: internal democracy, a limited salary scale, the primacy of labor over capital, profit-sharing, indivisible reserves, and an anchoring in the territory. This thinking inspired the creation in 1974 of an association, Partzuer ('Associated'), intended to provide an impetus to create a cooperative movement in the French Basque country, and the development of cooperative businesses from 1975. Their anchoring within the social economy enabled the founders of the

Basque SCOP[9] ventures to enjoy the support of the French cooperative movement and, incidentally, public policies relating to it. The movement thus took advantage of the incentivizing policies of the late 1970s (the SCOP Law of 1978) and the beginnings of the institutionalization of the social economy when the left-wing government took power in France in 1981 (Demoustier 2001).

This movement held that economic sovereignty within the territory and political sovereignty were inextricably related. The cooperative movement saw itself as a social movement, as was emphasized by the goals of the Lana, a workers' association. In 1982, Lana aimed to include cooperative enterprises within a consolidated model inspired by Mondragón. The creation of cooperatives was supplemented, upstream and downstream, by new instruments of local development (giving rise to Hemen Association in 1979) and a financial tool designed to attract popular savings (the Herrikoa venture capital company set up in 1980). All these initiatives thought of local development as a territorial and political problem. This was evidenced by the constant appeals for public subscriptions to provide seed capital for cooperatives and for the creation of new businesses via Herrikoa. The cooperative movement at this point was seeking osmosis between local communities and businesses, as in Italian industrial districts. This was based on a project to develop the Basque hinterland, something seen as an alternative to the 'alienation' produced by an economy based on an agriculture in decline, by tourism and by an exogenous industrial base. The Guipuzcoan model of diffuse industrialization was disseminated via training stays by the future founders of SCOPs to Mondragón in the 1970s and the presence of many southern political refugees in the French Basque SCOPs.

These operations, whether cultural and linguistic mobilizations, peasant mobilizations or social economy mobilizations, were distinguished by (a) a relatively unified conception of sovereignty based on strong unity between the political, cultural and economic 'fronts', (b) a relatively low impact on 'conventional' and electoral politics (Jacob 1994), and (c) a low level of institutionalization of mobilizations which were above all protest movements facing a hostile or indifferent attitude on the part of the state. However, while as a general rule the local political system was based on a self-reproducing system of interactions between the prefect and 'his' notables (Worms 1966; Chaussier 1996), the 1970s also saw the development of the first initiatives in favour of bottom-up local development involving elected officials, technicians and representatives of civil society. Soule, the easternmost province, was the innovator in this area, signing the first *Contrat de pays* (a development agreement associating municipalities, the region and the state) in the mid-1970s (Dalla Rosa 2006). Similar initiatives took place in the Mixe and Ostabarret valleys in the late 1970s and early 1980s. However, the main mobilization affecting cross-sector public governance would not take concrete shape until the late 1980s.

1990–2005: towards a sovereignty based on compromise

The second historical sequence, which began in the late 1980s, was characterized by a restructuring of public territorial action – a restructuring which would not be without its effect on sovereignist movements. Territorial institutionalization marked the beginning of a new stage in the Basque country (Chaussier 1996). It would take the form of a participatory and prospective approach involving state representatives, locally-elected officials and representatives of civil society. This fledgeling institutionalization was on the one hand a response to a strategy on the part of Basque social movements oriented towards the construction of development and identity as *public* problems, in the sense of 'a process in which a group of private and public actors interact in order to impose their representation of an issue, the interpretation which they derive from this, and go on to influence the direction of and the means for the action to be taken' (Lascoumes and Le Gales 2007: 74, author's translation). Contrary to all expectations, this process was initiated by the state via a development-oriented sub-prefect. Through this, the state intended to regain its role as a facilitator by conceding a minimum level of institutional recognition to a territory which at that time was shaken by social mobilization and political unrest. Seized upon by many local players who saw in it a window of opportunity, the process led to a new form of territorial governance. This would be a form of sovereignty based on compromise between *abertzale* and non-*abertzale*, and collaboration between the state, elected officials, the territorial administration and civil society.

A new model of territorial governance

Consultations led to the creation of the Basque Cultural Institute in 1990, the Basque Country Development Council (Conseil de développement du Pays basque) in 1994 and the Council of Basque Country Elected Representatives (Conseil des élus du Pays basque) in 1995. In 1997, the territory was recognized as a *pays* (country) within the meaning of the law of 1995, in other words a territory with a longstanding identity and traditions whose inhabitants share common geographical, economic, cultural or social interests. Thanks to the work of the aforementioned institutions, the first Development Agreement with the state was signed in 1997. In 2000, a specific Agreement for the 2001–2006 period was signed, marking the commitment of the state and local authorities towards local development. The process was repeated in 2005 with a new planning initiative, *Pays Basque 2020* (Basque Country 2020), which led to a new development contract in September 2008.

A new policy community was formed around the drive for territorial development. Policy communities bring together actors with three characteristics (Lascoumes and Le Gales 2007): they have skills and interests in an area of public action; they belong to circles which are different in nature (administrative, economic, academic, media, political, associative); and they have a high degree of commitment to playing an active role in the various phases of the problem definition, policy choices and the monitoring of implementation. The 'new territorial grammar' (Ségas 2004) which was then set up in the Basque country aimed to combine two types of governance (Enjolras 2010). The first was vertical, centred on public authorities, and attempted to manage a complex territory using incentives rather than coercive methods. The second was horizontal, based on a strong local dynamic of self-government and coordination between actors in civil society.

At the French national scale, the Basque experience was quickly seen as a laboratory for territorial governance in the sense that it saw 'situations featuring cooperation, with no order imposed by a hierarchy, and corresponding to the construction, management and representation of territories, especially as regards their economic or institutional environment' (Simoulin 2007). The Voynet Law of 1999 was itself inspired by the Basque experience in generalizing to all *pays* mechanisms such as the Development Councils established by the 1995 law passed by Interior Minister Charles Pasqua (Hourcade 2007: 7).

Enlistments, crazes and disappointments

While the new territorial governance model has undeniably produced horizontality and consultation in the conduct of public policy, what were the actual results in terms of institutionalization? Did the number of rules and procedures continually grow, and did they acquire greater precision and become genuinely prescriptive (Lascoumes and Le Gales 2007: 98)?

Firstly, a certain enlistment of activists from civil society can be observed in the new form of territorial governance. Significantly, the presidency and the general secretariat of the first Basque Country Development Council were taken on in 1994 by former leaders of the Basque workers' cooperative movement. These became development experts, above all playing a mediating role between the participation opportunities offered by the political and administrative sphere and the interests and values advocated by militant groups on the one hand, and organized interest groups on the other. This initial craze did not, however, mean that all institutional demands were translated into actual public policy.

The dynamics of institutionalization greatly varied depending on the sectors involved and the interplay between the scales at which they operated. The cultural and educational sector quickly appeared as one of the sectors most requiring public regulation at the territorial scale (requiring *ad hoc* policies) and at the national scale (requiring legislative changes). The meeting of supply and demand produced a gradual process of institutionalization. In 1990, cultural associations became federated within the Basque Cultural Institute, Institut Culturel Basque (ICB), which was publicly funded (by the state and local authorities) but had an associative structure. The ICB then became responsible for the conduct of coherent public action in Basque cultural matters, positioned at the interface between associations, elected political actors and cultural administrations. During the initial phase, the promotion of Basque culture and language were combined. Quickly, however, the pressure of mobilizations made it necessary for *language* policy properly speaking to become autonomous from *cultural* policy. In 2001, specific official arrangements were made for the language policy, which led in 2005 to the setting up of the Public Office for the Basque Language (Office public de la langue basque, OPLB). The OPLB consequently became responsible for carrying out sociolinguistic surveys, for the coordination of Basque teaching within the three school systems[10] and for the coordination of community networks promoting the Basque language, Euskera.

The actors within the cultural and linguistic movement chose from the out-set to adopt a critical engagement with these new institutions. Dubbed *eragileak* ('operators'), associations and federations of Basque schools, Basque courses for adults, the promotion of Basque in public life, and Basque language media made use of the new institutional opportunities to extend their resources and net-works. The use of cross-border cooperation schemes, including European ones (Itçaina and Manterola 2013), reflects this strategy. While remaining faithful to their function as tribunes, cultural operators pointed out the limits of an institu-tionalization which they considered incomplete. Within the Basque community, social movements called for clarification of procedures for the awarding of grants and contracting procedures undertaken by the OLPB and the ICB. Within French state institutions, the movement also called for new legislative and constitutional arrangements.[11] With the example of the Southern Basque territories in mind, many were critical of the fact that in the north, bilingual arrangements were based solely on volunteering. There were calls for making Basque language co-official, as well as imposing regulations on the use of Euskera.

Other circles, based on distinct scales of regulation, were less immediately sen-sitive to changes in territorial governance. Workers' cooperatives (SCOPs) were to be represented in the Development Council, but their issues were primarily focused on other arenas and subject to sectorial constraints.[12]

In agriculture, there were competing understandings about the level of govern-ment at which regulations should take place.[13] For the FDSEA union, the relevant scale was the Pyrénées-Atlantiques *département* (Chamber of Agriculture) and the national scale, where the Union was in a strong position. In contrast, propo-nents of peasant agriculture (ELB) argued that a specific territorial institution-alization was essential in order to address the specificities of Basque agriculture. This claim crystallized around the demand for a separate Basque Chamber of Agriculture, one distinct from the Chamber in the *département*. This discourse was well received by Basque farmers. On the one hand, the ELB, since its incep-tion in 1982, had continually improved its showing at farmers' professional elec-tions, gaining a slight majority among Basque farmers in 2001. Bolstered by this electoral legitimacy, the ELB adopted a posture of critical participation with regard to the new institutions that had been set up in the context of the new ter-ritorial governance to administer Basque agriculture.[14] Considering these institu-tional formulae to be unsatisfactory and powerless, in 2005 elements associated with ELB founded the alternative Chamber of Agriculture of the Basque Country (EHLG, Euskal Herriko Laborantza Ganbara). In its operations (services to farm-ers) and organization (opening out to consumers and environmentalists) EHLG offered a citizenship- and territorial-based approach to agriculture. Food sover-eignty and territorial sovereignty were thus merged into one and the same mobi-lizing discourse. Fearing a merging of these demands, the state and the majority union took legal action against the EHLG on the grounds of an infringement of the departmental monopoly enjoyed by the Pyrenées Atlantiques Chamber of Agriculture. In the end, these legal disputes were almost all won by EHLG and those supporting it, which served as a forum for the staging of a sovereignist peasant *and* territorial discourse (Itçaina 2011). In addition, the litigation contributed to a politicization of the cause which extended beyond the agricultural sector and strengthened a grouping of various sectorial demands (agriculture, university, language, public life) around the demand for territorial recognition.

From the point of view of civil society, the new model of Basque territorial governance gave rise to a number of questions. Disenchantment, which has frequently accompanied the participatory turn towards territorial governance (Arnaud and Simoulin 2011), was also present here. First, there was the image of a depoliticised territorial governance entrusted to development experts (Ségas 2011).[15] The Basque Country Development Council, in particular, has striven to gain acceptance for a discourse of expertise and territorial engineering, with the aim of producing a consensus. Secondly, there was an accumulation of uncertainties as regards the ongoing territorial reforms in France, notably regarding the disappearance of the *pays* and the recasting of decentralization.

2005–2013: the proliferation of imagined sovereignties

These two phases (the crystallization of a social movement, followed by a partial institutionalization of their demands within territorial governance) were followed by a third stage, corresponding to an increase in the 'imagined sovereignties' at stake. This change took place on the eve of a comprehensive territorial change, which would have its effects on the mobilization of civil society.

The territory fundamentally transformed

Changes in the relationship between social mobilizations and territorial governance must here be reframed in view of the global transformation of the Basque territory and, in the first place, of its socioeconomic context. Here as elsewhere, the crisis of the traditional territories was accompanied by the risk of a dissociation between places of production and places of consumption, as well as a disconnection between the origin of what is consumed and the destination of what is produced (Pecqueur and Itçaina 2012: 52). Moreover, territorial economy relied less on its productive base and more on other sources of income: salaries related to public-sector jobs, retirement benefits, social benefits or the income of secondary residents, particularly numerous on the Basque coastal zone. Those territories which raised residential income and those productive territories no longer necessarily corresponded to each other, leading economists to talk of a 'presential economy' (*économie présentielle*) (Talandier and Davezies 2009).

Particularly affected by this phenomenon due to its attractiveness, the Basque country intended above all to maintain a productive economy. One of the institutional responses was to recast territorial alliances in the form of inter-Communes and local collective development projects (such as the Collective Development Project of Lower Navarre). The other, complementary, response was to think in terms of competitiveness clusters. These were not based on productivity but on the concept of territorial specificity (Gumuchian and Pecqueur 2007), in other words territories' capacity to develop resources which are location-specific, and thus deeply rooted in the cognitive heritage of a particular place (Pecqueur and Itçaina 2012: 52). The work undertaken by the Basque Country Development Council from 2008 in order to legitimize the idea of a 'Basque country territorial brand', a quality mark intended for productions from all sectors, reflects this strategy. However exemplary they may have been, these initiatives would, however, bring actors involved in territorial governance up against the limits of the existing institutional framework.

A unified strategy: Batera and the territorial authority

The Basque territorial governance model, seen as exemplary in the years between 1990 and 2000, seemed to have stalled. For the Batera collective, which was set up in 2002 around the issue of the institutional recognition of the territory, 'while this mode of governance has enabled a continuous dialogue to take place between elected representatives and civil society, it has done nothing to respond either to the need for institutional recognition, or in any sense to the ambitions of the territorial project' (CTPB 2013: 5; author's translation). In particular, the 'Territorial Authority' (*collectivité territoriale*) was now seen as the most suitable institutional tool to meet the challenges posed by changes to the territory: 'the hyper-attractiveness of territory endangers social cohesion through pressure on land and real estate, and throws into question the economic potential at a time when the Basque Country has become a crossroads of exchanges and a crucible of European flows' (CTPB 2013: 5). Elected officials and actors in civil society have since 2010–2011 committed to a strategy favouring a territorial authority 'with a Special Status' (within the meaning of Article 72 of the French Constitution). In 2010, the Batera petition for a Basque Country Territorial Authority collected 35,000 signatures. Two thirds of Basque mayors voted in favor of it.

At the French national scale, the debate about the reform of local government took place in 2009–2010. A number of proposals were put forward by the Basque territory, but despite interventions by Basque parliamentarians, they were not taken into consideration. Worse, by removing legal support for the *pays*, the new decentralization reform made the Basque situation more delicate. Following a report by two legal experts, the Basque Country Development Council in April 2012, followed by the Council of Elected Representatives in November 2012, came out in favour of a territorial community with a special status at departmental level and with additional competences. The Territorial Authority would be based on three elements: an elected Assembly, an Executive Council politically responsible before the Assembly, and a forum for consultation with civil society. This formula would have greater democratic legitimacy and would enable a number of competences hitherto dispersed between state, region, department, inter-Commune cooperation and Communes themselves to be brought together. Early in 2013, coordination began among the five bodies representing the territory in order to take forward the Territorial Authority project: the Basque Country Development Council, the Basque Country Chamber of Commerce and Industry, the *Biltzar* (Assembly) of Communes and the Batera platform. The project quickly met with an objection to its admissibility on the part of the French government, as reiterated by Manuel Valls, then Minister of the Interior, during a trip in Aquitaine in May 2013: 'Neither a Basque Department, nor a Basque territorial authority, from the point of view of the Government, is on the agenda'.[16] On 27 June 2014, the Prefect of the Pyrénées-Atlantiques proposed two alternative institutional formulas to the Council of Elected Representatives: the '*pôles*' formula (a metropolitan area or an institutional body dedicated to 'territorial balance': *pôle d'équilibre territorial*) or a large inter-municipal institution for the whole French Basque territory. The initiative was received with skepticism given the attachment of the majority of Basque elected officials to the idea of a Territorial Authority with special status. However, and for lack of a better term, the same elected officials decided to support the second formula. In application of the new national regulation on territorial administration,[17] in the spring of 2016, 70% of the Basque municipalities representing 66% of the population voted in favour of a large inter-municipal institution covering the French Basque territory.

A new generation of socio-economic movements. . .

Comprehensive politico-institutional mobilization has been accompanied by socio-economic mobilization. The social economy, in particular, is intended to respond to the disconnection between production territories and consumption territories via a set of micro experiments to re-localize the economy. These new experiments were experiencing a resurgence in the 2000s, particularly in three areas. The first concerned microfinance, where the Basque country was innovating at the French scale as regards bodies offering micro-credit to women, Clubs locaux des femmes qui entreprennent (CLEFE), and to young people, Comités locaux d'épargne pour les jeunes (CLEJE), in the Soule area (Brana et Jégourel 2010). The second example concerned the development of short-travelled food distribution channels which generated new alliances between consumers from the coast and inland producers (Gomez and Itçaina 2014). Third, the agricultural sector was reorganizing its own production and marketing channels with a focus on small-scale collective solutions.[18] Finally, the movement to relocalize the economy affects monetary intermediation, with the launch of a complementary currency (the Eusko) in 2012 on the model of other European local currencies.

All these initiatives had four new features:

(a) The new generation of socio-economic movements was no longer based on a politicization limited to production processes, but a simultaneous politicization of production *and* consumption (Dubuisson-Quellier 2009). Ideologically speaking, this was no longer a time for an industrial Utopia for

the Basque interior, as it had been for the founders of the workers' cooperatives of the 1970s. Instead, there was a search for a balance between the productive economy, politicised consumption and environmentalist concerns.
In that sense, the new generation of Basque socio-economic movements
shared the characteristics of Sustainable Community Movement Organizations (SCMOs) (Forno and Graziano 2014), as being constituted by 'social
movement organizations that have the peculiarity of mobilizing citizens primarily via their purchasing power, and for which the main "battlefield" is
represented by the market where SCMOs' members are politically concerned
consumers' (ibid: 142).

(b) These SCMOs have brought into being an unprecedented alliance between
different sensitivities: not only *abertzale*, but also environmentalists, anti-
globalization activists, trade unionists and social Catholics. The concept of
food sovereignty has become a nodal point of these alliances between consumers and producers, who do not necessarily share the same approach to
territorial sovereignty (Gomez and Itçaina 2014). With the end of the political violence after 2010, these new socio-economic alliances have had some
political influence, their approach rubbing off on the alliances between
abertzale and left-wing groups, or the campaign by the Bizi! (Live!) movement during the 2014 municipal elections to get candidates to sign up for an
'Ecological Transition Pact'. As observed by Igor Ahedo (2014: 12), these
new alliances positioned the *abertzale* movement at the centre of the political
debate, thanks to these new proximities with a multi-cultural, altermondi-
alist, disobedient utopia, offering an alternative to the current development
model. Political nationalism indirectly benefited from this renewed socio-
economic and cultural activism that proved the know-how of *abertzales* in
matters of social innovation. If the *abertzale* electoral results in national elections remained relatively low,[19] they did far better in cantonal and, above all,
municipal elections.[20] Proximity played in favour of the *abertzale*, whereas
national elections were biased towards French national issues. In the Basque
country, the *abertzale* confirmed their position as the third political force,
with an increasing agenda-setting role on cultural and socio-economic issues.

(c) These initiatives have for the most part developed independently from the
public authorities. This development of 'bottom-up' initiatives can sometimes conflict with initiatives aimed at making a territorial resource. Thus,
actors from the peasant agriculture sectors within the Kalitaldea group have
withdrawn from the above-mentioned 'Basque Country territorial brand',
seeing it as a takeover of the initiative by the major agribusiness companies. However, this institutional distance did not prevent the civil society
organisations from repeatedly using various policy instruments to implement
their projects, notably the European and the bilateral cross-border schemes,
as a tool to develop the cooperation with their Southern Basque counterparts
(Itçaina and Manterola 2013).

(d) This new generation of socio-economic movements has experienced several learning processes: from French and transnational solidarity economy

networks, from participatory experiments, from the Global Justice Movements, etc. An interested eye is still kept on the southern Basque country, but the focus is more on participatory micro-innovations.

... neither dominant nor hegemonic within the territory

However, these experiments remain small-scale. In addition, within each sector, there is a clash of competing principles. Two examples from quite distinct sectors (agriculture and culture) illustrate this point.

In agriculture, to begin with, not all mobilizations can be reduced to the binary cleavage between the ELB (*abertzale*) and FDSEA (non-*abertzale*) unions. The end of the 2000s saw the emergence of a new type of mobilization rejecting not only the domination of the institutional order by the FDSEA and its agro-industrial allies, but also the discourse of both food *and* territorial sovereignty defended by the ELB. The milk strike of 2009 illustrates this third viewpoint. In the cow's milk sector, which is highly regulated at the European scale, protest was transnational. The milk strike of September 2009 was European, and in France had its highest participation levels in the Basque country. This was mainly a response to the EU's Common Agricultural Policy (CAP) and European integration, although the strike in the Basque country was also a sign of the emergence of a new voluntary and non-unionized player, the Association of Angry Independent Milk Producers, Association des producteurs de lait indépendants et en colère (APLI), the Basque offshoot of the European Milk Board. While the ELB union eventually supported the strike, the discourse of the APLI stood out for its rejection of the trade union's cleavage between the ELB and FDSEA, by a head-on attack on the European policy of liberalizing milk quotas and by a rejection of the inter-professional system of managing prices and volumes. The controversy which raged in the Basque country at this time (Itçaina 2012) combined local, national and European issues.[21] Interestingly, the dividing lines between actors did not exactly align themselves with the *abertzale*/non-*abertzale* cleavage. Unlike the EHLG, the APLI first appeared to be a category-based *interest* group (Hassen-teufel 2008), struggling to present itself as a territory-based *belief* group and establish alliances with other mobilisations.

Mobilizations concerned with culture and the Basque language have remained in principle more faithful to the *abertzale*/non-*abertzale* cleavage. But change is also occurring in this sector, on three levels:

(a) Cultural and linguistic issues have had a greater agenda-setting function as regards territorial institutions and the majority political parties. The decrease of political violence has undoubtedly led to more attention to issues related to the Basque language beyond *abertzale* circles.
(b) For cultural and pro-Euskera circles, this development has led to a two-part change as regards collective action. On the one hand, the move to institutionalize the promotion of Euskera and Basque culture has created a number of opportunities for activist bodies seeking support, together with new

career opportunities for community activists. Cultural circles have therefore engaged in a process of learning compromise and capturing institutional resources, even going so far as to adopt the depoliticized 'grammar' of territorial governance. On the other hand, institutional strategies are regulating the effects brought about by the professionalization of Basque culture and the emergence of a local and cross-border cultural micro-market. This market not only generates new forms of competition but also difficulties in times of crisis. Basque culture is gradually becoming a sector, with its own interests and constraints. But cultural and linguistic activists still intend to constitute a territory-based belief group upholding the general interest (the protection of the Basque language) and do not want to appear as a category group. In a sense, the French Basque country is reproducing, with a time lag, the internal diversification of the language mobilization observed by Ane Larrinaga and Mila Amurrio (2014) in the Spanish Basque country. According to these authors, two cognitive frameworks differentiated within the movement: 'one that was more political, which understood the language as being necessarily linked to power relations and politics and protest action, and another that was more cultural, and progressively managerialist; which tried to assign an autonomous space of activity to the language' (Larrinaga and Amurrio 2014: 9).

(c) These dynamics are far from developing in a consensual and depoliticized climate. The future of the Basque language and culture is anything but a technical issue to be left in the hands of territorial bureaucracies.

In 2013, the state attacked Communes which had directly or indirectly subsidized *ikastolak*, on the grounds that French law forbids public subsidies for private educational institutions (Falloux law of 1850). The public debate which then arose brought up to date not only the longstanding opposition between the state and the Basque movement, but divergences between the paradigms on which the three educational networks were based. The public network (Ikasbi and Biga bai parents' associations) promotes bilingualism within the republican state school system, implicitly aspiring to eventually integrate the other formulae into one single model. Euskal Haziak emerged from the Catholic approach to subsidiarity, within the context of the historic compromise through which Catholic education has been integrated within the French secularist model. The *ikastola* sees itself as the genuine *public* and secular Basque school system, despite its current private status due to the absence of any appropriate institutional structure. Especially in the 1990s, when there was broad support for moves to institutionalize cultural and linguistic policies, these three paradigms were able to unite. The earlier unanimity seems later to have given way to competition, which is a logical result of the institutionalization of linguistic policy. When Ikasbi criticizes Office Public de la Langue Basque (OPLB) for supporting the Seaska model at the expense of public education, this is not just an attempt to gain access to limited resources, but also to influence the linguistic policy design. Strategies aimed at gaining support from southern Basque institutions are also being modified by the new centralization of resources undertaken by the OPLB. However limited this may be, the ongoing institutionalization of the Basque territory in France has already changed the everyday political work of cultural and linguistic social movements.

Concluding remarks

Far from presenting the characteristics of a 'sovereign' or even a 'de facto' state (Bryant 2014), the French Basque country nevertheless represents an original case of a bottom-up process of territorial construction, characterized by an evolving interaction between a starting territorial institutionalization and powerful civil society mobilizations. Mobilizations of French Basque civil society since the 1970s have passed through three historical sequences. The first corresponds to a bottom-up structuring of a cross-cutting social movement, one at the same time economic, cultural and political, as well as one largely independent from institutions. In the 1990s, the new French Basque territorial governance led to some of these claims appearing more quickly on the institutional agenda. Beginning in the mid-2000s, faced with the limits of the 'Basque model' of territorial governance, civil society actors would call for a new territorial authority for the Basque country and would develop new socio-economic mobilizations. This unitary strategy, however, has struggled to mask the internal divisions between social movements which are continually working to articulate their sectorial interests with those of the territory as a whole. In other words, there is, without doubt, a 'territorial question' in the French Basque country that will certainly not be solved through ready-made institutional formulas. Rather, it is only through a discreet and long-run process of interactions between civil society mobilizations and multi-scalar policy-makers that a virtuous governance of territorial and identity issues will consolidate.

Notes

1 The author wishes to thank PRIO and the University of the Basque Country for their invitation to participate in this project, and Mike Fay for his help in translating this article.
2 These data consist of a) a qualitative survey of seventeen French Basque producer cooperatives and of several agricultural organizations ('Territorial Regimes and Economic Development' programme Sciences Po Bordeaux-Aquitaine, 2002–2006); b) a qualitative study of the dynamics of the Basque social economy (*Les formes de l'économie sociale et solidaire et les dynamiques territoriales* – DIIESES-Ministry of Employment 2004–2005); c) the 'Basque Identity and Culture in the Early Twenty-first Century' survey, EKE – Eusko Ikaskuntza – Gobierno Vasco (Baxok et al. 2006); d) an investigation of Basque farmers' mobilizations (GARNET European Network of Excellence); and e) a qualitative survey (with Jean-Jacques Manterola and Marc Errotabehere) on the social economy and cross-border relations (*Towards networked cross-border governance? The experiences of the third sector in the border territories in France and the United Kingdom* – Aquitaine Region, Sciences Po Bordeaux).
3 '*Politicization* occurs when actors explicitly employ values either to transform the meaning of an issue or in order to transfer its treatment to another site of negotiation' (Hassenteufel 2008: 21).

4 FDSEA, Fédération Départementale des Syndicats d'Exploitants Agricoles (Departmental Federation of Farming Trade Unions).

5 In 1963, the Jeunesse Agricole Chrétienne/Féminine was transformed into the Mouvement Rural de Jeunesse Chrétienne (MRJC).

6 'Peasant Agriculture must enable a maximum number of peasants distributed across the whole of the territory to make a decent living from their profession by producing on farms of human dimensions healthy, high-quality food, without posing a threat to the natural resources of tomorrow. It must work together with other citizens to make a living rural environment in a setting enjoyed by all'. Confédération paysanne, *'Qu'est-ce que l'agriculture paysanne?'* ('What is peasant farming?'), April 2010, www.con federationpaysanne-pdl.fr, retrieved 23 May 2013, author's translation.

7 Founded in 1979, Lurra ('Land') became Lurzaindia ('Protection of the Land') in 2013.

8 Like Mondragón, it was created by a Catholic priest. However, as emphasized by Zulaika (1988), there was also some resistance in Mondragón when some actors tried to extend the integral cooperative model to the *baserri* (farms), given the attachment to the family farmstead. In the French Basque country as well, what was developed among farmers was rather a partial cooperativism, limited to the shared use of equipment and commercial purposes.

9 Société coopérative ouvrière de production (Workers' Cooperative Production Company); French legal status for workers' cooperatives.

10 The three school systems were the associative immersion system of the *ikastola,* the bilingual public school system, and the private, Catholic, bilingual school system.

11 Asking for the ratification of the European Charter for Regional or Minority Languages, and for a new legislative framework for French regional languages, both debated in parliament in 2014; see Rochas 2010.

12 The movement for the creation of French Basque SCOPs slowed down in the 1990s following two highly-symbolic business failures.

13 Despite the continued decline in the number of farms, in the Basque country one finds a remarkable number (in the national French context) of young farmers setting up in business (Agreste Aquitaine 2013).

14 Key institutions were ICAPB (Institut de concertation agricole du Pays basque), set up in 2001, and the SUAT Service d'utilité agricole (Basque Country Agricultural Utility Service), set up in 2002 and again in 2005.

15 'Often also called "technicization", depoliticization is a type of political work which downplays values in favour of arguments based upon "expertise" and "efficiency"' (Jullien and Smith 2008: 21).

16 Sud-Ouest, 30 May 2013, author's translation.

17 Law of 7 August 2015 on the new territorial organization of the Republic (*loi NOTRe portant nouvelle organisation du territoire de la République*).

18 See the dynamic in the Aldudes valley, with the setting up of the Belaun agricultural cooperative (2008) and the CLPB dairy cooperative (2014).

19 Election results obtained by the Left *abertzale* coalition (EH bai) in the 2012 legislative elections: IV electoral district: (Oloron, Mauléon, Saint-Jean-Pied-de-Port): 6.80 per cent (13.8 per cent in the Basque part of the district) (6.32 per cent in 2007, 12 per cent in the Basque part), V. district (Bayonne): 5.28 per cent (5 per cent in 2007), VI. district (South Labourd): 9.78 per cent (9.09 per cent in 2007).

20 The first round of the 2014 municipal elections saw an unprecedented rise of the *abert-zale* voting. Leftwing *abertzale* reached good results in municipalities such as Urrugne (twenty-six per cent), Saint-Jean-de-Luz (twenty-six per cent), Ciboure (twenty-one per cent) and, above all, Ustaritz (thirty-eight per cent in the first round), which became the first municipality with over 6,000 inhabitants to be run by an *abertzale* mayor. As a result, eighteen municipalities had an *abertzale* mayor, and the *abertzale* played a pivotal role in bargaining between majority parties between the two rounds of voting. Left-wing *abert-zale* entered into alliances with the Socialist party in some municipalities of Labourd, while in Bayonne they united with the far left *Front de gauche,* thus provoking the defeat

of the Socialist candidate and the victory of the Centre-right. For their part, Centre-right *abertzale* of the PNB (Parti Nationaliste Basque) did not benefit much from this rise.
21 See also Welch-Devine and Murray's research (2011) on the economic constraints and opportunities that French Basque farmers faced before the 2003 reform of the CAP. Farmers have diversified their economic strategies in order to cope with a rise in rural tourism and second-home ownership, an expansion of leisure activities into an agricultural territory, and the implications that the uncertain future of the CAP has for small family farms in this area.

References

Ahedo, I. 2005. 'Nationalism in the French Basque Country', *Regional and Federal Studies*, 15(1): 75–91.
———. 2008. The Transformation of the National Identity in the Basque Country of France (1789–2006). Reno, NV: University of Nevada Press.
———. 2014. 'From the Margins to the Centre: The Emergence of the Territory in the Basque Country of France', paper for the conference *Basque Nationhood in a Globalizing World*, PRIO, ICIP, EHU-UPV, Bilbao, 28–30 May.
Arnaud, A.-J., and Simoulin, V. 2011. 'Gouvernance territoriale' [Territorial Governance], in R. Pasquier, S. Guigner and A. Cole, eds, *Dictionnaire des politiques territoriales* [Handbook of Territorial Politics]. Paris: Presses de Sciences Po, pp. 265–270.
Avanza, M., and Laferté, G. 2005. 'Dépasser la "construction des identités"? Identification, image sociale, appartenance' [Beyond 'Identity Building'? Identification, Social Image, Belonging], *Genèses*, 61: 154–167.
Baxok, E., Etxegoin, P., Lekumberri, T., Martinez de Luna, I., Mendizabal, L., Ahedo, I., Itçaina, X., and Jimeno, R. 2006. Euskal nortasuna eta kultura XXI. mendearen hasieran. Identidad y cultura vascas a comienzos del siglo XXI. Identité et culture basques au début du XXI. Siècle' [Identity and Basque culture in the early XXI c.]. Donostia-San Sebastián: Eusko Ikaskuntza, Sociedad de Estudios Vascos.
Berthet, T., and Palard, J. 1997. 'Culture politique réfractaire et décollage économique' [Refractory Political Culture and Economic Takeoff], *Revue française de science politique*, 47(1): 29–48.
Brana, S., and Jégourel, Y. 2010. 'Microfinance, acteurs et territoires: Analyse du secteur en Aquitaine' [Microfinance, Actors and Territories: An Analysis of the Sector in Aquitaine], in X. Itçaina, ed., *La politique du lien. Les nouvelles dynamiques territoriales de l'économie sociale et solidaire* [The New Territorial Dynamics of the Social and Solidarity-Based Economy]. Rennes: PU de Rennes, pp. 263–286.
Bray, Z. 2004. Living Boundaries: Frontiers and Identity in the Basque Country. Bruxelles: Peter Lang.
———. 2006. 'Basque Militant Youth in France: New Experiences of Ethnonational Identity in the European Context', *Nationalism and Ethnic Politics*, 15: 533–553.
Bray, Z., and Keating, M. 2013. 'European Integration and the Basque Country in France and Spain', in T. Mabry, J. McGarry, M. Moore and B. O'Leary, eds, *Divided Nations and European Integration*. Philadelphia, PA: University of Pennsylvania Press, pp. 127–156.
Brubaker, R. 2001. 'Au-delà de l'identité' [Beyond Identity], *Actes de la recherche en sciences sociales*, 139: 66–85.
Bryant, R. 2014. 'Living With Liminality: De Facto States on the Threshold of the Global', *Brown Journal of World Affairs*, 20(11): 125–143.

Carter, C., and Smith, A. 2008. 'Revitalizing Public Policy Approaches to the EU: Territorial Institutionalism, Fisheries and Wine', *Journal of European Public Policy*, 15(2): 263–281.

Chaussier, J.-D. 1996. *Quel territoire pour le Pays Basque? Les cartes de l'identité* [Which Territory for the Basque Country? The Cards of Identity]. Paris: L'Harmattan.

CTPB (Coordination territoriale Pays Basque/ Euskal Herriko Lurralde Koordinazioa). 2013. *Collectivité territoriale Pays basque: Un projet partagé* [The Basque Territorial Authority: A Shared Project]. Bayonne, CTPB, 27 April.

Dalla Rosa, G. 2006. 'La Soule: Entre exemple et exception' [The Soule: Between Exemplarity and Exception], in J. Palard and B. Gagnon, eds, *La Région et ses territoires: Stratégies et développement en Aquitaine* [The Region and Its Territories: Strategies and Development in Aquitaine]. Bordeaux: Confluence, pp. 223–247.

Demoustier, D. 2001. *L'économie Sociale et Solidaire*. [Social and Solidarity-Based Economy]. Paris: Syros.

Dubuisson-Quellier, S. 2009. *La consommation engagée* [Responsible Consumption]. Paris: Presses de Sciences Po.

Enjolras, B. 2010. 'Gouvernance verticale, gouvernance horizontale et économie sociale et solidaire: Le cas des services à la personne' [Vertical Governance, Horizontal Governance and Social and Solidarity Economy: The Case of Personal Services], *Géographie, Economie, Société*, 12: 15–30.

Etcheverry, M. 2008. 'Du bon usage de la gouvernance en Pays Basque' [The Good Use of Governance in the Basque Country]. Mémoire Politiques d'aménagement, Master 2 Economie de l'aménagement et développement local. Université Paris I-Sorbonne.

Forno, F., and Graziano, P. 2014. 'Sustainable Community Movement Organizations', *Journal of Consumer Culture*, 14(2): 139–157.

Gomez, A., and Itçaina, X. 2014. 'Utopiques alliances? La construction de la cohérence discursive des mobilisations autour des circuits courts en Pays Basque', *Lien Social et Politiques*, 72: 93–108.

Gumuchian, H., and Pecqueur, B. 2007. *La ressource territoriale* [The Territorial Resource]. Paris: Economica.

Harguindéguy, J.-B. 2007. 'Cross-Border Policy in Europe: Implementing INTERREG III-A France-Spain', *Regional and Federal Studies*, 17(3): 317–334.

Harguindéguy, J.-B., and Itçaina, X. 2012. 'Towards an Institutionalized Language Policy for the French Basque Country? Actors, Processes and Outcomes', *European Urban and Regional Studies*, 19(4): 434–447.

Hassenteufel, P. 2008. *Sociologie politique: L'action publique* [Political Sociology: The Public Action]. Paris: Armand Colin.

Heidemann, K. A. 2014. 'In the Name of Language: School-Based Language Revitalization, Strategic Solidarities, and State Power in the French Basque Country', *Journal of Language, Identity, and Education*, 13: 53–69.

Hourcade, R. 2007. Le Pays Basque en représentations ou les effets sur l'action publique d'un instrument de 'gouvernance' locale: Le Conseil de développement du Pays Basque [The Basque Country in Representation: The Policy Impact of an Instrument of Local 'Governance': The Basque Country Development Council], Mémoire Master Action et Espaces publics en Europe, IEP de Rennes.

Hunt, S. A., and Benford, R. D. 2008. 'Collective Identity, Solidarity, and Commitment', in D. A. Snow, S. A. Soule and H. Kriesi, eds, *The Blackwell Companion to Social Movements*. Oxford: Blackwell, pp. 433–457.

Itçaina, X. 2010. 'Appartenances linguistiques, identités collectives et pratiques culturelles en Pays Basque: Retour sur une enquête' [Linguistic Behaviour, Collective Identities, and Cultural Behaviour in the Basque Country: Revisiting a Survey], *Cultures et con-flits*, 79–80: 19–36.

———. 2011. 'Mobilisation territoriale autour d'un projet agricole en Pays Basque' [Terri-torial Mobilization Around an Agricultural Project in the Basque Country], in S. Béroud, N. Dompnier and D. Garibay, eds, *L'Année sociale 2011*. Paris: Syllepses, pp. 175–189.

———. 2012. 'The Contrasting Local Perceptions of Europe. The 2009 Milk Strike in the French Basque Country', *Cahiers du Centre Emile Durkheim/Centre Emile Durkheim Working Papers*, n°11.

Itçaina, X., and Manterola, J. J. 2013. 'Towards Cross-Border Network Governance? The Social and Solidarity Economy and the Construction of a Cross-Border Territory in the Basque Country', in K. Stoklosa and G. Besier, eds, *European Border Regions in Com-parison: Overcoming Nationalistic Aspects or Re-Nationalization?* Abingdon: Rout-ledge, pp. 169–187.

Itçaina, X., Palard, J., and Ségas, S., eds. 2007. *Régimes territoriaux et développement économique* [Territorial Regimes and Economic Development]. Rennes: Presses Uni-versitaires de Rennes, coll. Espaces et territoires.

Izquierdo, J.-M. 2004. 'Trajectoires nationalistes: Les nationalismes en Pays Basque fran-çais et espagnol' [Nationalist Paths: Nationalisms in the French Basque Country], *Pôle Sud*, 20(20): 47–61.

Jacob, J. E. 1994. *Basque Nationalism in France*. Reno, NV: University of Nevada Press.

Jullien, B., and Smith, A. 2008. 'Introduction: Industries, Globalization and Politics', in B. Jullien and A. Smith, eds, *Industries and Globalization: The Political Causality of Dif-ference*. Basingstoke: Palgrave MacMillan, pp. 1–28.

Keating, M. 2008. 'Culture and Social Sciences', in D. della Porta and M. Keating, eds, *Approaches and Methodologies in the Social Sciences: A Pluralist Perspective*. Cam-bridge: Cambridge University Press, pp. 99–117.

Keating, M., Loughlin, J., and Deschouwer, K. 2003. *Culture, Institutions and Economic Development: A Study of Eight European Regions*. Cheltenham: Edward Elgar.

Laborde, D. 1999. 'Politique culturelle et langue basque' [Cultural Policy and Basque Lan-guage], in P. Blanchet, R. Breton and H. Schiffman, eds, *The Regional Languages of France: An Inventory on the Eve of the XXIst Century*. Louvain-la-Neuve: Peeters, pp. 141–160.

Larrinaga, A., and Amurrio, M. 2014. 'The Meaning of Cultural Sovereignty in the Evolu-tion of the Ethno-Linguistic Movement of the Basque Country: From Politic-Cultural Activism to Intervention in Everyday Life', paper for the conference *Basque Nation-hood in a Globalizing World*, PRIO, ICIP, EHU-UPV, Bilbao, 28–30 May.

Lascoumes, P., and Le Galès, P. 2007. *Sociologie de l'action publique*. Paris: Armand Colin.

Leloup, F., Moyart, L., and Pecqueur, B. 2005. 'La gouvernance territorial comme nouveau mode de coordination territorial?', *Géographie, économie, société*, 7(4): 321–332.

Letamendia, F. 1997. 'Basque Nationalism and Cross-Border Co-Operation Between the Southern and Northern Basque Countries', *Regional and Federal Studies*, 17(2): 25–41.

Linz, J. J. 1986. *Conflicto en Euskadi* [Conflict in Euskadi]. Madrid: Espasa Calpe.

Oronos, M. 2002. *Le mouvement culturel basque, 1951–2001. 1. Ikas, Pizkundea, Euskal Konfederazioa*. Bayonne: Elkar.

Pecqueur, B., and Itçaina, X. 2012. 'Economie sociale et solidaire et territoires: un couple allant de soi?' [Social Economy and Territories: A Natural Couple?], *RECMA – Revue internationale de l'économie sociale*, 325: 48–64.

Pierre, T. 2013. 'L'officialisation de la langue basque en France: du droit à la différence au droit à l'égalité?' [The Officialization of Basque Language in France: From the Right to Be Different to the Right to Equality?], *Langage et société*, 145: 103–119.

Rochas, A. 2010. 'A l'épreuve de la diversité linguistique: Sociogenèse de la politique des langues régionales (1992–2008)' [Testing Linguistic Diversity. The Socio-Genesis of the Regional Languages Policy (1992–2008)], in D. C. Martin, ed., *L'identité en jeux: Pouvoirs, identifications, mobilisations* [Identity at Stake: Powers, Identifications, Mobilizations]. Paris: Karthala, pp. 361–377.

Ségas, S. 2004. *La grammaire du territoire: Action publique de développement et lutte politique dans les 'pays'* [The Grammar of the Territory: Development Policy and Political Struggle in the 'Pays']. Thèse en science politique. Pessac: Université Montesquieu Bordeaux IV.

———. 2011. 'Développement local' [Local Development], in R. Pasquier, S. Guigner and A. Cole, eds, *Dictionnaire des politiques territoriales* [Handbook of Territorial Politics]. Paris: Presses de Sciences Po, pp. 176–181.

Seiler, D.-L. 1994. *Les partis autonomistes* [Autonomist parties]. Paris: PUF.

Simoulin, V. 2007. 'La gouvernance territoriale: dynamiques discursives, stratégiques et organisationnelles' [Territorial Governance: Discursive, Strategic and Organizational Dynamics], *Droit et société*, 44. Paris: LGDJ, pp. 15–32.

Talandier, M., and Davezies, L. 2009. *Repenser le développement territorial? Confrontation des modèles d'analyse et des tendances observées dans les pays développés.* [Rethinking Territorial Developement? Confronting the Analysis Models and the Recent Trends in Developed Countries]. Paris: La Documentation française, Editions du Puca.

Urteaga, E., and Ahedo, I. 2004. *La nouvelle gouvernance en Pays Basque* [The New Governance in the Basque Country]. Paris: L'Harmattan.

Welch-Devine, M., and Murray, S. 2011. ' "We're European Farmers Now": Transitions and Transformations in Basque Agricultural Practices', *Anthropological Journal of European Cultures*, 20(1): 69–88.

Worms, J.-P. 1966. 'Le préfet et ses notables' [The Prefect and His Dignitaries], *Sociologie du travail* (July–September): 249–277.

Zulaika, J. 1988. *Basque Violence, Metaphor and Sacrament.* Reno, NV: University of Nevada Press

6 Sovereignty, capacity and democracy

The Basque case

Jule Goikoetxea

Democracy and sovereignty

We will study what sovereignty requires in order to be imagined. To that end, we will analyze how it is articulated and practised in the Basque democratization process. How is the relationship between the state and the community, which we call sovereignty, understood and realized within this stateless community? The underlying question is what does the Basque community need in order to govern and maintain itself across time and space as a democracy, and not just as a cultural community, in this global (capitalist) era? This question relates to the conditions for a community to become sovereign in twenty-first-century Europe. The objectives and ideas of democratic governance and popular sovereignty have always been to ensure that the 'people' reproduces itself as it decides. We will look at the political capacity and decision-making autonomy that is available to the Basque population in order to reproduce itself as a democracy.

Our premise is that in Europe, sovereignty is privatized, not popularized, while governance mechanisms are multiplied, not democratized. Accordingly, our *first hypothesis* is that demands for sovereignty are a consequence of privatization of public authority and decision-making, either by a foreign state or by private hands. The democratic structures and processes that should institutionalize Basque popular sovereignty are failing, both in Spain and the European Union, since the political capacity that should be used to realize the Basque population's demands (popular sovereignty) is being privatized and fragmented through the multiplication of the government or governance levels. However, along with globalization or global privatization, the democratization processes of recent decades have also had consequences at the local or national level, whereby new organizational logics have reproduced old national entities into new political subjects through a re-assemblage of territory, rights and authority. Our *second hypothesis* is that the Basque *demos* emerges within this general and antagonistic trend of privatization (carried out by the multiplication of government layers, in this case) and democratization (as a new assemblage of rights, territory and authority). The *third hypothesis* is that this new assemblage, the *demos*, requires popular sovereignty, since sovereignty in the twenty-first century is understood as political capacity for self-government, as will be seen by studying Basque sovereignty demands.

Sovereignty

Sovereignty has always referred to the contentious relationship between the state and the community. This relationship is one of coercion and cooperation. However, the state is just the form in which the community organizes itself in order to carry through its own decisions. What meaning does sovereignty acquire in a democratic context? *Democratic sovereignty* refers to the political capacity a community has when realizing its own decisions, amongst which is to reproduce or survive as a political community. We have shown (in Goikoetxea 2014) that democratic survival has its own conditions, requirements and objectives. Democracy is a type of political domination that has its own rules (Weber 2001), and thus certain types of authority, territories and rights (Sassen 2008). It is through regularized and common policies, institutions and hence practices that one can create a political unit and reproduce it as a *demos* (Goikoetxea 2013a). This democratic governance entails discipline and security in order to achieve both standardized welfare and efficient deployment of resources – human, social and economic (Foucault 1997). It calls for institutions with the political capacity to realize the population's political decisions. As Hinsley says, to the extent that the relationship between the state and the community requires regulation, in the sense that no political and legal system can work without the existence of coercive mechanisms able to impose obedience, the concept of sovereignty will be necessary in order to give legitimacy and justification to this regulating authority (Hinsley 1986: 199). We will show that any alternative for constructing a post-sovereign political unit in our current context is doomed to fail, because the modern state, and above all the welfare state, is based as much on popular sovereignty as it is on the efficient governance of the holder of this sovereignty: the population. To omit this reality is to ignore the fundamentals of politics and the political.

Sovereignty is thus a principle whereby a supreme authority must exist within the political community so that the political community can exist and act. Sovereignty implies a particular relationship or division between the state and the community, and so does democracy, where political legitimacy and authority may only come from the community. Here we will analyze how this relationship between the state and the community has changed and how, as a consequence, the sovereign principle must be re-thought.

The internal complexity of political communities has grown exponentially as the welfare state has developed. Consequently, the relationship between the state and the community has also become more complex. Political communities are becoming more integrated, and the state's functions are being multiplied at the same rate. This complexity makes the principle of sovereignty even more necessary, since its function is to articulate the relationship between the community and the state in order that they can both govern, and be governed, as belonging to each other despite being different (Hinsley 1986).

Without separation between the state and the community there is no sovereignty, and without mutual dependence between the state and the community, sovereignty has no function. We know that the function of sovereignty is to ensure the effective execution of power, and this function has to some extent been democratized. We have gone from the sovereign emperor – the Pope, the King – to the sovereign people. In democratic systems, this relationship must be between the community's political authority and the state's political capacity, and there is currently no democratic principle that legitimizes political action and decision-making other than popular sovereignty.

Through the description and analysis of certain selected practices, we will see how sovereignty is thought of, articulated and understood in the Autonomous Community of the Basque Country (ACBC). Since the global era is a process of de-democratization and ongoing privatization of popular decision-making and public authority, we will show that this process is linked to demands for sovereignty in the Basque Country.

Political capacity: the demos, the nation, the sovereign

Using the Basque case we will see that multi-level governance (understood as the governance system of the global era) has, *de facto*, led to the privatization of democracy and popular sovereignty. We agree with Sassen (2008) that the global era is characterized by national disassembling. We think, however, that too much emphasis is placed on global re-assemblage and too little on the new re-assemblages taking place at the local level. We will show that there is no global re-assemblage without local re-assemblage. Globalization and multilevel governance are the consequence of inserting old national capacities into new organizational logics, but these new assemblages are developed within new organizational logics by disassembling the national and re-assembling it in a new way, producing what we call the *demos*. So, we come back again to the first question about the conditions for the Basque nation to become a Basque democracy. As noted earlier, we will look at the political capacity and decision-making autonomy, and hence sovereignty, that the Basque *demos* has to reproduce itself as a democracy. All political identities, in order to reproduce across time and space, require resources and a certain level of institutionalization or formalization. Those identities with most resources are the ones we call hegemonic. The modern state is the organizational complex that has acquired, at least in Europe, the highest level of institutionalization and formalization. That is why the state is the reproductive nucleus of current political identities. Hegemonic political identities are those who are sovereign; they are those who have the highest political capacity available for realizing their demands and thus governing themselves. Those identities that have a state – that is, those structured nationals – have the most resources available for reproducing themselves across time and space as political subjects.

Therefore, we want to point out that the national is not just an identity; it is, above all, a political capacity. The structured national (Sassen 2008) is hegemonic, and hence sovereign. It is the structured national that is making available the global scale, and this cannot be achieved without re-structuring the local. *The structured national is the sovereign political identity, and it is a capacity that holds together the people and the state through a specific assemblage of rights, authority and territory.* However, after over three decades of democratization, new assemblages have emerged along with the capitalist global expansion. The *demos* is, in this connection, a new assemblage which requires some specific conditions in order to exist and to reproduce, and these may be contradictory or antagonistic with regard to the global and other former and current organizational logics, capacities and assemblages. According to our *third hypothesis* this clash between the antagonistic global re-assemblage and the local one leads to sovereignty demands especially by those who are not structured nationals but just nationals (without the sovereign structure, in other words the state). This is because only the structured national can decide how to reproduce, and hence to reproduce. *The problem which affects Europe is that those such as the Basque, who lack structure in their national capacity cannot constitute a* demos *or a new assemblage at a local level with the same capacities and resources as those Spanish nationals who are structured as sovereign.*

Democratization is a way of reproducing a nation – a political process that consists of including as many people as possible in the governance of the system by giving those people as equal as possible access to resources and opportunities (Tilly 2007). It is in this interaction between the state's capacity to intervene and control the population and the people's capacity to organize and articulate explicit demands for inclusion and equity, including demands for self-determination, that a people or a nation becomes a *demos*, and a political system becomes a democracy. That is why we say that new political subjects have emerged. They are different from historical nations, and different from the nation-state too, but determined by both of them. This is the case of Cataluña, which does not include the whole Catalan nation, and of the Autonomous Community of the Basque Country (ACBC), which does not include the whole Basque nation. Any 'people', understood as a group of plebeians or commoners, becomes a nation when it expresses the willingness to act and be recognized as a political subject or unit. Nationalism is, in these terms, a political practice and, like every collective practice, it produces and reproduces its own social object: the nation. In the same way, democratization produces its own subject and object: the *demos* (Goikoetxea 2013a).

What is the difference between the national, as the local assemblage of the last two centuries, and the assemblage that we call *demos* which has emerged within democratization processes in the last five decades?

The *demos* is an entity determined by the nation and the state, and hence by history, structure and culture, but it arises only within certain processes, such as the democratization we have witnessed in recent decades that may be described as a process of democratization, meaning a dynamic process that tends to institutionalize and realize popular demands by this very population (Hirst and Thompson 1996; Esping-Andersen 1990). It is not the first time it has occurred, but it is the first time it has done so massively and globally (Sassen 2008). These political communities that we call *demoi* are new assemblages of rights, territory and authority, determined by their national history but reproduced as political subjects that do not necessarily correlate with their historical nation. Accordingly, they demand sovereignty not on the basis of history or culture, but on the basis of their political authority to make political decisions. *This political authority is thought of as the basis of popular sovereignty* (see the electoral programmes of the Basque Nationalist Party and the coalition of Basque left-wing sovereignist parties).[1] The *discursive change* from the national right of self-determination to the individual right to decide based on the political authority the *demos* is thought to have shows the way in which democratization processes have had political, material, imaginative and discursive consequences, as pointed out in the *second hypothesis*. It shows how democratization is leading to new ways of understanding territory and of practising authority and rights, and *how these transform the ways in which sovereignty is imagined, demanded and realized.*

As we shall see in the sections that follow, *popular sovereignty* is currently understood as the political capacity a community has to reproduce as a *demos*, across time and space according to its own political decisions. That is why *popular sovereignty* cannot be realized without the state – without a complex of institutions able (or having political capacity) to intervene in existing non-state resources and activities of the population, and also able (or having political capacity) to represent this very population and integrate its demands into the governing process, and hence to effectively reproduce this population as a *demos*, as a democracy.

Privatization of political capacity: multilevel governance

We have said (in Goikoetxea 2014) that in Spain, political capacity is unevenly distributed amongst the supranational European institutions, with their growing legal densification; the Spanish central administration; and the unequal competences of the seventeen Autonomous Communities (ACs). This diverse and, in many cases, conflicting arrangement of political capacities directly affects the level of autonomy of the ACs, and hence differentiation, since these arrangements predetermine the sort of (re)production and (re)distribution of economic, social and cultural capital that take place within and amongst the ACs.

With regard to the European Union (EU), there are opposing interpretations of how the Union has affected the central state and national as well as local political capacities. The EU certainly does provide a new political and institutional framework for political participation by regions and minority nations. The disagreement arises between those who think that the EU has disempowered regions in their legal-constitutional power (Bourne 2008) and those who see it as empowering regions through relational sources of power such as cross-border cooperation (Börzel 2002: 48–54, Filibi 2004: 224–226). This chapter considers the legal-constitutional source of power to have paramount political and socio-economic consequences for democratization and the reproduction of European *demoi*. As regards the ACBC, eighty per cent of its competences have been affected by EU policy regulations, and even though policy implementation remains chiefly in regional hands, decision-making centres have been recentralized by the Spanish central administration, whereby the ACs, including the ACBC, have a risible level of participation and decision-making power (Aja 2003; Bourne 2008: 46–71; Blas 2012). Moreover, the Spanish party system is a two-party or majoritarian system, in which the government of the day needs the backing of one of the main nationalist parties, either the Basque Nationalist Party, Partido Nacionalista Vasco (PNV) or the Catalan Convergence and Union party, Convergència i Unió (CIU), in order to govern Spain when the party in power is in the minority. This means that the Basque population's demands are only satisfied – and only partially so – when the majority Spanish party needs the majority Basque party's backing. Otherwise, there is *no transfer of popular sovereignty* from the Basque population to the Spanish state, and even less to the European Union.

As previously argued (in Goikoetxea 2014), when it comes to meaningful political capacities in terms of political voice and decision-making power, the EU, by strengthening the central state's legal-constitutional power, has reduced the political capacity of the ACBC, which has, at the same time, been divested of the essential tools for driving its political economy, such as a real central bank. The introduction of the Euro and the European Central Bank has not only dispossessed the twenty-seven member states of the capacity to regulate their own economies, and hence their socio-economic policies, but has also directly diminished the ACBC's control over its own public finance system (Bourne 2008: 117–133) and hence over its own democratization process. We have discovered (Goikoetxea 2014) that the level of social interpenetration and territorial authority and legitimacy of Basque state institutions depends on their political capacity to control and distribute what the Basque population produces, and to include this very population in the governing process, or to realize the population's demands. *This is what consolidates the authority, territoriality and rights of the Basque demos, and this is also what would lead to its disappearance.*

The Statute of Autonomy of 1979 has not been fulfilled due to opposition from the Spanish central state. There are problems stemming from the precarious and highly unstable political capacity in almost every area, including compulsory and higher education, training, tax and finance systems, research and innovation, and social security. These problems have directly affected the process of democratization – that is, the amount and distribution of economic, social and cultural capital in the ACBC, and hence the level of socio-economic cohesion, that is, integration and equal access to resources and opportunities. Reducing the Basque state institutions' political capacity means weakening their level of monopoly, not only over authoritative law-making, but also over the production and reproduction of political reality, thereby hampering these institutions' capacity to satisfy the Basque population's expressed demands.[2] *The important point here is that sovereignty depends, in its material dimension, on the political capacity a community has to materialize its own political decisions or demands.*

There is no democratic justification for why some contemporary European political communities have more authoritative power, political capacity and/or sovereignty than others. In Europe, identities with state resources are those who reproduce themselves above other identities. That is why the voices and demands of the German, French and Spanish are materialized more frequently than those of the Basque. The same serves to explain why the Basque in the ACBC have more voice and political capacity than those in the Chartered Community of Navarre, and why the latter have more voice and political capacity than the Basque people of the northern Basque country in France (Ahedo 2016). This means that the fewer resources and the less institutional and constitutional power a political community has, the less sovereignty that community will be able to acquire, and hence the less reproductive power it will have for maintaining itself across time and space.

In this connection, the EU has not empowered regions, since institutionalized means such as cross-border and multi-level cooperation (i.e. the Atlantic Arc and trans-European networks), horizontal alliances (Bray 2011: 177–199, Filibi 2004: 226, 235, 244–258) and the Committee of the Regions (Filibi 2004: 227, 237, 246) do not have the authoritative and comprehensive character of legal-constitutional power, which applies to the whole political community and has the widest social, political and economic consequences compared to other types of powers or capacities (Sassen 2008: 96–102). According to our *second hypothesis*, this is how the EU and its member states are functioning as a platform for the privatization of popular sovereignty, and hence democracy (Bourne 2008; Kohler-Koch 2010). The democratic mechanisms that should institutionalize Basque popular sovereignty are working neither in Spain nor in the EU, since the political capacity that should be used to realize the Basque population's demands is being privatized through multilevel governance systems.

We conclude this first part by summing up *our hypotheses* and conclusions that, in Europe, sovereignty has been privatized, not popularized, and governance mechanisms have been multiplied, not democratized. As a consequence of the privatization of public authority and decision-making, *demands for sovereignty* have emerged.

A new assemblage of rights, authority and territory

We said that, along with globalization or global privatization, the democratization processes of recent decades have also had consequences at the local or national level, where new organizational logics have reproduced old national entities into new political subjects through a re-assemblage of territory, rights and authority. According to our *second hypothesis*, the Basque *demos* of the ACBC emerges within a general and antagonistic trend of privatization and democratization as a new assemblage of rights, territory and authority. And the last hypothesis pointed out that this new assemblage, in order to survive across time and space, requires sovereignty, understood as the community's political capacity.

We also pointed out that the internal complexity of political communities has grown exponentially along with the development of the welfare state. This makes the principle of sovereignty even more necessary, since its function is to articulate the relationship between the community and the state in order that they can both govern, and be governed, as belonging to each other despite being different (Hinsley 1986).

Territory

The predominance of liberal thinking has led many scholars to argue that democracy means one person, one vote. We have already shown (in Goikoetxea 2013b)[3] that this is not so. We will briefly illustrate again how the *demos* is different from a collection of individuals but rather consists of a particular collective assemblage of territory, rights and authority. Territory is as important as individuals with regard to democratization, and hence popular sovereignty. The reason is that public policies – welfare policies – are (except on rare occasions) implementable not individually, but collectively and territorially.[4]

Let us review our latest findings on the close connection that exists between democracy, territory and sovereignty. Table 6.1 (below) presents data from the year 2008, in other words just before the global crisis. Illustrating our argument, we show in the left-hand column the percentage of people who are active in the labour market. Here we see that the male population active in the labour market is

Table 6.1   Share of population active in the work force and with higher education

Year: 2008	Share of male population active in the work force (%)	Share of female population active in the work force (%)	Share of population 25–34 with higher education (%)
Total	**57.86**	**42.14**	**38.76**
Andalucía	**60.51**	**39.49**	**32.54**
Jaén	63.65	36.34	30.78
Málaga	58.45	41.55	26.15
Sevilla	59.58	40.43	42.17
Aragón	**57.79**	**42.23**	**42.02**
Huesca	58.58	41.44	38.39
Teruel	59.55	40.49	26.60
Zaragoza	57.34	42.67	44.78
Castilla y León	**59.87**	**40.13**	**42.72**
León	58.57	41.42	40.07
Palencia	61.23	38.85	46.38
Valladolid	58.12	41.88	49.01
Zamora	63.34	36.70	32.23
Cataluña	**56.22**	**43.79**	**39.20**
Barcelona	55.53	44.47	42.12
Girona	58.20	41.80	31.09
Lleida	57.36	42.67	30.44
Tarragona	58.40	41.60	32.11
Valenciana	**58.10**	**41.90**	**35.92**
Alicante/Alacant	58.35	41.65	29.46
Castellón/Castelló	57.73	42.26	34.64
Valencia/València	58.01	41.99	40.22
Galicia	**56.05**	**43.94**	**43.51**
A Coruña	55.86	44.13	47.95
Lugo	56.48	43.52	42.42
Ourense	56.72	43.26	37.80
Madrid	**55.04**	**44.96**	**47.79**
Navarra	**57.69**	**42.31**	**47.98**
País Vasco	**56.57**	**43.43**	**57.72**
Araba/Álava	56.81	43.18	60.29
Gipuzkoa/Guipúzcoa	56.09	43.91	61.96
Bizkaia/Vizcaya	56.81	43.19	54.72

Compiled by author using data from Instituto Nacional de Estadística [National Statistics Institute]

on average twenty-seven percentage points higher than the corresponding female population of each province. In some areas, such as Aragon, Valencia and Cataluña, the difference stands at an average of nineteen per cent, while in the ACBC the difference between males and females is only thirteen per cent.[5] However, what is even more remarkable is that the ACBC has the same rate of labour market activity (employment rate) amongst all its territories, whether urban or rural. If we look at the right-hand column, which shows levels of education, we notice that the capital of each Autonomous Community invariably has the highest educational level. In Andalusia, for instance, the difference between the capital, Seville, and Malaga is sixteen per cent. In Aragon there is a difference of eighteen per cent, and in Cataluña, twelve per cent. By contrast, in the ACBC there is a mere seven per cent difference. Moreover, the highest employment rate is found in Gipuzkoa, which is neither the capital nor the most populous territory.

In order to explain why socio-economic and political cohesion is higher in the ACBC than in other communities, the territorial distribution of political power (and capacity for material sovereignty) has to be taken into account. Had Bilbao (the most-populated city) been the capital rather than Gasteiz (in the least-populated territory), the urban concentration or centralization mechanism would have meant that, within the space of a few years, several hundred thousand people would have migrated from the other two territories (Araba and Gipuzkoa), leading to what has happened elsewhere in Spain. Since 1980, Madrid's population has increased by around forty per cent, and twenty-three provinces have lost most of their population, or seen it dramatically reduced.

From an analysis both of European varieties of capitalism (Hall 1999; Schmidt 2002; Hall and Soskice 2001) and of the distribution of population and Gross Domestic Product across European regions (see NUTS 2 and Eurostat Regional Yearbooks) one may draw the conclusion that policies of urban concentration or centralization are usually accompanied by a particular economic policy whereby most of the Gross Value Added comes from the traditional services sector, rather than from industry (Huber and Stephens 2001: 225; Pierson 2001). In the case of Spain, the main income within the traditional services sector comes from tourism, while industry represents only seventeen per cent. In the ACBC, however, industry represents a much larger percentage, contributing 1.86 per cent of the Spanish GDP with just 270,000 workers, while Spanish tourism accounts for ten per cent of the Spanish GDP though employing only three million people prior to the 2008 recession.

Nevertheless, we also see that a more productive economic structure and higher GDP, while it helps, does not necessarily lead to greater social cohesion.[6] Therefore, it is not only the production of wealth, but its redistribution that leads to higher cohesion. And yet it is not merely the distribution of economic capital, but also of knowledge or cultural capital that leads to high levels of social cohesion. *What we want to show is that a community's social cohesion and welfare depends on territorial cohesion.* The Basque industrial and technological restructuring operation turned out to be relatively successful in socio-economic terms because, in order to meet the high demand for skilled labour that the technological reconversion of the 1980s and 1990s entailed, the Basque Government managed to ensure widespread access to public higher education for all those living and working in Bizkaia, Araba and Gipuzkoa. What interests us is that the percentage of the population with higher education is very similar in all territories (Eurostat 2009, 2011, 2014). Having *similar rates of education in each territory* means that the restructuring of the ACBC's industrial network undertaken since the economic crisis of the 1980s and 1990s entailed neither massive displacements nor depopulation of any territory (Goikoetxea 1997), as happened in Spain as well as other European countries. Consequently, the higher levels of cohesion in the ACBC may be explained by the fact that, due to the federal system, the territories of Araba and Gipuzkoa are not politically or economically subordinated to the territory of Bizkaia. That is why those who live and work in those territories are not at a disadvantage with regard to social provisions, including higher education, vis-à-vis those who live in the most populous territory, or the ones with the greatest economic activity – as happens in Spain, and other countries such as France and the UK (Eurostat 2009).

All this means that social cohesion, socio-economic welfare and political equality, and hence democracy, is gained through – not merely, but necessarily – territorial cohesion. In other words, territory is one of the basic elements for democratization, and it is therefore constitutive of the *demos*.

Authority and rights

Rights are authoritative capacities. They are written political decisions that create capacities and also obligations vis-a-vis the community. Rights are meaningful in so far as they relate to a collectivity, and how that collectivity organizes itself, what it can and cannot do, how it may and may not behave, and what it can and cannot want (Hinsley 1986). Rights create political reality. They also shape and reproduce common beliefs and perceptions, shared interests and identities.

The political rights and authority of the Basque territories in the ACBC are ensured by the parliamentary representation system established by the Law of the Historic Territories. The system is articulated such that territorial representation is given greater importance than individual representation.[7] Thus, each territory sends the same number of members to the Basque Parliament. In line with this electoral system, prominence is also given to territory in the territorial parliamentary system (see Goikoetxea 2013b).

From 1979 up until the present day (except for 2009–2012, and then only due to the banning of the Basque nationalist and socialist party by the Spanish Supreme Court), Basque nationalist parties have always formed the Basque Government and also the three Territorial Governments (except for Araba in 1999 and 2007–2012). As we shall see, this is related to the political authority that they have been able to acquire.

The economic rights and authority of these territories is established by the so-called Economic Agreement (1981/2002). This financing agreement endows the three historic territories of Araba, Bizkaia and Gipuzkoa with legal rights to formulate, regulate and collect ninety-two per cent of all taxes. This financial autonomy means that the Basque territories have the right, authority and institutional capacity to establish the tax regulations applicable to the ACBC and to manage, settle and inspect all taxes levied. Following payment, each territorial government must hand over part of the revenues collected to the Basque Government,[8] who in turn has the obligation to pay a certain amount to the Spanish Treasury, which is referred to as the Basque Tax Contribution or 'cupo'.

As can be gathered from the above, the ACBC's federal system and the Economic Agreement do not subordinate either Araba's or Gipuzkoa's authority to Bizkaia's, nor are the ACBC's rights and authorities regarded as subordinate to that of the Spanish central administration. The state-wide parties, however, conceptualize the ACBC as a region of Spain, and hence they consider the ACBC's political, institutional and constitutional authority to be regional and subordinate to Spanish national authority – that is, subordinate to the structured national, which, as opposed to those non-structured nations, is considered to have sovereignty. Thus, sovereignty is linked to authority, and to structured political capacity – that is, to the state rather than the community or the people. *This means that for the state, state sovereignty no longer relates to popular sovereignty in the global era, while for the people, popular sovereignty is the legitimizing political principle of the democratic era.* The global era is based on the privatization of public authority and popular sovereignty either by a foreign state (a state which does not represent the community it governs) or by private hands, as in the case of the European Union – a system which is run by groups of people who represent private interests (Kohler-Koch 2010).

Political power has traditionally been identified with sovereignty, and sovereignty understood in its Hobbesian sense as the monopoly of the modern state. The state, as a sociological fact, is a complex of institutions that successfully upholds the claim to the monopoly over the legitimate use of physical force and over authoritative law-making (Weber 2001: 101; Poggi 1990; Hay et al. 2006). Underlying the notion of the state as a structure of coercion and cooperation there is still the Hobbesian idea of sovereignty as the unchallengeable and unified site of authoritative judgment – a political aspiration whose fulfilment is always a matter of degree.

As shown (in Goikoetxea 2013b), Spain is a highly illuminating example of how the divisibility of sovereignty (in terms of political capacities), downwards to the ACs and upwards to the EU, is transforming the modern nation-state (Hooghe and Mark 2001; Sorensen 2004; Keating 2006).[9] Co-sovereignty, in this sense, implies giving up political (military and economic) decision-making power to supra- or sub-state entities, and hence resources: the decision-making power and resources that states use not only to coerce, but also to meet the needs of the population upon whom their authority depends (Dunn 2000: 78–79). These needs, in contemporary democratic societies, include not only protection and security, but also welfare and hence social and economic cohesion and political inclusion: democracy. This means that *sovereignty may be divisible, but it cannot disappear, since a community without political capacities and an unchallengeable site of authoritative judgment cannot govern itself according to its own political decisions.*

We have seen that political capacity is essential for reproducing a nation as a *demos* and maintaining the *demos* across time and space. We have also seen that it is state institutions that currently have available to them the greatest political capacity and, thus, the capacity to create and reproduce political reality. It is reasonable to infer that the Basque political community's inability to govern itself as a state or structured nation has consequences in terms of democracy and welfare. According to our *third hypothesis*, this lack of political capacity has driven demands for sovereignty time and again. However, according to our *second hypothesis*, Basque demands for sovereignty have also been a consequence of the lack of political authority from the Spanish state which, in turn, is due to its having ignored the political-legal-constitutional demands. *This is a way of privatizing Basque public authority and popular decision-making* – in other words, privatizing the political rights, authority and capacity of the Basque demos. As a consequence, yet another new phase was opened up by Basque political parties when they proposed New Constitutional Futures for the Basque Country for 2015 (see Goikoetxea 2013a, 2013b).

Basque demands for sovereignty are often described as manifestations of 'ethnic nationalism'. Yet it is important to remember that only forty-seven per cent of the population have parents who were both born in the ACBC, while around twenty-five per cent are first-generation immigrants and around twenty-eight per cent have a parent originally from Castile, Extremadura, Galicia or Andalusia (Alvite et al. 2000; Aranda 2004). This suggests that the broad political support that existed for the New Statute of Free Association with Spain, approved by the Basque Parliament by absolute majority in 2004, was motivated not by the population's attraction to Basque ethnicity but rather by other causes related to the process of Basque democratization as noted in the *second and third hypotheses*.

Taking into account the high levels of cohesion in the ACBC, and the fact that 85.9 per cent of the population defends Basque self-government and 62.8 per cent wants it to be developed (CIS 2005–2013),[10] along with the fact that only eleven per cent think that the Spanish government has contributed most to improving the Basque Country (Bourne 2008: 34), it is obvious that the ACBC has met the needs of its population more successfully than the Spanish central state has. Therefore, the approval of the New Statute of Free Association by an absolute majority may be interpreted as a sign of the ACBC's growing success at upholding the claim to the monopoly of authoritative law making.

Thus, the demand for a status of Free Association was actually articulated not because the Basque community is a distinct nationality (in the non-political sense of a pre-given cultural unit), but because it is a federal political entity, a federal demos, which, due to its political and institutional functioning, has shaped, and most effectively met, the needs of its population, managing to uphold the claim to the monopoly of authoritative law-making more successfully than the Spanish state itself.

Demands for sovereignty

Let us recall the main rights, principles and areas of competence demanded in the latest Statute of Autonomy 2004 Reform Plan. In addition to the Basque people's right of self-determination (Preliminary Heading, Art. 1), we also find Basque nationality and citizenship (Preliminary Heading, Art. 4), a relationship with the Spanish state based on 'free association' (Heading I), a Basque judicial system (Heading II), direct representation in Europe (Heading VI) and exclusive areas of competence of Basque institutions (Heading IV, Arts. 46–51, 53, 54, 60) as follows: education, culture and language policy, social policy and social security, healthcare, economic policy, employment policies, industry, commerce and agriculture, tourism, tax system and financial policies, housing, the environment and natural resources, infrastructures, transport and public works, policing and public security. By contrast, we find a short list of exclusive areas of competence of the Spanish state (Heading IV, Art. 45): Spanish nationality and immigration laws, production, trading and possession of firearms and explosives, the monetary and customs system (non-EU), the merchant navy and control of air space, defence forces, the army and foreign policy (diplomatic services).

This is undoubtedly a partial picture, but nevertheless it illustrates very well how sovereignty is imagined by the majority of Basque political parties, the population's representatives and Basque institutions. It shows that what is at stake in demands for sovereignty is political capacity and autonomy – therefore, these are demands to deepen the democratization process of the *demos*.

The demand for sovereignty is worded as the 'Basque People's right of self-determination' (Preliminary Heading, Art. 1). This relates to the people's right to make their own political decisions regarding their political future and relations with other political communities. This demand for sovereignty is also worded as the 'right to decide', which is the right a community has to become a political subject if the people so wishes. Sovereignty is, however, realized through political capacities. This is why the longest part of the Plan for a New Statute is the one where the competences demanded are specified – and these competences are part of what we call political capacities.

The demand for sovereignty is thus thought of as the right the *demos* has to self-government, but it can only be achieved under two conditions:

(a) The community's political decision to become a political subject is what transforms this community into a political subject (subjective dimension of sovereignty). This is called performativity (see Austin 1962; Searle 1969), and political subjects are always performative.
(b) A community, in order to become a functioning political subject, needs to have political capacity (the objective dimension of sovereignty) so that it can realize the population's political decisions.

Whatever happens with rights, territory and authority also happens with the *demos* and with sovereignty. They are all social productions, discursive practices, and thus they are always constituted as two-dimensional: subjective and objective. Both dimensions are social dimensions, but the first one makes reference to those commonly held beliefs, perceptions, identities and interests that lead a community to perceive itself as 'evidently existent'. Social realities, in order to exist, require that the people (indeterminate but hegemonic) believe them to exist. As noted by Searle (1969), 'the five euro note would not have any value should the people (hegemonic) think it has no value'.

The second dimension relates to the institutional or objectified dimension of these identities, interests and beliefs. The subjective aspect of popular sovereignty and of the *demos* – that is, the people's belief and perception that a political subject exists – is the *sine qua non* of political reality. But this subjective dimension cannot be reproduced without the objective dimension, since the latter is the other *sine qua non* – that of social realities. Without the objective dimension of sovereignty and the demos, there is no place for a reproductive dynamic, and this is how political communities fade away.

In the Basque Country, sovereignty is articulated and understood as closely linked to democracy – as a condition for democratization. The nation-state is transforming itself in order to serve global capitalism and economic elites by privatizing public decision-making through strengthening the executive and judicial branches and weakening legislative, and hence public, authority (Sassen 2008). However, for democratization to take place, state institutions are paramount, since *the* demos *is an organized people able to take decisions and realize them by means of its institutions*. Democratization is thus linked to a process of empowering the people. This empowerment is carried out through a specific relationship between the state and the community. And, in order for this relationship to be democratic, it must rest on popular sovereignty, in other words popular authoritative decisions that legitimize state actions.

This way of thinking of sovereignty is a consequence of decades of democratization, which have come about following centuries of 'statalization' (Foucault 1997; Goikoetxea 2013a) of government and of society.

Conclusion

In saying that the *demos* is an assemblage of rights, territory and authority we imagine the demos as a legitimating device. Contrary to the way the European Union works, democracy cannot run on 'output legitimacy' (Moravcski 2002). Technical efficacy, economic efficiency and political transparency are mechanisms for reproducing, not producing, authority and legitimacy. It is popular decision-making that creates democratic authority and legitimacy.

The democratic institutionalization of popular authority and legitimacy makes available the reproduction of the very unit that confers this legitimacy: the *demos*. Were there no institutionalization of popular sovereignty, there wouldn't be any democratization. The reason why, in the northern Basque country, the reproduction of the Basque *demos* has failed is related to the lack of a mechanism for transferring Basque popular sovereignty to the state – in this case, the French state – and the Union. In the case of the Chartered Community of Navarre (CCN), there is also the lack of mechanisms for realizing Basque citizens' demands within this territory, not to mention at the Spanish and EU levels. Political decisions made by the Basque population are not transferable to the rest of the levels that constitute the multilevel governance system in place in Europe, the Union and its member states. *It is not interests that have to be clumped together level by level;, it is the democratizing dynamic that has to be reproduced on each and every level.*

Each government level or governance area, in order to materialize the population's demands, needs to be understood as an area of struggle. And it is within the contentious relationship between institutions and social mobilization that demands are articulated and integrated. It is this dynamic that leads to democratization, not the amalgamation of interests and identities. Identity and interests are the symbolic aspects of material practices, needs, and hence struggles. In order to articulate common demands and interests, contention is needed, since institutionalization comes about within this contentious dynamic between protest, demand and certification (Ibarra Güell 2000; Zubiaga 2012; Goikoetxea 2014). Since the Basque political community does not govern itself as a state, this democratizing dynamic disappears once it leaves the Basque territories, because there is no transfer of popular sovereignty, and hence of political decision-making and contention, to the state or the Union.

There is one way of thinking which holds that we are in a post-national and post-sovereign era. We would like to point out that the proponents of this 'new era' idea (see MacCormick 1999; Keating 2001) usually belong to a structured national that ensures them high socio-economic and symbolic status, provided by their sovereign state. We conclude that in twenty-first-century Europe there can be no democracy without popular sovereignty, and popular sovereignty cannot be realized without political capacity – and hence, state institutions understood as sovereign. Those who deny the existence of sovereignty do so simply because they already have it.

Notes

1 Electoral program of EAJ-PNV, see: www.eaj-pnv.eu/documentos/programa-electoral-parlamento-vasco-2012_14391.html; EH Bildu, see: http://ehbildu.net/es/elecciones/parlamento-vasco-2012/programa-electoral
2 See the Confederal Statute of Lizarra (1931); the Statute of Autonomy (1979); and the Statute for Free Association (2004), and for all the self-government demands made by the Basque Parliament since 1980 go to www.parlamentovasco.euskolegebiltzarra.org/eu and www.parlamento.euskadi.net/pdfs_actual2/tram014_ec.pdf
3 I want to thank *Ethnopolitics* for giving me the permission to reproduce here parts of the article 'Nationalism and democracy in the Basque Country (1979–2012)'.
4 See Goikoetxea 2013b and 2014 for a nuanced description of the Basque political, economic and social systems along with the public policies implemented since the 1980s.
5 See Esping-Andersen (1990) and Huber and Stephens (2001) for the consequences that active participation by women in the labour force has in determining the socio-economic model and welfare regime.
6 Source: BBVA-Ivie (2008); *España en cifras* (INE 2010: www.ine.es/).

7 Electoral Law 5/1990: Heading II. Electoral System.
8 This allowance is determined according to different variables: Relative Cost of Assumed Powers (competences), Provincial Revenue (GDP) and the tax burden imposed by each Provincial Council.
9 The single currency is a perfect example of this transformation.
10 When asked about the reform of the Statute of Autonomy of 1979, only 14.4 per cent think that it is unnecessary (CIS 2005: www.cis.es/cis/opencms/EN/index.html).

References

Ahedo, I. 2016. 'Iparralde: The Emergence of the Basque Territory in France', in P. Ibarra Güell and Å. Kolås, eds, *Basque Nationhood: Towards a Democratic Scenario*. Bern: Peter Lang.

Aja, E. 2003. *El estado autonómico: Federalismo y hechos diferenciales* [The Autonomous State: Federalism and Differential Facts]. Madrid: Alianza.

Alvite, P. 2000. *La inmigración extranjera en el País Vasco, II Congreso sobre la Inmigración en España* [Foreign Immigration in the Basque Country, Second Congress on Immigration in Spain]. Leioa: University of the Basque Country.

Aranda, J. 2004. 'La mezcla del pueblo vasco' [The Mixture of the Basque People], *Historia. Papeles de Ermua*, 6: 145–180.

Austin, J. L. 1962. *How to Do Things With Words*. Oxford: Clarendon Press.

Blas, A. 2012. *Euskal Estatuari bidea irekitzen* [Opening the Way for the Basque State]. Bilbao: Iparhegoa.

Bourne, A. K. 2008. *The European Union and the Accommodation of Basque Difference in Spain*. Manchester: Manchester University Press.

Börzel, T. 2002. *States and Regions in the European Union: Institutional Adaptation in Germany and Spain*. Cambridge, MA: Cambridge University Press.

Bray, Z. 2011. *Living Boundaries: Frontiers and Identity in the Basque Country*. Reno, NV: Center for Basque Studies Press, University of Nevada.

Dunn, J., ed. 2000. The Cunning of Unreason: Making Sense of Politics. London: Harper Collins.

Esping-Andersen, G. 1990. *The Three Worlds of Welfare Capitalism*. Cambridge: Polity Press.

European Commission. 2004. *A New Partnership for Cohesion: Convergence, Competitiveness, Cooperation*. Third Report on Economic and Social Cohesion. Luxembourg: Office for Official Publications of the European Communities.

Eurostat Regional Yearbook 2009 and 2010. *General and Regional Statistics*. Luxembourg: Office for Official Publications of the European Communities.

Filibi, I. 2004. *La Unión política como marco de resolución de los conflictos etnonacionales europeos: un estudio comparado* [The Political Union as a Framework for Resolution of European Ethno-National Conflict: A Comparative Study]. Bilbao: University of the Basque Country Press.

Foucault, M. 1997. *Society Must Be Defended*. Paris: Gallimard.

Goikoetxea, J. 2013a. 'Emancipatory Nationalism and Catalonia', *Ethnopolitics*, 12(4): 394–397.

———. 2013b. 'Nationalism and Democracy in the Basque Country (1979–2012)', *Ethnopolitics*, 12(3): 268–289.

———. 2014. 'Nation and Democracy Building in Contemporary Europe: The Reproduction of the Basque Demos', *Nationalities Papers*, 42(1): 145–164.

Goikoetxea, T. 1997. 'Modelo de Estado' [State Model], *XIV Congress of the Spanish United- Left Party*, Madrid.

Hall, P. A. 1999. 'The Political Economy of Europe in an Era of Interdependence', in H. Kitschelt, P. Lange, G. Marks and J. D. Stephens, eds, *Continuity and Change in Contemporary Capitalism*. Cambridge, MA: Cambridge University Press, pp. 135–163.

Hall, P. A., and Soskice, D., eds. 2001. *Varieties of Capitalism*. Oxford: Oxford University Press.

Hay, C., Lister, M., and Marsh, D. 2006. *The State: Theories and Issues*. New York: Palgrave Macmillan.

Hinsley, F. H. 1986. *Sovereignty*. Cambridge, MA: Cambridge University Press.

Hirst, P., and Thompson, G. 1996. *Globalisation in Question: The International Economy and the Possibilities of Governance*. Cambridge: Polity Press.

Hooghe, L., and Marks, G. 2001. *Multi-Level Governance and European Integration*. Boulder, CO: Rowman and Littlefield.

Huber, E., and Stephens, J. 2001. *Development and Crisis of the Welfare State*. Chicago, IL: University of Chicago Press.

Ibarra Güell, P. 2000. 'Los estudios sobre los movimientos sociales: estado de la cuestión' [Studies of Social Movements: State of Affairs], *Revista española de ciencia política*, 2: 271–292.

Keating, M. 2001. *Plurinational Democracy: Stateless Nations in a Post-Sovereignty Era*. Oxford: Oxford University Press, 2001.

———. 2006. 'Territorial Politics and the New Regionalism', in P. Heywood, V. Pujas and M. Rhodes, eds, *Developments in European Politics*. London: Palgrave, pp. 201–218.

Kohler-Koch, B. 2010. 'Civil Society and EU Democracy: "Astroturf" Representation?', *Journal of European Public Policy*, 17(1): 100–116.

MacCormick, N. 1999. Questioning Sovereignty: Law, State, and Nation in the European Commonwealth. Oxford: Oxford University Press.

Moravcsik, A. 2002. 'In Defence of the "Democratic Deficit": Reassessing the Legitimacy of the European Union', *Journal of Common Market Studies*, 40(4): 603–634.

Pierson, P. 2001. *The New Politics of the Welfare State*. Oxford: Oxford University Press.

Poggi, G. 1990. *The State: Its Nature, Development and Prospects*. Cambridge: Polity Press.

Sassen, S. 2008. *Territory, Authority, Rights: From Medieval to Global Assemblages*. Princeton, NJ: Princeton University Press.

Searle, J. 1969. *Speech Acts: An Essay in the Philosophy of Language*. Cambridge, MA: Cambridge University Press.

Schmidt, V. A. 2002. *The Futures of European Capitalism*. Oxford: Oxford University Press.

Sorensen, G. 2004. *The Transformation of the State: Beyond the Myth of Retreat*. New York: Palgrave Macmillan.

Tilly, C. 2007. *Democracy*. Cambridge, MA: Cambridge University Press.

Weber, M. 2001. *La política como vocación* [Politics as a Vocation]. Barcelona: Paidós.

Zubiaga, M. 2012. *Euskal Estatuari bidea irekitzen* [Opening the Way for the Basque State]. Bilbao: Iparhegoa.

7   Sovereignty revisited

The Basque case

Pedro Ibarra Güell, Iban Galletebeitia,
Mario Zubiaga, Jule Goikoetxea, Igor Ahedo,
Javier Alcalde and Pablo Aguiar

Rather than a conclusion, this chapter presents a *set of conclusions*. In the diverse chapters of this book, the experience of sovereignty has been discussed, the concept reconsidered, and the theory compared with reality, or the existing social perceptions of sovereignty. The concept of sovereignty depends on the context in which – and from which – it is experienced. It can thus consist in a social conviction (and even an emotion) linked to the desire for, and eventually the practice of, a collective decision. Conversely, it can also be proposed from an institutional space linked closely to political power. In the various territories of the Basque country where the experience and conceptualisation of sovereignty can be found, it is also affirmed in multiple ways.

From this perspective of diversity, we consider it appropriate in these *multifarious but also interlinked conclusions* to include the most relevant points of view, which are also very different from each other. The first part of this chapter – perhaps the most substantial part – describes the results of fieldwork on this question. From the social perspective, this is the most extensive and detailed approach. Next, within the description of the complex political scenario of the Basque country, we introduce approaches to the question of sovereignty that have a more political character. It seems appropriate to give a special mention to two specific (and even exceptional) factors that recur throughout the chapters of this book. One of them is the significance of ETA's violence, and its cessation, in the evolution of the demand for sovereignty. The second is the question of sovereignty in the territories of the French Basque country and Navarre. Finally, we close with a conclusion that transcends the more preliminary conclusions, drawing directly on the corresponding chapters of this book. This conclusion sets out a possible future political and social scenario in and for the Basque country, linked in the final instance to the prospects for sovereignty.

Social perceptions of sovereignty

As noted in chapter two on 'Changes in the Basque sovereignty demand', the purpose of our fieldwork was to test the hypotheses set out in the chapter. These hypotheses are confirmed by the results – *the conclusions* – of the fieldwork.

We conducted a series of interviews (more than fifteen) in an effort to capture the diversity of the population in terms of age, gender and livelihood, but with a common interest in the question of sovereignty. These are all people who participate, with different degrees of commitment and at different levels, in social mobilization and activities aimed at establishing sovereignty for the Basque country. On the basis of the chosen sample and the results obtained, it is not possible to establish a theory on the conception of sovereignty held by the Basque population. Our analysis deals with people who are concerned about this question because they believe that they do not live in a sovereign community and who thus, in principle, have a favorable attitude towards attaining sovereignty for the Basque country.

Initial conceptions

Establishing definitions on the basis of lived experiences is not an altogether simple task. For interviewees who 'experience' it, sovereignty is not so much about theoretical, legal-juridical definitions marking the limits and powers of a territory, but more about practical references to their everyday life and that of their fellow citizens. The experience of sovereignty is therefore 'something' that is situated more within the social than the political space. Apart from its static definition, it is above all something that must be carried out. Its conception is thus basically dynamic. Consequently, the proposed definitions would refer to moments of experiencing the *demand* for sovereignty.

Such a dynamic and at the same time popular vision of sovereignty appears explicitly or implicitly in the following definition: *'I relate sovereignty to the possibility of citizens deciding what we want to be in the future, and to our not wanting to leave that decision in the hands of the political representatives alone'.*

Decision-making capacity

Sovereignty and the right to decide are in a certain sense intertwined in the above statement. Sovereignty is when one decides, or when there is capacity for deciding, or when there are no external limits placed on that decision-making capacity. In this sense, sovereignty is not primarily a matter of governance – related to labor, economy, culture, etc. More importantly, sovereignty is exercised when a set of citizens have the capacity to decide on what it is they want to decide, without that decision having limits or frontiers. However, the interviewees also make it clear what the contents of decision-making are, or on what matters there should be self-government. That is, sovereignty is not only a question of deciding on the political status of the community, and affirming that the community should generically decide on its self-government, but also concerns what the community should decide on, or what exactly the self-government entails. One thus understands that the community, or its citizens, or more precisely the representatives of the community (and no one else), should decide on questions of politics, economy, culture, social life, and management of labor order, in other words, on everything that affects the daily life of the community. We could thus say that the predominant tendency in the interviews is to give content to the sovereignty based on the exercising of the right to decide. There is sovereignty when one decides without limits on all matters of general interest to the community.

A radical position

A conception that we could term more demanding arises in some of the interviews. In these interviews, sovereignty is not when a generic decision is taken on issues of importance to social life, but instead when the subject who decides on all these issues is the community as a whole. We could refer to this 'community as a whole' as 'the people'. For sovereignty to be exercised, 'the people' must not only have the capacity to decide on who their rulers are, but at the same time, they must decide that those rulers should regulate everything affecting their *collective* life. In addition, people must also decide on all aspects that affect their life as *individuals*. This implies, for example, that were sovereignty to be exercised, there would not be any economic elites who decided in practice on what must be done (and, in the final instance, be regulated) in the economy, especially in the financial and business world. Rather, 'the people' – in this case, workers as well as citizens – would exercise economic power. From this perspective, only then would it be possible to speak about popular sovereignty or full sovereignty.

   This 'radical' approach to sovereignty (which, as noted, is a minority position in the set of discourses and reflections analyzed) proposes that to exercise the right to decide or the independence of the community entails a set of measures to be implemented in the new situation of independence that would follow from the right to decide being exercised. In practice, this supposes the implementation of a popular and egalitarian form of sovereignty.

   As mentioned, the majority of interviewees consider sovereignty as an issue of capacity to decide, rather than of implementation. Thus, the majority establishes a principle of full self-government, but requires only that the self-government, represented by the corresponding elected institutions, is what decides on policy-making in fields such as the economy, labor, etc., without excluding any sections of the population. Each existing social, economic or cultural agency or power will hence take the decisions that correspond to its mandate or area of competence. There is thus no proposal for reforms in the agencies that exercise power, in which citizens constituted in a popular sovereignty would displace the present political representatives or social elites.

A popular conception

We nonetheless found that among the interviewees, there is a widespread belief that, for different reasons such as the relatively small size of the Basque community, and greater presence of 'left-wing' political forces, full self-government resulting from the exercising of the right to decide would produce, or develop into, a more egalitarian, more just and more participatory community. In other words, there is an expectation that the right to decide would ultimately result in a more popular sovereignty. Despite that the commitment to establish such a popular sovereignty is not understood as a condition for being able to exercise the right to decide, such sovereignty is considered to be a more-than-likely and desirable consequence of the right to decide.

Leadership

The popular character of governance that is proposed directly, or as a likely possibility, in the management of sovereignty once it is attained also appears in a systematic form in the definition of the collective subject that must set in motion the decision-making process to obtain that sovereignty. In this sense, a central leading role is given to social networks, or simply to society as whole, in mobilizing to achieve sovereignty (or independence) for the Basque country by exercising the right to decide. While the interviewees do not deny that political parties must also channel this process, a certain distrust of the leadership of the parties appears with greater or lesser intensity in nearly all the interviews. There is an understanding that an open process, without party sectarianism, would facilitate the collaboration of social groups that would otherwise remain apart from such mobilization. Such a process would encourage the creation of a sense of belonging to a community with a common identity.

In another section we observed the positions of political parties facing issues of leadership and mobilization, and their difficulties in achieving a convergence towards a common goal. What is striking is that party representatives are absent from the discussions and debates launched by activists. We stress that no disdain is felt towards the politicians, but there is an understanding (though perhaps not an explicit one) that the leading role must be in the hands of civil society. This is a leading role based on convictions. To cite verbatim: '*The main driving force for participating is the conviction that the decisions that affect the citizens belong to the citizens*'. Moreover, the acceptance of leadership by civil society is based on perceived ground realities such as the impact of recent mobilization against existing policies, and movements of outraged citizens.

As the above narrative suggests, this idea of sovereignty appears more as a proposal for better and more convenient self-government than a demand based on eternal and natural rights, and it is justified with arguments that are not at all essentialist.

What is the use of sovereignty?

Emerging from the demand to assert national sovereignty through deciding, the very concept of the nation – or more precisely, the assertion of Basque nationhood – is flexible, open-ended and, above all, based on subjective will rather than objective elements.

To the question of 'how is the nation to be understood?' informants responded, '*As a community of people who share a physical space that is aware of itself as a nation with the will to self-government*'. This describes a space to which access is absolutely open. One is a member of a national community insofar as one affirms one's feeling of belonging to it, with no other requirement. This opening up is permitting the convergence of interests, in allowing for a broad-based mobilization towards the 'right to decide', including not only citizens with strong nationalist convictions, but also those with a weaker nationalist consciousness, and others who understand that, for a particular community to demand sovereignty, it is unnecessary to feel like a nation. The last affirmation ties in with another argument presented in this set of interviews: The right to decide, and to exercise this right to achieve full sovereignty, is rooted in basic democratic principles. Therefore, the collective practice of deciding on a community's self-government is legitimate or justifiable in any democratic society.

Another argument with a strong presence, and a similarly practical character, is that there are socio-economic benefits in achieving sovereignty. By exercising the right to decide, one would thus have a better life in the Basque country. Better, that is, from the usual perspective of more work, more social services, more security, more public participation and more institutional efficiency. Interviewees made forceful claims along these lines: '*[to exercise the right to decide in order to secede is] the only way to survive the Spanish state, which will otherwise drag us into complete human, economic and ecological destruction*'.

The dominant discourse does not establish an improvement in the community's conditions of life as something inevitable. However, it does establish a credible possibility for substantial improvement, at least in the longer term. Moreover, the majority of interviewees maintained that self-determination makes sense mainly because of its utility, or convenience, whereas questions of principle are of less importance. In short, we did not hear many affirmations of pure principle, such as: '*I believe the population of the Basque Country should have the right to decide independently, whether we are going to live better or worse*'.

Is sovereignty equivalent to self-government?

Finally, it is useful to mention a somewhat different conception of sovereignty. Indeed, some of the interviewees maintained that they were already experiencing sovereignty, at least in some respects. This is not entirely unexpected in a context such as the Basque country, where there is a participatory culture (and on occasion practices) in the resolution of collective affairs, together with a relatively high level of self-government as offered by the Spanish model of autonomy. However, it is worth noting a very clear qualification on the part of this section of interviewees, which is that the present degree of self-government is not what they expect of a fully sovereign community, nation or people. Moreover, while acknowledging their ability to make certain decisions on social or economic issues in a collective way, they perceive this as different from and less than the ability to act as a sovereign community.

From political to social sovereignty: proposing a shift in the perspective

We will now see how, after starting out from a more political – more conventional – perspective, our findings direct us to shift towards a more social perspective.

In drawing conclusions from the fieldwork, and on the basis of other chapters in this book, we have observed that the concept of sovereignty has evolved. This is the case in the world at large, and in the Basque country in particular. The evolution has proceeded from a decidedly political, classical perspective to arrive at the orientation we have just described, which has a decidedly more social character. Material reality reflects the discourse of identity, whether of individuals or social movements. In the Basque case, industrial development has given rise to a comparatively strong Basque economy, while also generating the features of a strong sense of belonging to a Basque collective identity. As described by J. Azurmendi (1996), the notion of 'Christian personalism' provides a key to this sense of identity: a Basque pride in being a strong community from the perspective of being industrialized, modern and advanced – as a community at the forefront of technological development. Since the mid-1950s, the development of the Basque employee-owned Mondragón Corporation illustrates the progressive way of making up the Basque people from a social, democratic and universalistic perspective. Mondragón is a highly networked, broad-based and decentralized enterprise, widely known as a prime example of a successful cooperative enterprise model.

A sense of nationhood resting on a unique modernity or progressive identity has to be constructed on very different terms than a belonging based on romantic traits such as a unique traditional culture. The first sense of nationhood corresponds well to the current Basque scenario, which appears as a more pragmatic nationalistic political identification and strategy, promoting political options that are geared towards maintaining and developing achievements of economic success. The second sense of Basque nationhood can also be found, comprising strategies that are more essentialist, and ultimately more socially divisive.

The state as starting point

We should recall that the evolution of the concept of sovereignty runs parallel to the process of the formation of the modern state. Sovereignty, or supreme and original political power, is an essentially problematic discourse insofar as it condenses the tension between power understood as the expression of the will of the political community itself, and power defined by the capacity of a ruler or state institution to make its will effective. This tension is expressed in two, closely connected ways.

In the first instance, the shaping of the modern state shows the evolution of the concept towards greater democratization. That is, precedence is taken by the 'protected consultation' or the field of an equal, general and protected citizenry with respect to the arbitrariness of public powers whose formation and will are increasingly subject to popular decision-making. However, as seems obvious, democratization is a process that is impossible to close, which is why the tension between popular decision-making and government action cannot be eradicated.

Moreover, this unfinished ideological evolution equally affects both constituted states and nations in which there is a demand for statehood. Thus a second problematic field for the concept of sovereignty is opened up from the moment when there are *demoi* that, conceiving themselves to be sovereign and lacking political power or a sovereign state, are nonetheless integrated in sovereign states with fragmentary *demoi* that do not conceive themselves to be sovereign in a unanimous and homogeneous way.

Thus, in this second assumption, the claim is centered on the demands for sovereignty that certain political communities and, in some cases, their institutions, make to an already constituted sovereign state. Here, the demand for sovereignty is expressed as mobilization for political change, and can be analyzed with the characteristic analytical instruments of new social movements.

Sovereignty and mobilization

In recent years, the classic agenda has been updated with the Dynamics of Contention model proposed by Doug McAdam et al. (2001). These authors observe that in every process of mobilization, irrespective of its content and scale, similar mechanisms and processes can be detected, albeit linked in different ways.

In nationalist contention – that is, contention related to the demand that a nation without a sovereign state makes to a sovereign state containing several nations within it – certain relevant and interrelated processes can be highlighted: the formation of discursive categories that shape the subjects of the contention, the political polarization that derives from those categories, and innovation in the repertoires of mobilization connected to both. In this sense, the discourse around the demand for Basque sovereignty has been expressed in recent years in a discursive formation – Basque nationalism – that has evolved over time, defining what could be said (and not be said) at each moment.

In recent decades, what Basque nationalism has said or imagined in relation to sovereignty has been connected to certain *topoi* or discursive places that made it possible to activate the mechanism of attributing threat and opportunity in an efficient way and, at the same time, led in one way or another to innovation in the repertoires of mobilization. This evolution was analyzed on the basis of studying the principle daily newspapers of the two big families of Basque nationalism.

And democratic society . . . as the point of arrival

Going more deeply into something that was noted in the final part of the previous conclusions, we can affirm that the presence of categories like 'the right to decide' has been considerably strengthened in recent years, giving shape to an 'imagined Basque sovereignty' that separates from the classical national-identitarian aspects to connect with the will of the plural Basque *demos*. As a consequence, the 'Basque nationalist' category becomes weakened in favor of new categories like the 'pro-sovereignty' category which enable the appearance of new axes of polarization that are transversal with respect to pre-existing national identities. Similarly, the primacy of the 'will of the Basque citizenry' as key to resolving the demand for sovereignty is progressively separated from traditional, culturally centered contents, while greater relevance is given to socio-economic aspects of welfare. In this evolution there is, to a certain extent, a confluence in the discourses of the two ideological families of nationalism.

A complex political scenario

In our qualitative research we have detected that civil society is experiencing sovereignty – or better put, its lack, or the desire to obtain it. Deciding about everything that concerns us would appear to be an exercise of imagining arrival at the final scenario. This nonetheless conceals or avoids the incoherence between such an attainment and practice, reproduced daily, without channels of hegemonic legitimation, working in parallel (or with the same rhythm) in the institutional and the socio-economic field.

Sovereignty is constructed or deconstructed on a daily basis, in competition with other discourses and political proposals: within the civil, institutional, economic and social fields, and with the guarantee of a central government that certifies the existence of a sovereign subject that is able to decide. One of the keys in the Basque case is the lack of daily materialization of that final scenario. The only practical attempt to proceed to or take steps towards a new, real, institutional sovereignty was started on the initiative of the Basque Parliament led by Lehendakari Juan José Ibarretxe, with his well-known 'Ibarretxe Plan'. Ibarretxe's proposal for shared sovereignty, or 'freely associated status', was channeled through the Basque institutions and rejected by the Spanish government.

Divergent strategies

(a) **Lack of disarmament or a final end to ETA.** The enormous complexity of leaving the past behind means that EH Bildu, a coalition that was democratically constituted under the juridical purview of the Spanish state, is unable to carry out normal political activities such as seeking agreements and consensus with other parties.

(b) **Political parties.** There is a crisis of mediation between civil society and political institutions, and of decision-making by representation. The political parties find themselves in a buyers' market, which is clearly demonstrated by the articulation of civil society movements around populist reasoning.

(c) **Stability.** The Basque nationalist party, PNV, is the only party that can provide the central government in Madrid with a guarantee of stability in the Basque country. In the not-yet-normalized Basque community, agreements between constitutionalist and nationalist forces are impossible without the PNV in the role of main protagonist. The political branding of Bildu as an associate of

ETA has made agreements between PNV and the left-wing nationalist forces almost impossible.
(d) **Hegemony.** The PNV is the key, central and hegemonic party in the dynamics of the Basque dispute. However, the discursive articulation of political sovereignty is currently based on a less than likely agreement between nationalist parties (PNV and Bildu) and constitutionalists, with the newly founded party PODEMOS as an unknown factor.

We are facing a multifaceted and complex political dispute. On the one hand, there is a clear parallel between the civil society agenda and the institutional agenda, which together make up the collective political agenda of the Basque community. On the other hand, there is no synergy and confluence above and beyond the Autonomy Statute of 1979. Constitutional reform would only entail a new pact between the state and PNV. This is very different from the Scottish and Catalan cases, given that both the dynamics of the actors and the historical processes are radically dissimilar. There is no Basque movement or party like the Catalan 'Junts pel Sí'.[1] As a consequence, strategies for imagining (or denying) sovereignty are also very different.

In the Basque case, we find two versions of Basque national consciousness. On the one hand, there is a moderate form represented by PNV and its alternative proposal for shared sovereignty, which is open to pacts based on dialogue, consensus and bilateral relations with the Spanish state. On the other hand, there is a radical subject with an enemy syndrome represented by ETA, justified as an articulation of popular will, and using protest, mobilization and repertories of violence to demand recognition of the right to decide.

And now, in the post-violence scenario, there are pro-sovereignty majorities beyond the nation that are not yet articulated. Attempting to explain what this means, there are two versions. One posits a moderate subject that wants dialogue, consensus and agreement, and puts forward the concept of the *foral* nation. As with the PNV, its objectives are economic agreements, quotas and pacts, and perhaps adjustments to the Constitution. The other posits a radical democratic subject engaged in peaceful protest and mobilization to achieve dialogue, consensus and agreement as a people. With the end of violence, this subject comes together around statements such as: '*Together we will think and decide what we want to be, and as Basque people, we have the right to decide*'.

The proposal of the Spanish state is neither to reform nor change the Constitution, as long as the two majority parties are in agreement. At the time of writing, change is unlikely given that Partido Popular and Ciudadanos have an absolute majority in the government.

Divergent dynamics

In two other contemporary cases, namely Scotland and Cataluña, we observe that sovereignty demands have been articulated (both discursively and practically) by the creation of instruments, artifacts and even quasi-official organizations that have guided, supported and at times sought to dominate the political sphere. In grassroots movements, civil society and, above all, in fields of strategic action (the institutional field and the field of political and social economy), these sovereignty demands have been capitalized on and crystalized into a national logic. These dynamics are what hegemonically reproduce and create the orders of legitimate authority in contemporary society. In the institutional field, the mediation of democratic or popular sovereignty demands has simultaneously replenished civil society, creating parallel spirals of strategic action that in turn generate denser networks of popular sovereignty in the field of organized civil society. Meanwhile, the universal discourse continues to have an effect in the Scottish and Catalan cases. We could categorically say that the prior ability to exercise sovereignty makes it a possible exercise, and that it materializes through reciprocal feedback among four fields of strategic action: organized civil society, alliances of political parties, institutions oriented toward civil society demands and, facing these, a central government that recognizes a political subject with sufficient sovereignty potential, or aptitude to decide what it wants to be.

In our research on the Basque case, we see that civil society is doing what it can in favor of a universal discursive articulation that, in broad terms, takes up the demands and yearnings for more sovereignty of the Basque people. The channeling of the pro-sovereignty strategy is still focused on emotions, given that in the Basque case there is a lot of prior trauma, among the general public as well as political activists and their families. So, among other objectives, the popular pro-sovereignty initiative Gure Esku Dago functions as a balm for the deep psychological wounds borne by citizens in general. Surfeit, repetition, excess, monotony, more repetition . . . partisanship in electoral politics is widely repeated in the current critique of political parties as legitimate representatives of the people and accountable to the popular will. It would seem to us strange or exceptional for anyone to attain higher degrees of sovereignty simply through civil society activation and popular activity without the feedback of the other fields of strategic action we have mentioned.

A decisive change

In all of this evolution in the perception of and demand for sovereignty, the role of ETA's violence (and also that of the state) has had a decisive function. Until a short while ago, it defined a period in which the politics of sovereignty – in the *hardest* sense of the term – was fundamental. On the other hand, ETA's definitive cessation of violence redirects the leadership of the demand for sovereignty towards civil society. As noted previously, the fundamental role of ETA in this whole process requires that we make a succinct reflection on some basic aspects of its trajectory and the current consequences of its operational disappearance. Some of these reflections appear in other chapters, and others, which we also consider relevant, are incorporated into these final conclusions.

Political violence has been present in Euskadi for decades. To the violence exercised by the Francoist regime must be added, starting in 1968, the violence practiced by ETA and later by paramilitary organizations created under the shelter of the Spanish state. With over a thousand mortal victims this is the most bloody and violent political conflict of the Spanish state in the second half of the twentieth century. If we widen our lens to Western Europe as whole, the death toll of the Basque conflict is exceeded only by that of the conflict over Northern Ireland, with over three thousand deaths.

Focusing on Euskadi, more than four decades of ETA operations had a decisive influence on the political debate. Besides the direct consequences for the victims themselves, another type of impact should be considered, namely the effects on the population in general. We will highlight some consequences:

Polarization: The violent actions, whether exercised by ETA or the security forces and state apparatus, generated severe social confrontation. The violence gave rise to polarization in which the sides both claimed that 'you are either with me or against me'. For anyone who did not clearly identify with either of the two sides, this created enormous difficulties.

Restriction of political participation: Many people withdrew from political participation, either due to fear of ETA or obstacles to participation that were created by the state. In 2002, the Organic Law of Political Parties was approved. This would subsequently give legal cover to the banning of Batasuna on the pretext of failing to explicitly reject violence as a political instrument.

Sequestering of debate: As the terrorist organization defended certain political aspirations, the independence of Euskadi and the creation of a socialist state, these goals, especially the first, became taboo proposals on the Basque political agenda. Thus, the political forces and social agents opposed to independence took recourse to accusing anyone who might make any proposal in favor of independence of connivance with terrorism. In practice, this seriously limited and sequestered the political debate.

On 20 October 2011, ETA announced 'the definitive cessation of its armed activities'. Very briefly, we will indicate some keys to understanding this decisive event. The Northern Irish model of putting an end to violence had proved successful. Terrorism was discredited since the eruption of Islamist (nihilistic) terrorism. Civil society no longer feared the consequences of taking a position against violence. Finally, the patriotic left realized that terrorist violence did not contribute towards the goal of independence for Euskadi, but hindered it instead.

Until today, official restorative efforts have focused on the direct and indirect victims of violence. In our view, it is all of society that needs to heal. There are issues, such as the treatment of the prison population, over which there is deep division. Besides, there are questions that require a more inclusive treatment, among which the following can be highlighted: recognition of all victims, and the asymmetry in their treatment; elaboration of a memory that is inclusive; and recognition of the suffering caused, by *whoever* caused it.

With respect to the debates 'frozen' by terrorism, grassroots initiatives like Gure Esku Dago[2] are positing the legitimacy of the citizenry to determine their future and exercise their right to decide. It is not surprising that the majority of Basque politicians fail to offer their support or encourage such proposals. The contemporary Basque political class was socialized in the setting of violence. It may be that in order to break the taboos, a generational change is required to enable the debates that were previously not possible.

Overcoming the scenario of violence might take generations. It also requires questions related to transitional justice to be tackled. In recent decades there has been a proliferation of analyses and developments of this type of justice. In fact, Euskadi has expertise in developing tools for transitional justice, some experience in their application, and people with the capacity to implement them. Unfortunately, there is still a lack of political will on the part of the Spanish government to address issues related to transitional justice. With the April 2017 unilateral disarmament of ETA, a great step has been taken towards finally overcoming the long legacy of political violence in the Basque country, despite that it is a unilateral move forward, or perhaps precisely because it is unilateral.

Sovereignty, political conflict and power

The following reflections (or conclusions) directly frame the question of sovereignty in the political conflict (or confrontation) between the Basque nation and the Spanish state in the Basque country today.

Party political confrontation

Confrontation between Basque nationalists and nation-wide parties has been labelled by the latter as one of 'nationalists versus constitutionalists' (Habermas 1994; Müller 2006). This labelling reflects a long-standing incompatibility between constitutional systems and historical rights-based foral regimes, best exemplified by the Basque case. For Herrero de Miñon (1998), one of the fathers of the Spanish Constitution, this opposition expresses different conceptions of the *corpus politicum*: the first based on the homogenization and centralization of powers, and the second on differentiation and decentralization (Tilly 2000; Burgess and Vollaard 2006). Closely related to this opposition is the antagonism between the diverse patterns of relationship set up by the Autonomous Community of the Basque Country (ACBC) vis-à-vis the central state. Basque 'nationalists' understand this relationship as being between two equal political entities, whereas Spanish 'constitutionalists' understand it as one of subordination. These incompatible conceptions of the ACBC, and the confrontation caused by the antagonistic patterns of political relationship, have turned attempts to further Basque social, political and economic interests as interests on a par with those of the Spanish central state into 'minority nationalist' demands, and thus into something that must be opposed at all costs. This was demonstrated again with the Spanish Congress and Court's rejection of the New Statute of Free Association (2004) and the 2008 popular consultation (STC 103/2008), respectively, both approved by absolute majority in the Basque Parliament. As a result, the major fence that divides political allegiances in the current political landscape is the one between Basque nationalist parties – who defend the Basque political system's development according to its renewed foral and federal structure – and the state-wide parties, incapable of defending it in these terms. It is therefore reasonable to argue, following Goikoetxea (this volume) that underneath this confrontation between Basque and Spanish nationalists, there is a divergent development of the democratic system.

State-building and democracy-building

This raises the question of the connection between state-building and democracy-building. According to Tilly (2000), the degree of democratization depends on the degree to which the state can translate citizens' expressed demands into the transformation of social life. As Tilly (ibid.) points out, this cannot happen without significant state capacity, which leads us to the concept of political capacity as the material key for democratization.

Political power is often associated with sovereignty, understood in its Hobbesian sense as the monopoly of the modern state (MacCormick 2000; Sassen 2006). However, non-state political communities such as the ACBC do also have political power and a high level of institutional materiality, which means that they do also (set out to) create unchallengeable and unified sites of authoritative judgment. For this reason, instead of sovereignty, the concepts of political power and political capacity have been used. As noted earlier, political capacity refers to the levels of institutionalization and territorialization that a community – and, in this case, a set of Basque organizational structures – has been able to achieve. This concept of political capacity sheds light onto the double dimension of the demos: the object and subject that emerges in a democratization process. This means that the demos of a democratic system has two dimensions, the materialized or objectified one – apparent in state institutions (including political parties, trade unions, etc.) and socio-economic structures – and the embodied or subjective dimension that refers to 'dispositions of the agents who operate these institutions or fight against them' (Bourdieu 1985: 739).

Following this line, Basque democracy-building will require a continuous (re) production of not only economic, social and cultural capital, but also the symbolic capital by means of which a distinct demos is represented and reproduced. Depending on the Basque institutions' political capacities and the system of multi-level governance that these are embedded in, Basque public politics and policies will differ, thereby determining the future type of reproduction of the Basque demos in both its material, socio-economic dimension and its subjective and discursive dimension The reason why Goikoetxea (this volume) does not give pre-eminence to the cultural over the socio-economic in the reproduction of political distinctions is because of the assumption that nation-building in twenty-first-century European democracies are carried out through demos-building processes. Conversely, both reproduction practices concerned with nation-building and demos-building are currently embedded, in every detail, in the same socio-political processes and structures and justified through identical economic and political discourses and strategies.

The issue of territory: Iparralde and Navarre

The symbolic process of building sovereignty in the ACBC rests on the activation of three elements. Firstly, it is draws on the administrative and political recognition of a territory in the form of an Autonomous Community that the Constitution itself recognizes on the basis of certain historical rights and the articulation of an independent taxation system. Secondly, and more importantly, it relies on the shaping of a pro-sovereignty political subject that transcends party politics in order to begin to root itself in civil society. And finally, it grows out of the recent articulation of a sovereign horizon that is feasible in the medium to long term, taking concrete form in efforts to define an imagined reality *after* the attainment of sovereignty.

Nonetheless, we see a very different reality in the Basque territory in France, Iparralde, as described in the works of Itzaina (1998), Gurrutxaga (2005) and Ahedo (2016). On the one hand, the French state has staged a sequenced process, first state-building and later nation-building, which has greatly weakened Basque identity until recent times. This process, combined with the lack of recognition of the territory as such, explains the difficulties for the emergence of a nationalist movement. When such a movement nevertheless emerged, its first task was to give symbolic importance to the territory. The role played by the Basque nationalists in the dynamic in favor of a Basque administrative area (a department), and in public development and territorial planning policies, explains the key agenda-setting position that the nationalist movement has been achieving over the last decade. Thus, in the electoral scenario the movement conditions local majorities by its support or opposition. In parallel, the symbolic emergence of the territory enables the Basque movement to widen the axes of adhesion of the local citizenry to the nationalist project, insofar as it is no longer perceived as necessary to meet criteria such as 'knowing the language' or 'having blood ties' in order to identify as Basque. Nonetheless, although the nationalist movement in the French Basque country has managed to make a territory lacking institutional-political recognition 'exist' in the minds of the inhabitants, it has not managed to articulate either a political subject or a sovereign horizon in terms of state articulation. This, however, does not mean that the nationalist movement of Iparralde is not structuring a new political subject and a new horizon. It only means that it is not structuring it in state terms, but in terms of local community, which we see as the first step towards national and later state structuring.

In the case of the Chartered Community of Navarre (CCN), the existing plurality of identities described by Blas (this volume) also shows us a reality very different from that of the ACBC (see also Bard 1982). In this case, Navarre is visualized by significant sections of the population as a periphery of the Basque periphery, which activates a sense of foral identity in opposition to Basque identity. Equally, the complex historical, social, cultural, linguistic and geographical reality of the territories of Navarre combined with the diverse positions found with respect to 'Basqueness' explains the nonexistence of a uniformly shared territorial imaginary. However, a new political majority has recently been articulated that has tried to give concrete form in this territory to the yearnings for change facing the exhaustion of the Spanish political system. This has taken concrete form in the unity of action between nationalists and the newly emergent formations. A new alternative political subject is thus being shaped. Nevertheless, while it may be favorable to the right to decide, this alternative political subject is not demanding sovereignty. Moreover, a rival Navarrist political subject is trying to impede the articulation of a Basque-Navarrese community. An expression of this is the recent commitment by Partido Popular president Mariano Rajoy to alter the transitory provision of the Constitution that would enable the annexation of Navarre into the ACBC.

Conclusion: looking back, and towards the future

The demand for Basque sovereignty has evolved. There are multiple causes for this evolution. While it is impossible to definitely establish a direct connection between certain external and internal contextual mechanisms and cognitive mechanisms with a discursive character, it seems clear that this evolution is in keeping with certain *general* external trends. These include the end of the Cold War and subsequent changes of frontiers, the process of building Europe itself, new forms of managing national conflicts in democratic contexts, and a global change of paradigm of political action among anti-system left-wing forces.

At the same time, and relatedly, we should also consider domestic trends that explain this evolution: failed expectations in relation to Spain's decentalization process, cessation of violence by the armed organization ETA, electoral competition between the two families of Basque nationalism (combined on occasion with joint actions and strategies) and the prominence of trade unions in the demand for sovereignty. More recently, the economic crisis and its elitist management have strengthened the demand for popular (or citizen) sovereignty, for individual decision-making capacity in a world where the supposedly sovereign citizenry has been deprived of any meaningful possibility of self-determination.

With respect to the Spanish case, the Basque country lost its sovereignty as a state in the time of the Kingdoms of Navarre and Castile 500 years ago. Since then, it has not achieved more than limited degrees of sovereignty in the form of pacts, agreements and certain quotas. This sovereignty by agreement was always in the interest of guaranteeing the sovereignty of a modern state, in this case the Spanish state. Once again, we see that pacts are always made from the *a priori* of power, in a win-lose logic, where the asymmetry will always be hierarchical. As in many other historical narratives, throughout the episodes of disputes and conflicts of different intensity there is always a division into two communities: those who have a state and those who do not have one, or have lost one. Stated differently, there is always a division between those who win the war and those who lose. In different periods the two sides label each other as republicans and

Francoists, Francoists and opponents of the regime, constitutionalists and nation-alists, and (very gradually) as democrats and democrats. Today we can define them as two democracies (Euskadi/Spain) that find themselves in competition and in an always-asymmetrical relation in the dilemma of competing and disputing their sovereignty over the demos or elector subject that supports, sustains and maintains them, which is the Basque imagined community. It is clear that this relation between the representatives of each community (people or nation) can take different forms. Three types (or categorizations, as Hirschman would say) can be the options of each demand (or discursive articulation): (a) exit, (b) voice and (c) loyalty.

Let us first consider (b) voice. If we look at the widespread (indeed global) his-tory of decolonization, we find many peoples who have attained their own state thanks to decolonization processes and self-determination endorsed by the United Nations. Over the course of many centuries as an imperial world power, Spain also lost many colonies. However, it does not seem reasonable to call the Basque country a Spanish colony, given that the aristocracy and a large part of the Basque bourgeoisie, as well as the Spanish bourgeoisie, have actively collaborated and to a large extent designed and created the present-day system of the Spanish state of autonomous communities, in which the Basque and Spanish communities live.

Broadly speaking, we can clearly see that the possible future alternatives could be that of exit (a) (secession) or of loyalty (c). However, the latter would be on condition that the political representatives of each people manage to find the appropriate discourse to convince their citizens of a hypothetical change (or non-change) in the degree of Basque sovereignty. This will depend exclusively on the democratic principle (b) (voice) of correctly channeling the different demands of each citizen and of obtaining (or not) some consensus (or avoiding polarization) on whether (or not) the Basque people has the right to be a differentiated sover-eign subject. In today's Europe, the question is whether a national project – with-out political violence, articulated with the endorsement of a social majority and broad popular support – may decide on its own future and constitute itself into whatever is decided upon. This is the challenge that we are facing. The democratic dilemma is served.

Notes

1 Online at: www.juntspelsi.cat
2 Online at: gureeskudago.eus/es/

References

Ahedo, I. 2016. 'Iparralde: The Emergence of the Basque Territory in France', in P. Ibarra Güell and Å. Kolås, eds, *Basque Nationhood. Towards a Democratic Scenario*. Oxford: Peter Lang, pp. 253–280.
Azurmendi, J. 1996. 'Pensamiento personalista en Euskadi en torno a la guerra' [Person-alist Thinking in the Basque Country Around the War], *Revista Internacional de los Estudios Vascos*, 41(1): 77–98.

Bard, R. 1982. *Navarra: The Durable Kingdom*. Reno, NV: University of Nevada Press.

Burgess, M., and Vollaard, H., eds. 2006. *State Territoriality and European Integration*. London: Routledge.

Bourdieu, P. 1985. 'The Social Space and the Genesis of Groups', *Theory and Society*, 14(6): 723–744.

Gurrutxaga, I. A. 2005. 'Nationalism in the French Basque Country', *Regional and Federal Studies*, 15(1): 75–91.

Habermas, J. 1994. 'Citizenship and National Identity: Some Reflections on the Future of Europe', in B. Turner and P. Hamilton, eds, *Citizenship: Critical Concepts*. London: Routledge, pp. 341–358.

Herrero de Miñón, R. M. 1998. *Derechos históricos y Constitución* [Historical Rights and Constitution]. Madrid: Taurus.

Itzaina, X. 1998. 'Le debat autour du territoire de l'eglise en Pays Basque: a la fronteriere du politique et du religieux?', in A. Borja, F. Letamendia and K. Sodupe, eds, *La construcción del espacio vasco-aquitano: Jornadas Euskadi-Aquitania, Bilbao, 13–15 de noviembre, 1997*. Bilbao: Universidad del País Vasco, pp. 149–164.

MacCormick, N. 2000. *Questioning Sovereignty: Law, State and Nation in the European Commonwealth*. Oxford: Oxford University Press.

McAdam, D., Tarrow, S., and Tilly, C. 2001. *Dynamics of Contention*. Cambridge Studies in Contentious Politics. Cambridge: Cambridge University Press.

Müller, J. W. 2006. 'A "Thick" Constitutional Patriotism for the EU? On Morality, Memory and Militancy', in E. O. Eriksen, C. Joerges and F. Rödl, eds, Law and Democracy in the Post-National Union, ARENA Report 01/2006. Oslo: Arena, pp. 375–400.

Sassen, S. 2006. *Territory, Authority, Rights: From Medieval to Global Assemblages*. Princeton, NJ: Princeton University Press.

Tilly, C. 2000. 'Processes and Mechanisms of Democratization', *Sociological Theory*, 18(1): 1–16.

Index